UNDERSTANDING BIG GOVERNMENT
The Programme Approach

Richard Rose

Centre for the Study of Public Policy,
University of Strathclyde

Sponsored by the European Consortium for
Political Research / ECPR

SAGE Publications
London   Beverly Hills   New Delhi

SAGE Publications Ltd
28 Banner Street
London EC1Y 8QE

 SAGE Publications India Pvt Ltd
C-236 Defence Colony
New Delhi 110 024

SAGE Publications Inc
275 South Beverly Drive
Beverly Hills, California 90212

British Library Cataloguing in Publication Data

Rose, Richard, 1933—
    Understanding big government.
    1. Political science
    I. Title
    350   JF201

ISBN 0-8039-9778-7
ISBN 0-8039-9779-5pbk

Library of Congress Catalog Card Number 83-051198

Printed in Great Britain by
J. W. Arrowsmith Ltd., Bristol

CONTENTS

TABLES

FIGURES

ACKNOWLEDGEMENTS

To understand contemporary government takes time. In the face of promises of great benefits or disasters, we must wait to see what happens. The results are often very different from what is expected. This is particularly true today. Political systems have not collapsed as was sometimes forecast in the midst of economic difficulties in the 1970s or in the 1968 student protests. Nor have all political problems been resolved, as was optimistically forecast in the early 1960s. In the Western world post-1984 government is not about to be transformed into the totalitarian system envisioned by George Orwell's nightmare reflection of Soviet and Nazi totalitarianism.

The original impetus for the research reported here came from a discussion about the crisis of government organized by Rudolf Wildenmann for the European Consortium for Political Research at the Werner-Riemers Stiftung, Bad Homburg, Germany, in 1975. The more I listened to cosmopolitan scholars talk about 'the' crisis, the more I puzzled about the causes of their anxiety. Clearly, something was troubling people, but what was it? It was heartening to have Giovanni Sartori there to confirm my suspicion that discussions without definitions of terms were unlikely to prove fruitful.

In reaction, I outlined a paper that sought to state precisely and analytically under what conditions and to what extent citizens had good reason to be worried about developments in government. The paper was published in English as 'Overloaded Government: the Problem Outlined' (Rose, 1975), and at greater length in Italian as 'Risorse dei Governi e Sovraccarico di Domande', *Rivista Italiana di Scienza Politica* (5, 2, 1975). I have returned to the subject since in many different contexts, as the citations of this book show.

Trying to comprehend contemporary government is a big task, given the variety of ways in which different Western nations respond to problems common to all of them. Hence, my research into overloaded government was undertaken under the auspices of the European Consortium for Political Research, and sponsored by the Volkswagen Foundation. The Volkswagen Foundation grant made possible a series of Workshops at the European University Institute, Florence; the Free University, Berlin; the

Fondation Nationale des Sciences Politiques, Paris; and the Centre for the Study of Public Policy of the University of Strathclyde, Glasgow. Altogether, these workshops generated more than 50 papers from a dozen countries, each examining problems from a particular analytic and national perspective. A collection of papers written by Paolo Farneti, Max Kaase, Dennis Kavanagh, Rudolf Klein, Jan Kooiman, Jacques Leruez, Don S. Schwerin, Peter Self, Artur Wassenberg and myself was published as *Challenge to Governance: Studies in Overloaded Polities* (Sage Publications, 1980).

Like government itself, the network of institutions and individuals involved in this collaborative research project has grown bigger and bigger. The European University Institute, Florence, invited me to give a series of seminars at the Institute in 1977 and 1978 with Dennis Kavanagh. A well-timed Fulbright Professorship led B. Guy Peters and myself to collaborate in an intensive study of the conflicts between increasing costs and benefits of government, published as *Can Government Go Bankrupt?* (Basic Books, 1978).

Understanding government is a continuing task. Work on the concluding stages of this book was greatly facilitated by grant HR 7849/1 from the British Social Science Research Council for a programme of research concerning the growth of government in the United Kingdom. This grant particularly assisted thinking about the role of laws and the systematic analysis of taxation in Chapters 3 and 4. It has also provided an impetus to move from considering ideas on a broad European canvas to its logical complement, finding what can be learned by the detailed test of generalizations in a single country. Terence Karran and Denis Van Mechelen have been of great help in this.

Continuing discussions within the Centre for the Study of Public Policy have been a ready source of stimulus. Particularly helpful comments on drafts of the manuscript were received from: Douglas Ashford, Klaus von Beyme, Sabino Cassesse, Frank Castles, Bernard Cazes, Andrew Dunsire, Hugh Heclo, Arnold Heidenheimer, Christopher C. Hood, Peter Jackson, Rudolf Klein, Johan P. Olsen, J.P. Owens, Edward Page, B. Guy Peters, Peter Self, Daniel Tarschys and Aaron Wildavsky.

In addition, June M. Roberts has been extremely competent in running successive changes in this manuscript through an Olivetti word processor, and Dr Rachel Henderson assisted greatly in copy-editing and proofreading.

While many people have contributed to the making of this book, I myself am solely responsible for the evidence and interpretation that follow. Given that the subject matter is in some respects controversial, the curious reader might wish to know the point of view of the author. Analytically, the approach is akin to that of a budget-examiner. Budget examiners start from a recognition that contemporary government is big in benefits and big in costs. The acceptance of the contemporary mixed economy welfare state as a fact may jar with the political commitments of the old and new Right. The emphasis upon fiscal constraints in funding the welfare state in the 1980s may jar with the political commitments of the old and new Left. The Right is correct that government cannot grow without limit; resources are always constrained. The Left is correct that the welfare state programmes making government big will not readily be abandoned in a democracy.

Big government is a major political issue today, but to understand this issue does not promise a single solution. In a very real sense, many issues of government are incapable of a final solution; they are conditions of existence. In so far as actions recommended to deal with difficulties are political, then they will not be consensual, for politics is about conflicting values. Political conflicts must be coped with; they cannot be eliminated. Social scientists can diagnose problems, and suggest the consequences of choosing between alternative policies. But the logic of the social sciences is not sufficient for political prescriptions. In a democracy, professors should defer to politicians who have the legitimacy that comes from popular election.

To devote great attention to problems of political economy is not to put material values first. Government is founded upon the necessity for public order in society, and democratic government is founded upon the desirability of popular consent. The history of Europe shows that government does not have to be big to be bad. Petty tyrannies have little to recommend them, except that they have harmed fewer people than totalitarian behemoths. My own experience in researching Northern Ireland has provided ample evidence that civil rights, including collective order and political rights, are the most important political values by which governments, big or small, should be judged.

Richard Rose
Centre for the Study of Public Policy
University of Strathclyde

INTRODUCTION: GOVERNMENT IN THE 1980s

Government is big in itself, big in its claims upon society's resources and big in its impact upon society. By every conventional measure, government looms large in the life of every Western nation today; governments differ from nation to nation only in their degree of bigness. Because government is dynamic not static, it can grow bigger still. Whether or not big government is regarded as a big problem, it is certainly a major issue of politics in the 1980s.

Big government is a fact of life. The scale of government today is very different from that confronting philosophers as different as Thomas Hobbes, Thomas Jefferson, John Stuart Mill and Karl Marx. To argue in favour of 'small is beautiful' is anachronistic and Utopian. The circumstances that have brought about the growth of government appear irreversible. Nor are other institutions of society, such as business corporations, trade unions or universities, likely to decline in size. The question confronting policy-makers is not whether government ought to be big, but what significance should be attributed to its present size.

Historically, the growth of government represents a great triumph of the modern Western state. The creation of big government has been the product of less than a century. In the middle of the nineteenth century, government's activities were relatively few; maintaining public order and defending national boundaries were the primary concerns. In the course of the twentieth century, government's activities have expanded in scale, in subject matter and in variety (Rose, 1976a). Government has grown far beyond the minimalist conception of the Nightwatchman state to become the central institution of the mixed economy welfare state. Institutions of government designed for a traditional agrarian society have adapted to the claims of industrial and post-industrial societies. In addition, Western governments have also greatly increased popular support; oligarchic or authoritarian regimes have been superseded by representative institutions of governance.

Because the growth of government has occurred more or less in parallel with the expansion of the franchise, big government can be praised as the necessary means by which the majority of individuals in a society have democratically mobilized against the traditional entrenched powers of elites (Rokkan, 1970). It can be praised as evidence of individuals learning to co-operate to provide collectively for their needs. The immediate causes of the growth of government — the provision of education, health and pensions — can be welcomed as 'good' goods, providing major benefits for nearly every family in society (Rose and Peters, 1978a: Chapter 3). The benefits of big government are popular. A wide-ranging survey of public opinion in Western nations concludes, 'Active government involvement in providing a basic level of economic and social well-being for the citizenry is everywhere a matter of majority public acceptance' (Coughlin, 1980: 25).

Big government can be attacked as bad government, and even as a threat to individual liberty. The provision of benefits to citizens is said to be proof of the state leading its subject down *The Road to Serfdom* (Hayek, 1944). While accepting the collective provision of some services by the Nightwatchman state, critics attack contemporary government for going far beyond the provision of defence and police protection. If the government were to confine its duties to those of the Nightwatchman state, it could cut its expenditure by two-thirds or more (Seldon, 1979: 71). Arguments for doing so start from the assumption that the market is a more efficient means of allocating society's resources than government (Wolf, 1979; Savas, 1982). It is argued that the expansion of public expenditure could even kill the goose that lays the golden tax egg, reducing the rate of economic growth. Marxists agree with market economists that big government is a symptom of big trouble. Some Marxists see the expansion of government's activities as a sign of the coming collapse of capitalism (O'Connor, 1973); other Marxists see the inability of government to sustain expansion in the face of fiscal constraints as a sign of impending collapse (Gough, 1982).

Size is an important characteristic of government, but it is not all-important. Even though the size of government varies greatly among Western nations, complaints about big government are everywhere voiced. Complaints are heard where government is relatively small because the population is small, for example, in Ireland and Sweden. It is particularly puzzling that complaints about relatively big government are specially vociferous in the

United States. By the conventional measure of government spending as a percentage of the national product, the United States has a relatively small government. Spending at all levels of American government in total accounts for 33 percent of the national product, against an average among Western nations of 39 percent (OECD, 1982a: Table 6.4). By this standard, in the Western world American government ranks in the bottom quarter for size.

Many problems of contemporary government concern small numbers of people. For example, only a relatively few of the 56 million people in Italy — some politicians, judges, policemen and journalists in public life — have been wounded or killed by terrorist violence. But the authority that is being attacked is meant to maintain public order for all. Violence in Northern Ireland is confined to less than 3 percent of the population of the United Kingdom; it is none the less an attack upon the political authority of the British Parliament. The seizing of 52 American hostages in Iran in 1979 captured the attention of the President, even though the hostages were a trivial proportion of Americans at home or abroad.

The great bulk of the polemics about big government is about government per se, and not about the size of government. Both free market economists and collectivists argue from a priori assumptions about what is assumed to be right and proper. The virtues or faults of government are only incidentally a function of scale; they are assumed to be intrinsic to the nature of government. If government actions are viewed as intrinsically good, then the more that government does, the better society will be. If government is thought of as bad, then the bigger that government becomes, the worse will be its effects upon society. There is no consensus, within nations or internationally, about whether a given amount of government is too much, not enough or just about right.

Identifying the questions

Understanding big government is the object of this book. To understand big government requires far more than the glib assertion of political values or the too-clever-by-half deduction of consequences from untested and over-simple assumptions about government in the abstract. To understand the scale of government requires attention to questions of broad theoretical significance; it also requires an open-mindedness about the variety of answers that can be offered by the experiences of Western nations.

First of all, it is necessary to define what is meant by the term 'government'. To speak of government is a bit like speaking of an elephant, for each can be identified by any one of a large number of different-size characteristics. Government has a multiplicity of attributes. Not only is it a formal organization, but it is also an active process of mobilizing laws, money and public employees to produce public policies. Each of these attributes can be measured separately. To a surprising extent, the answer to the question 'how big is government?' depends upon the definition and measures employed.

Second, it is important to distinguish between questions of size and of growth. Bigness is not an inevitable characteristic of government. It reflects a very long process of growth. Whatever the measure, the past century has been a century of the growth of government. Moreover, most of that growth has occurred in the recent past. The governments of most Western nations have more than doubled in size since the early 1930s, and some have doubled in size since 1945. But past growth is not proof of future growth. In the 1980s it is particularly important to consider the direction of possible change. Under what circumstances can government remain relatively static, or even contract? Yet such is the size of government that, even if it contracted, it would still remain big.

Third, it is necessary to shift from a static to a dynamic analysis in order to identify the causes of the growth of government. Economic change, social change and political change — whether intended or unintended — can cause government to grow. Many influences are immediate and palpable, but others are buried in the past, for contemporary government did not become big overnight. The multi-dimensional character of government means that no one theory is likely to account for all types of change. Nor will every change be in the same direction, or at the same tempo. To identify why government has become big does not mean that continued growth is inevitable. Some causes of growth may be unique, such as the momentum provided by the Second World War and national reconstruction afterwards. Other causes, such as the demographic push that encouraged the postwar expansion of education, can be reversed, implying contraction of a major government programme.

Finally, this book seeks to identify pervasive political consequences of big government. The most important concerns of government are qualitative not quantitative, maintaining effectiveness and political consent. Expanding or contracting the size of government will alter its effectiveness only in so far as there are economies or diseconomies of scale. A big government is not ipso facto more capable of doing what politicians want; many constraints upon government are independent of size. Nor can popular consent to government be taken for granted. This is demonstrated by the histories of Germany, France, Italy and Austria in the first half of the twentieth century — and in the 1960s by the 'near misses' of the United States in the Deep South and in the Vietnam War. Is big government more likely to enjoy the consent of citizens because of all the benefits it provides? Or is it more likely to lose the consent of citizens, because of its costs, political as well as economic?

The first chapter of this book considers the complex meaning of big government, problems of measuring its size and following its dynamic course. The second chapter considers purported causes of the growth of government, and hypotheses that warn of baleful as well as benign consequences. The next three chapters review government's three principal resources: laws, taxes and public employees. Each resource is significant and different. For example, taxes are levied upon everyone in society, but the benefits of a job on the public payroll are enjoyed by only a limited fraction. Laws can sometimes demand compliance and sometimes confer benefits.

Government organizations, the subject of Chapter 6, play a central role in mobilizing resources and delivering public programmes. The seventh chapter reviews the variety of government programmes, and the extent to which the size of government is best considered in terms of what government does (its programmes) rather than what it is (a set of organizations) or the resources it mobilizes. The final chapter considers big government not only in terms of the priorities of governors, but also in terms of the priorities of ordinary citizens.

Many of the most important conclusions of this book are negative, for many assumptions about the size and growth of government are not borne out by the facts.

● Parliaments are *not* increasing the rate at which they add laws to the statute books, nor are contemporary societies much affected by the dead hand of laws enacted long ago (Chapter 3).

● The increase in taxation has been caused more by inflation than by an expansion of government's share of the national product (Chapter 4).

● The great majority of public employees are *not* remote bureaucrats cloistered in the national capital; public officials principally deliver education, health care and other services to households nationwide (Chapter 5).

● The number of government organizations does *not* multiply endlessly, and in the past three decades Western countries have been reducing the number of major government institutions (Chapter 6).

● Government programmes that have been growing most have *not* been novel programmes of dubious effectiveness and controversial aims, but rather well established and well accepted public policies providing pensions, health care and education for tens of millions of people (Chapter 7).

To disprove many commonplace assertions is not to suggest that big government is without problems. In the 1980s virtually every Western government faces big problems arising from the growth of government. The most pressing problem is that government's spending commitments threaten to expand at a pace faster than its fiscal resources. The perennial problem of meeting the costs of government is very different when government claims upwards of half rather than 10 or 25 percent of the national product. The world economic recession means that policy-makers cannot rely upon high levels of economic growth to meet the costs of big government. In Hugh Heclo's (1981: 397) evocative phrase, in the 1980s it is no longer possible to have 'policy without pain'.

Governments have managed to sustain a large panoply of programmes since economic difficulties became evident in the early

1970s, and have done so without losing political authority. But there has been a rising anxiety and uncertainty about fiscal problems. Economists too are uncertain about the foundations of political economy. The Swedish committee awarding the Nobel Prize in Economics has hedged its bets about economic fundamentals. The prize has been awarded to such exponents of the free market as the American Milton Friedman and to proponents of centralized state planning such as the Russian Leonid Kantorovich; and in 1974 there was a joint award to the Swedish socialist, Gunnar Myrdal, and to the Austrian anti-socialist, Friedrich von Hayek.

The capacity of governments to cope with fiscal problems — albeit at a rising cost in unemployment, inflation and economic growth — reflects the great wealth of contemporary Western societies. This wealth has been used by hard-pressed governors to buy time. But we do not know how much time we need to buy, and whether existing resources of government are sufficient to meet future claims. The present pressures upon government may be temporary, but so too is a leak or a crack in a wall. It can be attended to, remain as it is, or get worse.

The strategy of analysis

To answer questions about big government one must think big. This volume integrates research across a considerable span of time, space and public programmes. Inevitably, one must sacrifice details in order to gain breadth. Because the scope of government is both great and complex, it makes sense to view government as a whole. The characteristics of big government can then be anatomized by a strategy of analysis that makes comparisons between the experience of many nations, of different times in the post-1945 world, and of different public programmes. Although the scheme sounds complex, the results can be easily understood. For example, a comparison of changing patterns of health and education expenditure in Western nations involves all three strategies of analysis.

The first step is to determine the nations to be included in comparisons. A global review of all countries in the United Nations will identify many political differences that correlate with gross differences in national product, such as literacy; poor governments and governments of underdeveloped nations tend to be smaller governments (cf. Taylor, 1981). But to conclude that there is a poverty or literacy threshold affecting the size of government tells us nothing about prosperous, literate Western nations that have long been above that threshold. Moreover, the countries analysed must not be too different in qualitative terms, lest quantitative analysis points to misleading conclusions. For example, quantitative analysis may find similarities among Eastern and Western European nations (Pryor, 1968) in health or education expenditure as a percentage of the gross national product, but this tells us nothing about qualitative differences between Soviet-style and Western European governments.

Because the problems of big government are common to advanced industrial societies, they cannot be explained away as the fault of individual politicians, the choices of a particular party or the flaws of one nation's character. Equally, this means that the problems of big government cannot be resolved simply by seeking a wise leader or the correct party. Because the problems are systemic rather than personal, they will not easily be removed by a single election result. In larger as well as smaller European countries, the causes of national difficulties are often outside rather than inside national boundaries. A national government that spends money recklessly to win an election cannot expect foreign governments to accept the burden of resolving its resulting problems.

To understand big government, we must pose questions common to the experience of many Western nations. Where differences are found, we must explain the causes of variations, and consider the consequences too. Inevitably, the extent of geographical coverage must vary with the problem at hand. For some purposes, such as the analysis of taxation, statistics compiled by the Organization for Economic Co-operation and Development (OECD) are at hand for up to two dozen industrial nations scattered across four continents. For other topics, such as the scale of government legislation, there are few systematically comparative data available. One must seek evidence from countries sufficiently varied to provide a reasonable test of the robustness of generalizations. Particular attention is concentrated upon the largest nations of Europe — Britain, France, Germany and Italy — as well as Sweden, where the welfare state has flourished specially, and the United States, where it has flourished less.

A distinctive feature of this volume is the integration of European and American experience. To permit an ocean to confine intellectual inquiry to a single continent is to practise insularity on a continental scale. A generation ago, differences in the levels of affluence between America and European countries might have been advanced as an argument against comparison. In the past two decades European and American standards of living have been converging. Even more important, the economies of the OECD nations are increasingly involved with each other in an interdependent world economy.

To write about big government in a comparative context is not to claim that all countries are identical in their characteristics or in the size of government. Comparisons can identify variations between nations as well as similarities (cf. Dogan and Pelassy, 1981). Some problems are unique to a single society; for example, there was nothing in Europe in the 1960s to match the trauma of the Vietnam War in American political life, or in the 1970s matching Watergate. In the uncertain world of the 1980s, it would be a brave policy-maker who would contemplate the problems of another country and smugly proclaim: It can't happen here.

Second, this book spans the dynamics of four decades. The big governments that exist today were not created as the result of a single election outcome. Nor are they simply to be explained as the consequence of centuries of historical evolution, for governments assumed their present scale only in the post-1945 era. Too much historical concern can obscure the distinctive properties of the present, just as concentration upon current events can hide the fact that many properties of governments are not the conscious choice of the governing party of today, but the unintended consequence of inertia forces persisting from the distant past.

To understand big government we must look backwards and forwards. Government on the scale that we know it today did not exist 50 years ago. The very idea of bigness is changing. Anxieties about the growth of government were voiced in the mid-nineteenth century by liberals when government was far smaller than it is today. Contemporary concern is very much a phenomenon of the 1970s and 1980s; it was not characteristic of the 1950s and 1960s. Important as it is to understand the past for its own sake, it is even more important to understand the past as prelude to the future. Past decisions — about taxing, spending and public employment — persist; laws and organizations give them continuing force. Inertia commitments of present-day government limit its scope for future choice. An understanding of the past also demonstrates that current circumstances are neither inevitable nor unchanging. Since the end of the Second World War, Western governments have gone through four distinctive periods.

In 1945, some Western nations mobilized resources on a grand scale, because of the exigencies of war. The contraction of government by postwar demobilization in Britain and America is a striking demonstration of the fact that the growth of government is not inevitable. Political and economic reconstruction was the first priority in the war-ravaged countries of Western Europe. Older people who today worry about maintaining affluence in youth worried about finding the bare means of sustenance amidst the ruins of war. France did not regain its 1929 level of production until 1950, and Germany did not return to its prewar high until 1953. Political reconstruction took longer. Italy secured a new Constitution in 1948 and Germany in 1949. Austria was not freed from military occupation until 1955, and the current French Constitution dates only from 1958. Security — against external military threat as well as internal subversion — was a principal preoccupation of major Western nations in the 1950s. The longer the duration of peace and order, the more attention politicians could give to economic prosperity.

The 1960s was a period of affluence and political optimism. With the confidence of youth and riches, President John F. Kennedy opened the decade by proclaiming that the United States had infinite resources to spend in pursuit of its political aims. In Europe too political optimism was widespread. Governments found that sustained economic growth offered treble affluence: a larger gross national product meant that there was more money to raise individual earnings and increase welfare state programmes simultaneously. This was noticeable not only in historically prosperous industrial societies, such as Germany and Britain, but also in Italy and Ireland, where a peasant way of life was giving way to urban prosperity on Europe's economic periphery. The chief political protest of the time — the 1968 student revolt — was not against poverty, but against the alleged consequences of affluence (Barnes, Kaase et al., 1979).

Every Western nation was richer in 1980 than in 1970, but the economic difficulties of the 1970s raised the spectre of ungovernability. A leading American scholar and political activist, Samuel P. Huntington (1974: 166), argued, 'Post-industrial politics could be the darker side of post-industrial society', and castigated social scientists for averting their gaze from this prospect simply because it was 'unpleasant'. Citizens too expressed anxiety about the future. The median citizen of the European Community reckoned that there was almost a 50-50 chance of civil disorder (*Euro-Barometre* no. 8, 1978: 28-35). Analytically, the idea of ungovernability is a nonsense. The question is not whether we shall be governed, but how? A modern Western society can no more do without the authority of government than it could do without money (Rose, 1979).

In the 1980s economic difficulties have produced fiscal stress. Yet they have also shown that Western governments can cope with many political challenges facing them. France and Italy have demonstrated the flexibility of their representative institutions; the Fifth French Republic has its first socialist president, and the Republic of Italy has had its first non-Christian Democratic premier. In Spain, Portugal and Greece authoritarian regimes have been replaced by popularly elected governments. Western European communist parties have retreated from their historic role as alienated parties of combat, and seek integration in national political systems. Right-wing extremist parties poll derisory votes, when they appear at all. It is in Eastern Europe, for example Poland, where the challenge to established authority is greatest. Western governments show continuing evidence of their legitimacy, even though they do not demonstrate full effectiveness in managing their economies.

To understand big government a third dimension of comparison is necessary: comparison across a range of public policy programmes. The constitutional structure of Western governments was developed initially when government delivered few policies. The change in the scale of government is less a change in what government is, a set of formal organizations, and more a change in what government does, delivering the multiplicity of programmes that constitute the contemporary welfare state. Government is big today because major programmes — education, health, pensions and military defence — make big claims upon society's resources. National Parliaments tend to remain constant in size, but national budgets do not. The pressures to enlarge budgets rarely reflect institutional change; they are usually demands to increase the scale of programmes, particularly major social welfare programmes.

When government is disaggregated into different programmes there is no necessary reason why all its programmes should grow at the same rate, or grow in the same direction. A government that is big in aggregate can be growing bigger in some programmes, while other programmes simultaneously remain static or contract.

Public programmes differ in the claims that they make upon resources. For example, pensions policies and financing the national debt are money-intensive. Education and health programmes are labour-intensive, requiring large numbers of public employees. Marriage and divorce policies are law-intensive. In this book, attention will be focused upon government programmes that account for the great bulk of public employment and public expenditure in Western nations today.

Comparing different programmes within one country is likely to reveal major differences, just as comparing the same programme across national boundaries can reveal similarities. Pension programmes have many things in common throughout the Western world. Within an interdependent international economy, energy programmes also have much in common. Together, cross-national cross-programme comparisons can test the extent to which there is more in common between the same programme in different countries than there is between different programmes within the same country.

Understanding the differences between government yesterday and today, between governments at home and abroad, and between growing and static programmes of government does not promise an end to the problems of government. But it is a beginning. Without understanding the nature, the causes and consequences of big government, it is impossible to defend what is good in the present against unwarranted criticisms, or to protect the future of government against unwanted and unintended consequences of growth.

1 TAKING THE MEASURE OF GOVERNMENT

In order to understand big government, we must first of all know what government is. Conceptualization comes before quantification. In order to measure the size of government, we must be able to identify the presence of government. What is it that distinguishes governmental from non-governmental institutions?

Government is first of all a set of formal organizations. Organizations give structure and continuity to the activities of government. The distinction between government as persisting organizations and government as elected politicians is the difference between the ephemeral and the durable. Elected officeholders come and go, whereas the organizations of government are meant to last as long as a constitution endures — or even from one regime to another, as the experience of France, Germany and Italy illustrates. The centrality of politics differentiates the structure of government from other types of formal organizations in society.

Government organizations are here defined as formal administrative structures established by the constitution or public laws, headed by officials elected by citizens or appointed by elected officials and/or principally financed by taxation or owned by the state. This definition of government emphasizes the importance of constitutional authority, confirmed by popular election, and the claims of public sector organizations upon tax revenue; Chapter 6 gives further elaboration.

The existence of government implies the presence of private sector organizations that are not a part of government. Contemporary Western countries are mixed societies as well as mixed economies. Major private sector organizations, whether profit- or non-profit-making, are important in society. However, the fact that government organizations, profit-making corporations, trade unions and non-profit-making bodies such as universities are all part of the same society does not mean that they are interchangeable.

The public and the private sectors cannot exist in isolation; the two are interdependent in a mixed economy welfare state. Government raises large sums in taxes from the private sector, passes laws that regulate what private sector organizations can and cannot do, and spends money in ways that affect their interests (see e.g. Aharoni, 1981; Weidenbaum, 1970). Private sector organizations receive many benefits from the public sector, not least the guarantee of public order.

The existence of relations between public and private sector organizations no more abolishes the differences between them than does the existence of diplomatic relations between America and Russia. To talk to foreigners does not deprive an individual of his passport. A government organization is no less a part of government if it influences the private sector, nor does a private sector organization lose this status if it lobbies government. Only a totalitarian society would recognize no difference between the two types of institutions, considering everything as part of the state.

Government is also a set of programmes. We judge government by what it does (delivering a multiplicity of programmes) as well as by what it is (a set of organizations). Governing involves the mobilization of laws, money and employees and the conversion of these resources into programme outputs. Resources are needed to give substance to policy intentions; big government requires big resources.

In addition to knowing what resources government commands, we also need to identify the programmes for which resources are used. The growth of government does not occur in general, nor does it involve the same amount of growth in each organization. Growth occurs in specific programmes of government, and depends upon programme and resource specific characteristics as well as upon generic features of government. The programmes of government are multiple. Big governments are concerned with measures intended to promote health, education, housing, income security, a better environment and industrial growth, as well as the classic programmes of the Nightwatchman state concerning law and order, foreign affairs, and military defence (Rose, 1976a).

We cannot test statements about the size of government without measuring what government does. Because programmes involve a variety of resources and organizations, the activities of government are not reducible to a single homogeneous measure. Theoretical economists may assume that government produces an undifferentiated stream of welfare, but anyone else will notice very big differences between programmes in their purposes and in the mix of resources that they mobilize.

The first section of this chapter identifies the essential elements of the complex structure of government. Given this knowledge, the next task is to consider the conceptual and practical problems of measuring the size of the different elements of government. This is necessary in order to determine which governments are big, and how big government is today. Whatever the size of government at any given moment, this size can change. In the course of time, a government can grow bigger, contract or remain much the same in size. The third section examines the dynamic patterns of change in government.

Disaggregating government

Government can be seen as a whole only by breaking it up into the parts that constitute the complex idea of government. The constituent elements can then be related to each other in a model that represents what government is and what government does. A model of government should first of all be capable of application to many countries; it should not be confined to one country's unique institutions. Second, the elements should be defined with sufficient clarity so that it is possible to get some measures of their size. The grand abstractions of political systems analysis, phrased in a language remote from everyday government, are not appropriate here. Third, the number of constituent elements should be limited, in order to concentrate attention upon fundamentals of government. To elaborate elements endlessly is to gain detail at the cost of comprehension. Finally, the separate elements should be explicitly related in the model as they are in the process of governing.

At a very high level of philosophical abstraction, government may be reduced to a single undifferentiated whole. But this tells us very little about what government is, let alone what it does. The European conception of the state implies a unity of sorts, but this is not the unity of a monolithic organization. Germany or Austria is no less a state because it has a federal constitution than is unitary France or quasi-unitary Italy. Marxist theories treat the state as a monolith, but empirical studies of interest groups recurringly document conflicts within government. To deny the existence of such conflicts would be to argue that there is no politics within government. Yet even in the Soviet Union, where ideology and actions combine to concentrate power, there are many conflicts within government (Tarschys, 1977). If ever a state is a unity, it should be so in international relations, given unity in international law, and a national interest to advance. But empirical studies of foreign policy emphasize that even in moments such as the 1962 Cuban missile crisis in the United States, organizations within government dispute what should be done collectively to advance a notional national interest (Allison, 1971).

By definition, a model of government identifies a number of different attributes; it also identifies their relationship. The model of government employed in this book is narrower than the familiar model of the political system developed by David Easton (1965), which follows the liberal assumption that the initial impetus to action comes from popular demands. Here the organizations of government are the central motive force; government has made demands upon subjects for centuries before recognizing the right to voice demands through the ballot. This book is thus concerned far more with what goes on within the black box of government than are models of the political system in general.

In simplest terms, government organizations do three things:

(1) *mobilize resources*: the resources that government mobilizes — laws, tax revenues and public employees — are in part extracted from society (e.g. tax collection) and in part produced within government itself (e.g. laws);

(2) *combine resources into programmes*: the combination of government resources requires political authorization, whether expressed by a conscious decision of the government of the day or by a law enacted generations ago; and administrative action by a particular organization within government, for a Department of Defence and a Pensions ministry each has a distinctive mixture of programmes and mixture of resources;

(3) *deliver programme outputs*: the delivery of goods and services to citizens intended to benefit from them is the justification of most programmes of contemporary government.

Government organizations are multiple, and each is concerned with many programmes simultaneously. Because the activities of government are continuing, organizations are simultaneously mobilizing resources, combining resources into programmes, and delivering programme outputs. The process of government is literally non-stop; all parts of the model are at all times important. The parts of the model are inextricably linked. Resources are not mobilized in a vacuum; they are required to constitute programmes. Programme outputs do not disappear; they have an impact upon society that in turn affects the level of resources available to government in future. The study of the impact of government policies upon society is a subject that deserves (and has received) many books on its own. This book concentrates attention on the impact of different elements of government upon each other.

The five elements in this model of government — laws, tax revenues, public employees, public organizations and public programmes — constitute the five core topics of this book (see Figure 1.1).

FIGURE 1.1

A simple model of government

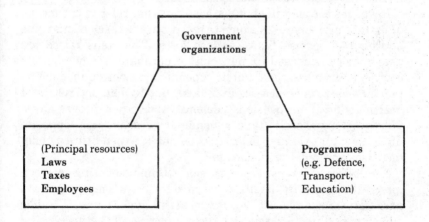

1. Laws. Laws are a unique resource of government. Whereas taxes usually claim less than half a country's gross national product and government employees constitute about one-quarter of the labour force, government enacts 100 percent of the laws of a society. Government requires laws to authorize the activities that constitute programmes. Laws limit the discretion of popularly elected politicians as well as that of bureaucrats. For example, a conservative administration cannot ignore welfare state legislation; if it does not like such measures, it must secure the repeal of established legislation. In a complementary way, a socialist administration cannot build a socialist society without first spelling out in legislative form how this is to be done, and winning legislative approval for its intentions.

2. Public revenues. Government raises money in a multiplicity of distinctive ways. Taxes come in many forms; income taxes, sales taxes and taxes on tobacco differ in their nature and in the revenue that they yield. In an inflationary era, taxes levied in fixed money terms will have a different rate of growth from taxes expressed as a percentage of income or sales. Although public revenue and public expenditure are both measured in money terms, the two are categorically different. Revenues are part of the cost of government, and expenditures are usually viewed as benefits.

Revenues are classified under headings that refer to the means of extracting money — income taxes, profits tax, sales and value added taxes, excise taxes, and so forth. The sums raised are usually not earmarked for particular programmes; they go into a common pool of revenue. Public expenditure is determined not so much by how revenues are extracted, but by characteristics of health, education, pensions, defence and other programmes. Moreover expenditure and revenue may change in opposite directions; for example, in a recession public expenditure usually increases and public revenues fall.

3. Public employees. Laws are not self-implementing, nor can money be spent by itself. A large number of employees is a necessary resource of every modern government. Public employees differ greatly in their functional characteristics, including high-level policy advisers and administrators, refuse collectors, teachers, postmen, soldiers, nurses, coal miners and so on. From musicians and cooks to economists and lawyers, there are few occupations that do not have some members working in the public sector. Many occupations are exclusive to government, such as soldiers and judges. There are even more types of public employees than there are public programmes.

4. *Organizations.* Organizations are central in government. Laws are enacted, taxes paid and employees engaged by the active initiative of government organizations. Government is not a single organization but a complex of organizations. Some organizations are fundamental, being authorized by a constitution, for example, Parliament, courts of law and an executive. Some organizations are established and can be abolished by statute, such as local government and nationalized industries. Within central government, there are functional divisions into ministries concerned with defence, finance, foreign affairs, health and so forth; each ministry in turn is subdivided into a variety of operating agencies and bureaus. Many goods and services of government are delivered by local authorities, special purpose welfare and health agencies, or nationalized industries.

5. *Programmes.* Organizations combine the resources of government into 'programme' outputs. The term programme is used instead of the more familiar term 'policy', because of the multiple and vague meanings that the term 'policy' has come to have. A policy can mean anything from an issue of concern to government (e.g. unemployment), or an intention to do something about a given issue (e.g. a policy intended to achieve full employment) to a very specific programme of activities, authorized by law and committing money and personnel to a specific government agency (e.g. a programme providing job-training for 16- to 18-year-olds). Every programme makes some claims on all three of government's resources — laws, money and public employment — and requires organization to carry it out. By contrast, policy issues and policy intentions can be free-floating, without any claim on government resources or any organizational anchor.

Linking the five constituent elements of government emphasizes their interrelationship and interdependence. A change in one element in the model will affect other elements. If programmes are to grow, then the resources that government

mobilizes must grow. If there is an influx of revenue as a
consequence of economic growth, then there will be more money to
finance more public employees, more laws and expanding
programmes. Change in organizations can affect the efficiency and
effectiveness of programmes. Each element of government has its
own distinctive properties, affecting its measurement and rate of
change. We cannot reduce the measure of government to a single
element, because its constituent parts are varied. There is a
multiplicity of answers to the question, 'what grows when
government grows?'

How big is big?

To ask 'How big is government?' is easy. To answer the question is
difficult, and the answer may even be misleading. Government has
many properties, of which size is only one. In the first instance we
identify government in terms of nominal qualities, for example,
whether or not its rulers are chosen democratically. Only after this
is done can we turn to ordinal questions, such as: Is one
government more or less representative than another? Last comes
quantification, such questions as: How many members sit in
Parliament? Because the programmes of government are multiple,
there is no assurance that everything can be reduced to a common
measure, whether money, votes or other easy-to-count objects.
Judging the size of government should follow from one's idea of
what government is. In the words of a leading polimetrician (that
is, an expert in constructing political measures), Ted Gurr, 'All the
most interesting variables are nominal.'

To answer the question 'How big is government?' we need to
measure separately five different elements: laws, tax revenues,
public employment, government organizations and public
programmes. Knowing what we want to measure does not tell us
how to measure government. The short answer is: we must
measure different parts of government differently. The measures
of different parts of government are not commensurable: to add
laws and taxes would be absurd. The evidence that will be adduced
in subsequent chapters provides a second reason for not reducing
all elements of government to a single measure or element. The

elements of government differ in how they are measured, they
grow at different rates, and sometimes they change in different
directions.

Two measures of government's resource claims are routinely
reported in quantitative terms: the amount of money that
government raises in taxes, and the number of its public
employees. Public revenue is the only element in our model of
government that is normally measured in money terms. Each unit
of money is of equal value. A tax of £100 is ten times a tax of £10,
and a tax of 100,000 lire is ten times bigger than a tax of 10,000
lire. Measuring public revenues presents a minimum of problems.
However, substantial and uneven inflation means that money is
not of constant value. A pound will not buy the same amount of
goods in 1985 as it did in 1975 or in 1965. Any comparison of public
revenues across time changes meaning, depending upon whether it
is expressed in current money values, or whether an attempt is
made to deflate the actual amount collected in order to take
account of changes in purchasing power.

Money values also lose simplicity when comparisons are made
cross-nationally, for $10 does not equal £10 or DM10. In a period of
fixed exchange rates, different currencies could be converted to a
single currency, usually US dollars. But since exchange rates were
allowed to float in 1972, the value of the dollar, the pound and the
Deutsche Mark in relation to each other changes every day. Even
if a standard currency unit is adopted, a given amount of money
has a different significance in relatively prosperous Germany or
Sweden than in a society with less wealth, such as Italy or Ireland.

Public employees are the second resource of government that is
readily suited to quantitative measurement. We can add up the
number of people on the public payroll to arrive at the total
number of public employees. By making comparisons with past
national figures, we can determine whether public employment is
growing, contracting or remaining much the same in size. There is
not even a problem of discounting for inflation, for an individual
worker remains a constant unit, whatever the currency or number
of noughts in his wages.

The size of public employment has limited meaning by itself. To
be told that there are 18 million public employees in the United
States — a number larger than the total population of six

European Community countries — is of uncertain significance. This figure must be related to the total labour force of the United States, in order to understand the relative importance of public employment within America. Turning an absolute number into a percentage figure fundamentally alters judgements. Instead of America having the biggest government among major Western nations because it has the most public employees, it is seen to have the smallest, because the percentage of the labour force in public employment (18.8 percent) is lower than in any other major Western nation (see Table 5.2).

Even though tax revenues and public employment can each be quantified they cannot be compared, for the measure used for revenue — money — is not commensurable with that used for public employment — people. We can no more add together money and people than we could add tanks and typewriters. It can be misleading to assess the size of all programmes by using just one measure, for programmes differ in their degree of labour-intensiveness. To expand education means hiring more teachers, but to increase spending on pensions requires only a minor alteration in the computer program that generates pensioners' payments.

Laws, organizations and public programmes are much harder to quantify. We can count the number of laws enacted each year or on the statute books, and we can count the number of government organizations and programmes. But this is not likely to tell us much that we want to know. For these elements of government, nominal differences are the most important differences. We do not want to know how many laws a government has enacted in a year, but which laws. We do not want to know how many organizations a government has, but what the organizations are, and what they do. We do not want to know how many programmes a government is responsible for, but the names and content of these programmes. Once we know the subject of laws, organizations and programmes, we can then proceed to analyse their political significance.

The measurement of public programmes is distinctive, because every programme of government draws upon a mixture of three resources: money, manpower and laws. Since two of these resources are readily quantifiable, it is possible to speak with some precision about programmes in terms of the amount of money they require, and the number of public employees involved. We would expect to find programmes such as education and health big in their claims on both public money and public employment, and programmes concerning art museums or international student exchange making relatively small claims on public funds and public employment. The tables and prose in Chapter 7 report the extent to which government programmes are big in terms of both of these quantifiable resources, or make major claims on one resource but not another.

To say that a given programme is important because of the amount of money or manpower devoted to it is to put the cart before the horse. The causal connection is almost invariably the other way. Because a given programme is important, it is therefore able to make big claims upon the resources of government. However, programmes that make a small claim upon money and manpower are not necessarily unimportant. For example, the courts of law cost little to maintain and employ few people, but they carry out a classic defining role of government. A country's diplomats are far fewer and cost less money than its armed forces but this does not mean that diplomacy contributes less to a country's security than does armed force.

Whatever the measure, care is needed in interpretation. This is most evident in comparative analysis across national boundaries. We do not say that the government of Britain or Germany is nearly 150 times bigger than that of Luxembourg, simply because the population of Britain or Germany is that much larger than the population of Luxembourg. Nor would we think of British or German government as small just because the population of these countries is only one-quarter that of the United States. Anyone who complained about big government would not accept as reasonable a suggestion to move to Luxembourg or Ireland, the countries in Western Europe with the smallest populations; bigness is not just a function of the total population of a country.

The effects of population differences can be controlled by measuring the scale of government in per capita terms. We can judge the amount of taxes collected per capita, or we can examine the percentage of young people going to university, or the proportion of total employees working in public employment. By discounting the effect of population, we find that the two OECD countries with the largest populations, the United States and Japan, are among the smallest governments in terms of a variety of measures of government's size.

The size of government is relative. It is most immediately related to historical trends within a country. Given appropriate evidence, we can say that the government of France is bigger today (or less small) than it was a century ago. Equally, we can speculate about whether government will grow bigger in future, maintain its present size, or grow smaller. If we treat the present size of government as the norm, because it is familiar, then any reduction in size can be said to make government smaller, just as past increases have made government larger. Taking the current size of government as the statistical norm does not mean that it is necessarily desirable in a normative sense too.

In this book each chapter will devote careful attention to concepts and measures. Ideas come before quantities. Unless we know what we are talking about, no measure is of any use. A clearly defined qualitative concept can focus our attention upon what is important about big government, and a quantitative indicator can misdirect attention because of its spurious connotation of precision. The intrinsic properties of numbers are a constant, but their instrumental utility varies according to the subject at hand. The fact that all elements of government are not equally amenable to quantification does not alter the importance of those that are harder to measure.

The most sensible analytic strategy is to establish first of all the extent to which quantitative data can be obtained to indicate the scale of each of the elements of government. The next step is to use these indicators to establish orders of magnitude. Once some measure is available for one point in time, comparisons can be made with a country's own past and with other countries today in order to assess the direction and rate of change in government's size. It is thus practicable to distinguish big from small governments, and big from bigger governments. Recognizing the point at which to stop quantifying is also important. As the noted statistician, John Tukey, has argued: 'Far better an approximate answer to the right question, which is often vague, than an exact answer to the wrong question, which can always be made precise.'

Patterns of change

To speak of big government is to imply that there is a time when government was (or could again be) small. The further back in time we go, the smaller we would expect government to be. Interesting as it would be to compare the growth of government from its origins to the present, this is neither practicable nor desirable. It is not practicable because there is no agreed point from which to date the origins of a national government. Any attempt to apply the same measure in different countries will place the origins of European governments centuries apart. *The World Handbook of Political and Social Indicators* (Taylor and Hudson, 1972: Chapter 2) uses three different definitions of the origin of government: the year of national independence, the year of adoption of the present constitution; and the period of consolidating modernizing leadership. Using multiple measures of the national origins of government confounds centuries of history. For example, France has been independent since the creation of a recognizable French state in late medieval times; yet its present constitution dates only from 1958. The United States is unusual among Western nations in having a clear date for the establishment of government. But to note that the American Constitution has persisted since 1789 does not mean that American government has remained unchanged since George Washington's time.

To understand the dynamics of big government, we must guard against considering too much as well as too little of the past. The influences upon big governments are not necessarily the same as factors causing small governments to become big. Industrial-ization and urbanization may explain changes over a century or more (Flora, 1975), but that does not mean that a post-industrial society will necessarily have a government contracting in size, or that the flight from the cities will produce less government. This book is about big government today, and whether or not it is growing bigger still.

When examining patterns of change in the size of government, the first need is to ascertain the direction of change. In the past century, government has grown larger in most measurable respects. But this is not proof that future change will invariably take the form of further growth. In most Western nations, in reaction against past patterns, there are some political groups actively seeking to make government contract. Logically, the size of government could take any of three directions: it could grow bigger still, it could contract, or it could remain much the same in size. Whether government grows or contracts, the rate of change can be steady, or it can accelerate or decelerate through the years.

1. Growth of government
When government increases in size, three different patterns of growth can be distinguished. Government grows in a *steady*

linear fashion if the annual rate of increase is much the same from year to year. Very simple models of the growth of government, for example, government growth as a function of continuing bureaucratic pressures, imply that the scale of growth is steady, and steadily upward. A nightmare vision of the growth of government sees it growing at an *accelerating* rate, its size growing faster from one year to the next. The reasons for accelerating growth may be malign, an uncontrollable bureaucracy accelerating its demands, or positive, government catching up in the provision of public programmes after a period of austerity. *Deceleration* means that government continues to grow, but that the rate of growth in the near future will be less than that of the recent past. The bigger government is, the slower its rate of growth, for example, the higher the level of public revenues, the more difficult it will be to raise taxes higher still. A decelerating rate of growth may also reflect a saturation of demand; once the coverage of a national health service reaches 100 percent, there is no further scope for expansion.

2. No change in the size of government

Two very different patterns can result in no change in the size of government over a period of time. If a measure of government shows no change at all over a period of years, then it can be described as *static*. But maintaining a static pattern in a world of change and flux is not easy; for example, a government may wish to keep interest rates steady, but economic pressures may cause interest rates to fluctuate. A *cyclical* change involves a more or less regular growth and contraction in government. The long-term result is nil change, because the ups and downs tend to cancel out. For example, government seeks to hold the level of unemployment constant over a period of years, but expects unemployment rates to fluctuate up and down from month to month. Government will not try to keep any one programme constant by sacrificing other programme goals; it may accept a rise in unemployment when inflation is perceived as the greatest difficulty, and seek to reduce unemployment when inflation is decelerating. Because of frequent reversals in a cycle, there is a big difference between a cyclical and a static pattern, even though both involve no long-term growth in government.

3. The contraction of government

In so far as government is able to sustain political pressures reducing the size of government, there can be a steady linear contraction in government. Opponents of big government hope that their efforts can make government contract at an accelerating rate. As its presumed benefits are increasingly apparent, the rate of contraction would speed up. But efforts to contract government may run into increasing opposition, thus causing a deceleration or even a levelling-off of the size of government. For example, demobilization of the military will be carried on for a few years after a war but at a decelerating rate; otherwise, the whole of the armed forces would be disbanded.

4. Incrementalism, chronic instability and discontinuities

A common feature of these rates of change is that they are *incremental*, involving regular and predictable changes. This is most true of linear models with unvarying rates of change. It is also true of cyclical patterns, since the reversals in direction that characterize a cycle are predictable, occurring at a regular tempo, albeit in different directions. Accelerating and decelerating rates of change can show predictable regularity, and statistical equations may readily describe their progress. The political rationale for incremental change is that politicians find that the simplest way to resolve problems facing them is to make relatively small changes. Even a radical government can find that the institutional resistances to change are such that it can make haste only slowly (Braybrooke and Lindblom, 1964; Dempster and Wildavsky, 1978).

To describe a change in size as 'incremental' is not to say that it is of little political significance. Changes in inflation rates, interest rates or unemployment normally involve a shift of only a few percent, but can have a big impact. If interest or unemployment rates rise from 5 to 10 percent, this is a doubling of inflation or unemployment. If small percentage changes are applied to a gross national product of trillions of Deutsche Marks or billions of pounds, seemingly small changes can add up to a lot of money. Predictable regularity has nothing to do with absolute size; inflation in Italy has been more incremental than in Britain, for Italian inflation in the 1970s was steadier, but the annual rate of inflation was much higher.

Two non-incremental forms of political change go well beyond the occasional shift between predictable patterns. In the absence of predictable regularity in government, *chronic instability* involves abrupt shifts in year-on-year rates of change, and a more or less random reversal of direction (Rose and Page, 1982). Just as a change must be reasonably steady for a decade or more in order to be classified as predictable, so too instability must persist for a lengthy period in order to be classified as chronically unpredictable. In a period of economic difficulty, public revenue and public expenditure may reflect chronic instability.

The biggest changes in government, even if the least frequent, are *discontinuities*. When this happens we cannot plot patterns of change as before, because of a shift in what is being observed. For example, the shift from peace to war is a discontinuity in the activities of government. Discontinuity arises from a change in the goal of a programme — for example, altering the object of education policy from selecting bright children for special instruction to a policy of educating all children in a common curriculum intended to promote social equality. Discontinuities also arise when threshold levels are crossed in a seemingly incremental pattern of change. If prices increase by 2 or 3 percent a year, then we say the consumer price index is changing incrementally. But if price increases rise to 15 or 25 percent, then we speak of inflation.

A multiplicity of patterns does not mean that all are equally probable. Today, there is far more discussion of the growth of government than of contraction. Yet change in government need not involve growth; changes can occur in opposing directions, and follow different patterns. Before we can decide whether theories of the growth of government are in fact true, we must carefully measure whether government grows.

This book provides a very robust test of theories of big government for three reasons. First it does so because government is disaggregated into five different elements, and is not simply treated as if it could grow in only one dimension and direction. Second, considerable attention is given to the measures of the size of government, to avoid the casual confusion of big numbers ('billions raised in taxes') with big government ('40 percent of national product raised in taxes'). Third, this study views the size of government in a dynamic perspective: we want to know not only how big government is today, but how much it has been growing in the past, and what pattern of change is likely in future.

2 CAUSES AND CONSEQUENCES OF BIG GOVERNMENT

Big government is a long time in growing; its laws, institutions and programmes are the product of centuries of history. In England, the oldest law on the statute books dates back to the thirteenth century. In America a constitution designed in the late eighteenth century to serve 13 small ex-colonies continues to regulate political institutions of a mammoth 50-state regime. Even when a new constitution is enacted, as in postwar Germany, Italy and France, the new regime inherits a great assemblage of commitments and resources from predecessor regimes. The very name of the Fifth Republic of France emphasizes its continuity with four predecessors since the end of the eighteenth century.

The past is a given; at any particular point in time a government cannot alter what has already been done. However much it may wish to change things — to make government smaller or bigger — it must start with what it inherits. The inheritance consists of a set of organizations, some of which are embedded in the country's constitution; a statute book laying down laws and procedures for directing public employees, raising taxes and combining resources into programmes; and a variety of programmes with beneficiaries and clients. Government organizations institutionalize the past, carrying its influence forward into the present; they are reinforced by processes of political socialization that condition individuals to expect great continuity from year to year in what government does.

The past constrains the present size of government. The bigger government is the greater the constraints, for there is less scope for new initiatives and fewer unmobilized resources. The longer programmes are in place, the harder it is for opponents of big government to de-institutionalize them by repeal. In the words of Daniel Tarschys (1981: 11), a Swedish scholar and politician, 'We have become more and more governed by old decisions.'

Most programmes of governments are not chosen by today's governors. Ronald Reagan did not choose to preside over the biggest budget deficit in the history of the United States government, nor did Margaret Thatcher choose to preside over a growing public sector in Britain. Equally, their Democratic and Labour predecessors did not choose to preside over rising unemployment and inflation. Problems of government that make the headlines today often reflect the influence of events occurring before the government of the day entered office. A contemporary government has so many institutionalized commitments that its own inertia will carry it forward from year to year. To alter the course, let alone reverse the direction, of government is not a task that can be achieved in the relatively short period of time between one general election and the next.

A government that is already big is, by definition, very different from the government of a relatively small-scale nineteenth-century liberal state or the contemporary government of a Third World nation. Theories of modernization are meant to explain how we got here from there; but because they treat the present as the end-point in a government's adaptation to industrialization and democratization, they are not addressed to the next step on the endless journey of government (Rose, 1968; Flora, 1975). The importance of the past does not mean that the future is predetermined.

A combination of theories is required to explain the multiple characteristics of big government. To search for the cause of big government in a single theory is to misunderstand what makes government big. Just as the size of the gross national product is the sum of many different goods and services produced, so the size of government is the sum (or byproduct) of many different activities undertaken by government, each with its distinctive scale and determinants. Moreover, different elements of government may change in opposite directions: for example, tax revenues can increase while the number of government organizations are contracting. No mono-causal theory is likely to explain all changes in government, for, as Heclo (1981: 392f.) notes, it is the conjoint result of a 'kind of mutual check and balance among principles' which reflects the 'tolerated contradictions' and 'mutually inconsistent priorities' of politicians in aggregate.

Running — or running after — a big government is very different from being the head of a government whose tasks could be discharged in a morning, as was the case in the Westminster of Disraeli and Gladstone, or the Washington of Theodore Roosevelt. The problems of directing a big government are multiple. Big government presents challenges to citizens as well. In this book, two consequences of big government are given special attention. A major concern of governors is whether or not big government remains effective government: does growth increase or reduce effectiveness or have nil impact? Effectiveness concerns citizens as would-be beneficiaries of government programmes, and as taxpayers too. In a democracy citizens have a further concern: is big government more or less dependent upon popular consent? Has the growth of government reflected greater responsiveness to citizens, or induced greater remoteness?

The purpose of this chapter is to review the theories that purport to explain why different dimensions of government are big, and to review consequences reckoned to flow from the growth of big government. The first section reviews a variety of economic and social influences upon the size of government. But social and economic changes do not by themselves lead to big government; political actions are necessary too. Political influences upon government's size are reviewed in the second section. The chapter then considers ways in which the size of government may alter its effectiveness, and also how big government can affect popular consent.

Economic and social influences upon the size of government

In response to the growth of government, theories of big government have burgeoned (see e.g. Tarschys, 1975; ACIR, 1981: Chapter 5; Larkey et al., 1981). The most general of theories are usually propounded in the timeless and universalist language of theoretical economics. With considerable logical rigour the theories deduce hypotheses to predict how politicians and citizens should act, and consequences of their actions. But the very generality of these models is usually self-defeating, creating analysis in the abstract without any consideration of the institutional inheritance that at any point in time constrains the actions of politicians. Just as geology is a science based upon the specific historical characteristics of different parts of the earth, so government is grounded in the accretion of commitments through the years. As Larkey et al. (1981: 203) note, abstractions unrelated to historical institutions run the risk of being no more than 'recreational mathematics'.

To search for the cause of big government in a single conscious choice in the past or present is to misunderstand the historical process. It is to reduce government to a near-sighted historian's concern with that which is found in Cabinet papers, newspaper reports or interview transcripts. In fact, the size of government reflects the interaction of conscious choices, unanticipated events, and long-term political, social and economic processes. Of these influences, some are clearly political — for example, welfare legislation and tax legislation. By contrast, others are relatively remote from governmental determination — for example, the number of young people born a decade or more ago tends to determine the number of pupils entering secondary school today. Many measures that influence government reflect events occurring over a quarter or half a century. Contemporary programmes of the welfare state can have their origins in choices made around the time of the First World War, which have taken half a century or more to reach full maturity.

Time is the central concept in theories of the growth of government, because the direction, the pattern and the scale of growth is revealed only in the course of time. Whereas it is not always easy to disentangle cause and effect in the analysis of contemporary conditions, one can be certain about their temporal priority. Actions taken yesterday can influence government today, but the opposite cannot be the case. In the creation of big government, there is always a yesterday. For any given observation about the size of government, we can always take one step backward in time to seek an explanation in what went before.

Since the days of the Greeks, grand theories have been constructed describing the dynamics of government, and predicting what will happen at the next stage. The most familiar stages-of-growth model is that of Karl Marx; the withering away of the state is its final stage. Grand theories of the stages of growth attempt to do too much with too little. A few simple influences are meant to be of universal importance, and irresistible power. Moreover, the pattern of political change is meant to be the same for each country. While Marxist models are usually clear about the ultimate destination of government, they are often weak in explaining, or explaining away such facts as the failure of capitalist states to collapse. Theories of political change that focus on the sequence of events leading to the modern state are unclear or contradictory about what happens next in the government of 'post-industrial' society (cf. Huntington, 1974; Inglehart, 1977).

The conventional historian's approach to explaining the growth of government is to examine in detail events within a single country for a period of time. This approach emphasizes nation-specific influences upon the size of government. The most casual review of the twentieth-century histories of Britain, France,

Germany, Italy, Sweden and the United States will reveal many differences. Three nations have had constitutional continuity, but France and Italy have had three constitutions each and Germany, four. There have been major differences in the response of national governments to major crises such as the Depression of the 1930s, which was met by Franklin Roosevelt's New Deal in America, by Hitler in Germany, by Mussolini in Italy, by a socialist government in Sweden, and by stand-pat conservatives in France and Britain. World wars have also had very different effects. Britain and America have twice been on the winning side; Italy and France have been with the victors once and the defeated once, Germany has lost two wars, and Sweden has twice remained neutral. Political culture is often used as a shorthand concept describing the residue of historical values and beliefs that reflect national differences transmitted from generation to generation.

However, the most important feature of contemporary Western governments is not that one is British, another French and a third German, but that all have bigness in common. It is the common commitment to government management of the economy and a range of welfare programmes that distinguishes contemporary mixed economy welfare states from their predecessors, and makes national governments similar. To explain the growth of government in nation-specific terms is to overlook a fundamental point. All governments were small a century ago, and all Western governments are big today.

Because the rise of big government is common to Western nations, the logical and parsimonious approach is to start by seeking explanations that are stated in language applicable across national boundaries, yet are not so general that they apply indiscriminately to every government, big or small. Nation-specific reasons are required to explain deviant cases — for example, the absence of a national health service in the United States. But first of all we need to see the broad sweep of influences that have commonly affected governments from Finland to Australia.

Because this book combines cross-national and cross-time analysis, it is possible to examine models that are both general and conditional. They are general in so far as statements are made about what to expect of government under specified conditions. They are conditional, inasmuch as there is no assumption that the same conditions will be met in every Western nation. This method can be used, for example, to see whether cross-national differences in rates of economic growth lead to differences in the size of government.

When Western governments have a multiplicity of constituent elements with different patterns of change, a variety of theories are offered to explain the cause of big government. If each theory is generalized from a single historical case, then each will be true in at least one context. But none will be true in all circumstances. To assert that one theory would explain the heterogeneous activities of Western governments is presumptuous at best, and misleading at worst.

The approach adopted here is to assume that a variety of influences affects the size of government. Influences can vary in their significance for particular elements of government, for specific programmes, and at different times. None of the economic, social and political influences can claim to be all-important. Influences are set out separately for the sake of exposition. But it is important to recognize that it is their combined impact that determines the size of government.

Economic growth. A very familiar explanation of the growth of government is that it follows from the growth of the national economy; the greater the size of a country's gross national product, the greater the size of government, at least in so far as size is measured in money terms or determined by money resources. This is a supply-side explanation of the growth of government: the more money there is available in society, the more public revenue the government will mobilize. So stated, the proposition seems obvious. But the non-obvious, even contentious, question that follows is: Does government grow at the same rate as the economy as a whole, in which case there would be no reason to worry about fiscal stress, or does it grow faster or slower than the economy?

Two decades ago American writers argued vigorously that government would grow more slowly than the economy. The central thesis of J.K. Galbraith's *The Affluent Society* was that government expenditure would be kept at a minimum as an economy expanded, thus leading Galbraith (1958) to predict the paradox of private affluence and public squalour. Regarding popular aversion to taxation as axiomatic, Anthony Downs (1965) proceeded to explain 'Why the Government Budget is Too Small in a Democracy'. These theories were very restricted in place, reflecting the free enterprise mentality of Americans, and in time reflecting the relative stagnant levels of public expenditure in the

United States in the Eisenhower era, a pattern different from Europe then or now. The popularity of such theories not so long ago is a useful caution against assuming that contemporary theories of the inevitable growth of government will remain in fashion.

Today, social scientists usually assume, with considerable supporting evidence (e.g., OECD, 1978), that government tends to grow faster than a country's gross national product. The classic exposition of the thesis is found in the writings of a late nineteenth-century German political economist, Adolph Wagner (1877; 1890). Wagner's 'law' is often interpreted as a simple statement about economic growth leading to government growth. In fact, it was 'a law of increasing state activity' (Peacock and Wiseman, 1961: 17): government's desire to expand military, economic, and social services was expected to lead it to seek more public revenues. Wagner, a *Kathedersozialist* and subject of Bismarck's Reich, saw the state as an active agent promoting society's wellbeing.

A correlation between growth in the economy and growth in government leaves open the question of which is the cause. Government may grow faster as a consequence of economic growth, the economy may grow more slowly as a consequence of government's growth; or their relationship may only be a coincidence. Conventional Keynesian economics prescribes that government should expand faster by deficit financing when economic growth slows down, in order to stimulate economic growth. It is sometimes forgotten that Keynesian economics can prescribe a contraction in the government deficit when the economy grows too rapidly. In theory, Keynesian demand management could leave the relationship between government and the economy more or less constant. Politicians, however, practise one-eyed Keynesianism, expanding government expenditure when the economy slows down, but not cutting it back when the economy picks up (see Rose and Peters, 1978a: 135ff.; Lindbeck, 1976). Given the inability of conventional Keynesian policies to deal with economic difficulties since 1973, some economists now argue that Keynesian policies are a cause of the economy growing more slowly than government (Buchanan and Wagner, 1977).

Particularly relevant today are theories that hypothesize a deceleration or levelling off in the size of big government. Herber (1967) has postulated a three-stage progression: (1) government is relatively and absolutely small in a subsistence economy; (2) it grows relative to the economy as the economy increases its capacity to finance services that government is specially suited to provide; and (3) it levels off when the demand for such public services as schools, roads and military defence is satiated. The basic point of Herber's model, which has not been confirmed by political events since publication in 1967, is that the past rate of growth in government is not to be treated as a constant in future projections (see also OECD, 1978).

Explaining the growth of government in terms of economic growth implies that a contraction in the economy ought to be matched by a contraction in government. This has not been the case in the past decade. One reason is an artefact of the conventional measure of size. A contraction in the gross national product will, ceteris paribus, make government appear to grow, if the measure of size is the ratio of a constant (public expenditure) to a contracting figure (the gross national product). A second reason is political. In periods of economic contraction, government is expected to increase expenditure in order to counteract the consequences of recession. The failure of anti-spending politicians such as Margaret Thatcher and Ronald Reagan to reduce the size of government in part reflects counter-cyclical expenditures on unemployment benefits triggered by economic recession.

Consumer demand. The readiness of economists to analyse the growth of government has led to the proliferation of market-oriented theories of politics, which reduce the actual complexities of a mixed economy to a simple theoretical model of a market with only consumers and producers. The political rationale for doing so is that there is (or should be) voter sovereignty as there is (or ought to be) consumer sovereignty. In fact, government does not operate like a producer in the market. Its revenue is coerced by taxation; it is not provided voluntarily by the consumers of its services. The distribution of programme outputs depends upon political bargains in which each potential recipient is not able to determine what he or his family receives.

Buoyant revenue. Another theory of economic growth leading to government growth sidesteps the complex question of government choice and consumer preferences. It is based upon a technical feature of revenue systems, namely, that revenue will increase when activity in the economy increases as long as (and because) tax rates are unchanged. Most taxes are not levied as a fixed sum, but as a percentage of income or sales. If the economy grows by 10 percent, a sales tax of 5 percent will yield 10 percent more revenue. By doing nothing, government can increase government revenue painlessly from the fiscal dividend of economic growth. If an economy grows by 20 percent in the life of a Parliament, then, at its end government revenue can increase 20 percent and the take-home pay of an average citizen can increase by 20 percent too. Income tax, the major tax in most Western countries, is inclined to increase public revenue faster than the economy grows, because it is progressive; as income rises, a progressively higher proportion of income is paid in tax.

For the past decade public revenues have been buoyed up far more by inflation than by economic growth. Because taxes are levied in current money values, an increase in income resulting from inflation will increase tax revenue, as if it had been produced by real growth. Inflation rates of 10 percent or more a year have generated very large increases in the money value of public revenue, without any proportionate increase in the provision of public goods and services. In so far as taxes are progressive and rates are not indexed, then inflation will push taxpayers into higher and higher tax brackets.

Buoyant costs. If the costs of government rise faster than the costs of producing goods and services in the private sector, then as long as government is committed to producing the same volume of goods and services (that is, a constant amount of education, health and housing), the size of government will slowly grow as a proportion of the total national product, owing to this relative price effect. A study of OECD nations from 1950 to 1970 found that the median overall price increase for government expenditure was 170 percent, compared with an overall national price increase of 101 percent (Beck, 1976, 1979; Heller, 1981).

A variety of reasons can explain why government costs rise faster than costs in the private sector. The most parsimonious is offered by William Baumol (1967). Productivity in the service sector increases more slowly than productivity in manufacturing; in so far as government is more a producer of services than is the private sector, government's costs will rise faster, and thus account for more of the national product. The relative price effect is not a proposition alleging the inefficiency of government services. It is an empirical proposition that applies as and when: (a) government programmes are disproportionately in the service sector; (b) the growth of productivity in the service sector is lower than in manufacturing; (c) public sector wages are comparable to private sector wages that reward workers for productivity increases; (d) the government continues to provide public services at a level that is constant in volume terms.

An alternative interpretation of the rising cost of government is that it is caused by governmental inefficiency. Inefficiency is said to result from the fact that most government activities are non-market, that is, public goods and services are usually not sold to individual consumers who signal their demands by purchasing these services. Most activities of government are financed by taxes unconnected with the goods and services that they finance. Wolf (1979) hypothesizes that non-market failures of government will occur because of the substitution of the goals of public officials for consumer wants; diseconomies of increased scale; and the externalization of costs of compliance upon citizens. Savas (1982) has catalogued a variety of American examples, such as refuse collection, where public services may be undertaken more cheaply by private contractors setting prices in competition with each other. In so far as these critics of big government are correct, the growth of government increases benefits for public employees much more than it increases benefits for citizens.

Important as economic changes are, they are only one dimension of a complex of changes in society. To concentrate exclusively upon economic change is to reduce both the causes and consequences of government growth to a one-dimensional analysis of the cash nexus. Since the dominant values of government are political and social rather than pecuniary, this is inadequate. Two very specific types of social change are potentially important influences upon the size of government: demographic change and changes in social structure.

Demographic change. Many government programmes are directed at particular age groups, such as education for children, and pensions for the elderly. Many programmes have an age-related distributional bias: health care goes disproportionately to the elderly, and crime increases with the proportion of young people in a nation's population. When laws establishing public programmes make a citizen's age the prime determinant of entitlement to education or a pension, then the size of the programme is determined by the number of youths or elderly who can claim this benefit. The more children there are, the more schools need to be built; and the more elderly people there are, the more money government must spend on pensions. In such circumstances, a government does not need to take any decision to increase the scale of these programmes. As long as it does not repeal laws entitling people to these benefits, then the programmes are bound to grow.

A striking feature of demographic trends is that they can reverse. It can confidently be predicted that public provision of pensions will grow in the 1980s in nearly every Western nation, because of the growth in the proportion of the elderly people in the population. At the same time, in most Western countries there will be a contraction in the proportion of the population of school age (OECD, 1979: Table 2.3). In so far as demographic factors are the sole determinant of programmes, this implies a contraction in education, a major programme of the welfare state. It is an open question whether education services, which expanded rapidly in response to an earlier baby boom, will contract in proportion to the fall in the number of youths to be educated.

Changes in social structure. Welfare services existed before the creation of the welfare state; many of these services, such as care of the elderly and the sick, were provided within the home or by religious and charitable foundations. Social changes have led to an alteration in relationships between generations and in the tendency of women to remain at home to look after families. The rise in the proportion of women going out to work has led to a demand for public care for children, whether in schools or nurseries, and removed a source of voluntary care for the elderly. Today, women who once cared for children or elderly parents as unpaid family workers are often public employees caring for children as teachers, or looking after the elderly as nurses or social workers (Rose, 1983c).

An increase in education can increase demand for public goods and services. A more educated population can demand more public goods and services, such as education for their children and social services for the elderly. As more educated people tend to have higher incomes, they have more discretionary income to pay for such programmes.

Historically, urbanization has had a major impact on the size of government, for people living in cities require services not needed in the countryside, and are far better placed to make their demands effective politically (Newton, 1980). In contemporary Western societies, population movements within metropolitan regions from cities to suburbs and back — and from urban areas to the small surrounding towns — create pressures for the expansion of government. The relative burden of maintaining central city services increases as the number and average income of city residents drops, while the cost of maintaining roads, bridges, libraries and other central place services remains constant or increases. New suburbs have no backlog of social investment; they require many public facilities to be built at present-day inflated capital costs. People who move to small towns and the countryside may retain a desire for higher standards of public services than their rural neighbours have been content with, thus increasing demand for public services in areas that are no longer rural. The interregional movement of population can have similar effects upon public services. Even if total population remains constant in size, the movement of people around a country can increase the total demand for public services.

Many social changes affect government only indirectly. A decline in the proportion of the population in the working class will, if occupation is a principal determinant of voting behaviour, depress the vote for socialist parties. In so far as this causes a socialist party to lose an election it would otherwise have won, and in so far as the victorious party pursues different policies, then changes in social class structure may indirectly cause changes in government activities. Such a theory is about political change influencing the size of government, for the crucial condition is said to be a change in party control of government for which socioeconomic change is neither a necessary nor sufficient condition.

Political influences upon the size of government

Political change cannot be reduced to social change. The kinds of changes that can be explained or predicted are often obvious to the point of banality: modern bureaucracies require a substantial degree of popular literacy, and welfare states a substantial degree of wealth. Concern with a broad sweep of history can dismiss as mere details what is important here and now — the character and scale of governments that are relatively similar in socioeconomic conditions, all being members of OECD; similar in political fundamentals, having free elections; and yet different from each other in the scale of their resources.

It is far more difficult to specify *how* politics influences government than to decide *whether* politics influences government. By definition, political action is a necessary if not always a sufficient condition of government action. This is true whether the initial stimulus comes from economic or social changes and is simply mediated by political institutions, or whether political initiatives are the primary stimulus to government action.

Two very different types of political influences can influence the size of government. The first set concentrates upon values and wants: government is the size it is because it provides what people value and want. The second set emphasizes the long-term compounding of established inertia commitments; government is the size it is because of a process of events compounding through the years. The first set of explanations faces the present and future: government is and can be whatever size influential groups want. By contrast, the second set faces the past: the size of government today is a reflection of past events more than present choice; the outcome is unwanted or unintended by any individual or group.

Values

To attribute influence to political values is to put purpose back into politics. The actions that make government big are explicable in terms of purposeful values. Before asking the interest group question — What are politicians getting out of this? — the approach poses the question — What are politicians getting at? A generation of realist and behaviouralist analysis, as Anderson (1978: 34f.) notes, has meant that 'the latent functions of political activity have all but driven the manifest functions of politics from the eyes of social scientists'. To correct this imbalance, Anderson stresses the need, 'first of all, to understand what policymakers think they are doing in their own terms'.

Values can be very broad; a desire to have a more or less equal distribution of income in society is not the object of a single programme, but the over-arching rationale for a wide variety of government activities. Values can also be very narrow; for example, a local conservation society can seek to apply land-use planning regulations to conserve a limited number of buildings in its municipality. In addition to differing in breadth and specificity, values can also differ in the extent to which they are readily amenable to quantitative analysis or involve 'priceless' judgements. If it is assumed that the desire to end poverty is the value that motivates a programme, then it is necessary to have a quantifiable measure of this value, in order to know whether or not the programme is succeeding in this intent. It is usually far easier to state values in words than to measure values with numbers.

Many books invoke the concept of political culture in order to explain observed differences between countries by differences in cultural values. Changes from one stage to another in the development of the welfare state may be correlated with changes in values. For example, Heclo (1981: 386f.) relates the changes in the welfare state in the past century to changes in the priority given such values as liberty, equality and security. King (1973) explains the absence of the welfare state in America by reference to the presumed individualist values of Americans, for which the absence of a welfare state is evidence. The danger of this strategy is that a correlation between government actions and values can reflect the influence of institutions upon values as well as of values upon institutions. In trying to employ values as an explanation for the size of government, there is always the danger of treating the present size of government as proof that this is what people value.

Because governments with very different values are often similar in scale, many properties of government cannot be reduced to explanation by values. Government on the scale of the contemporary welfare state is *not* simply a reflection of democratic, egalitarian values. One striking example is the rise of the welfare state in the Second German Reich under the patronage of Bismarck and Kaiser Wilhelm, well before its rise in liberal-democratic Britain. The welfare state could be introduced by a regime as 'a defence against full political citizenship', as well as in consequence of egalitarian values (Flora, 1981: 72f.). Even more striking is Pryor's (1968) analysis of public expenditure in Eastern and Western Europe in the postwar era, showing that communist and anti-communist regimes similarly devote substantial resources to such welfare state programmes as health and education.

Wants and demands

Political wants and demands can be treated as the primary determinant of the activities and scale of government. Wants are not an object of moralizing; they are more akin to interests than to values. When actively articulated, wants become demands for government action. In a simple model of democracy, demands are meant to determine what government does. The question then becomes: Whose wants and demands are most important?

What the voters want. In liberal democratic theories, the wants of voters are meant to be of greatest importance, but empirical research undertaken by liberal democrats has shown that there are many obstacles to translating popular wants into public policies. Surveys show that voters do not have opinions about many major issues confronting governors, and that those with opinions often divide, thus giving no clear guidance for action. Moreover, where clear majority judgements exist, they may be a retrospective endorsement of a successful measure, without assurance that repeating the action would guarantee success and therefore popular approval. Moreover, the views of mass publics can change in reaction to the success or failure of particular programmes and politicians. Public opinion is far more volatile than the institutions of government (Paldam, 1981: 194). A programme or institution established in the belief that it is what the voters want can persist and grow, even if it becomes unpopular.

Whereas public opinion surveys typically ask voters to evaluate a single programme, the size of government reflects the sum total of many separate programmes. It must reflect the costs of government as well as the benefits. The British Gallup Poll finds no agreement among voters about where the line should be drawn between costs and benefits. It asks respondents to state a preference between three different courses of government action: increasing taxes and welfare services; decreasing taxes and welfare services; and leaving things as they are. In the life of the 1979 Thatcher government, the median respondent usually favoured leaving things as they are, but the largest single group usually favoured increased growth in government's taxing and spending. There is no consistent and clear majority for any one policy (Rose, 1983a: Table 1).

What politicians or bureaucrats want. Some theories of politics assume that the size of government reflects the activities of self-interested people with the maximum opportunity to influence government, namely, politicians and bureaucrats. In this model (Schumpeter, 1952; Brittan, 1975), politicians are entrepreneurs bidding for votes in single-minded pursuit of the goal of election or re-election. In the absence of a budget constraint in election campaigns, it is in the short-term interest of both candidates and voters to push the bidding up, thus increasing the scale of government's activities, as election pledges are redeemed. The self-interest of bureaucrats is said to favour the growth of government too (Niskanen, 1971). It increases the responsibilities of individual bureaucrats and the benefits they are credited with providing, thereby raising their power, status and salaries. Politicians promise to increase the scale of government activities at election times for their own interest, and bureaucrats working in the interest of bureaucrats enable them to deliver their promises.

While many politicians and bureaucrats often have an interest in the expansion of government, this need not always be the case, either in theory or practice. In theory, entrepreneurial politicians could seek popularity by promising to cut taxes and spending when this appeared popular, as has been done by many right-of-centre politicians in the face of economic difficulties, most notably Ronald Reagan and Margaret Thatcher. Bureaucrats do not benefit from the expansion of the largest spending programme of government, the provision of old-age pensions; the money finances computer-written checks to pensioners, nor the wages of public officials. Moreover, there are costs as well as benefits in a bureaucrat making his bureau bigger, and risks in promoting the growth of government when this can be controversial or mobilize effective opposition (cf. Holden, 1966).

To construct a theory of the growth of government on the self-interest of individuals is to turn politics into an asocial or antisocial activity. It is also to ignore the constraints that institutions impose upon individuals who hold office within them, and the constraints that the expectations of society place upon the individual pursuit of overt self-interest. In fact, neither politicians nor bureaucrats can do whatever they wish. They are confined by laws, by their own past commitments and by established institutions and expectations, as well as by party political competition.

What parties want. Whether viewed as intermediaries for popular preferences or as originators of programmes, parties are central in representative government. Before thinking of government changing size, we can think of it changing hands with the swing of the electoral pendulum. Elections determine which party controls government, and the party in control is supposed to determine what the government does. From such a perspective, left-wing or socialist governments should make big government bigger still, as socialists favour collective action by the state, and right-wing or bourgeois governments should make government contract, or keep it small (Castles, 1982a).

In contemporary Western countries the distance between Left and Right is less in practice than in theory. The creation of big government has been compatible with the dominance of Christian Democrats in Italy and Socialists in Sweden, and with the alternation of Conservative and Labour governments in Britain. There is empirical evidence to suggest that Catholic parties, proclaiming a social as well as a Christian ideology, do as much to advance big government as any other type of party, if only because they must 'buy' popular support with programme benefits. Socialist parties do not always promote bigger government, and in the face of fiscal difficulties a Labour or socialist government may be better placed to plead 'necessity' as an obstacle to expanding public programmes (Wilensky, 1981; Castles, 1982b). Parties may prefer vague rhetoric to ideology; for example, the campaign that brought the Spanish Socialists to office in 1982 was simply *por el cambio* (for a change); the direction and extent of change was not specified.

Theories of the partisan determination of public policies ignore the many influences upon government that are stronger than parties. The result of a single election does not overturn all past commitments of government: these remain institutionalized in the administration, budget and laws that incoming politicians are sworn to uphold unless or until they can alter them. Nor does an election alter the interest group structure of society. Business firms and trade unions have a permanent stake in the government of a mixed economy, and will continue to press their conflicting demands whatever party is in office. Last and not least, the election of a party to power does not alter the international constraints upon the management of a country's increasingly open and vulnerable political economy (Rose, 1980a: Chapter 8). In so far as government policies change from time to time, circumstances specific to a particular parliament or administration can be of greatest importance (Beck, 1982).

What interest groups want. This model assumes that government is very segmented: each interest group is reckoned to dominate a particular ministry, a particular group of politicians and a particular set of programmes. Because programmes provide benefits disproportionate to the direct cost to the beneficiaries, each interest group will want to increase the scale of its programmes. The simple interest group model, however, ignores the extent to which different institutions of government tend to check each other. This is most evident when departments compete with each other for money to finance their programmes. It also ignores the extent to which interest groups are antagonistic to each other, each seeking to veto the demands of the other. A business lobby may capture a Ministry of Industry, but a trade union lobby can capture a Ministry of Employment. Given that the policies of greatest impact usually require the active or passive consent of many ministries — and of government and Parliament collectively — there are many opportunities for interests to veto each other's claims, thus resulting in what some critics have described as pluralistic stagnation. If interest groups are more or less balanced, each cancelling out the influence of another, then their strength should tend to keep government of constant size.

Neo-Marxist writers argue that one interest does in fact dominate government, namely, a more or less narrowly defined capitalist class. Marxist writers (e.g. O'Connor, 1973) argue that capitalists want government to pursue expansionist welfare state programmes, in order to prevent a crisis of under-consumption arising from low wages; to provide minimum social benefits necessary for an educated and pacific labour force; and to legitimate income inequalities by buying off potentially discontented workers. The money spent to legitimate government reduces the profits available to capitalists, thus threatening a crisis of under-investment and the collapse of capitalism. The evidence that Marxists cite to sustain their doctrine of the state as a tool of capitalists can also be cited in support of the hypothesis that government grows bigger because it does what people want. Moreover, free market writers claim that the growth of these programmes promotes Soviet-style socialism.

To explain the size of government as a reflection of political wants and demands is to assume a close fit between these demands and what government does. The scale of government at any one time is believed to reflect the articulate demands and contemporary choices of individuals and groups, whether only one group is meant to be dominant, or the promotion of big government is reckoned to reflect a combination of interests. The ideological dominance of the mixed economy welfare state is not permanent, but is grounded in specific historical circumstances.

If government is said to be the size it is because people want it, this implies that groups can lobby effectively to reduce the size of government. A shift in values to emphasize personal relations as against impersonal bureaucratic relations, or to 'small is beautiful', would reverse the demand for welfare state programmes. If voters decide that they want less government rather than more government, then politicians may adapt accordingly. The incentives for bureaucrats to favour a reduction in the size of government are fewer, but if public resources are reduced, then it becomes in the interest of bureaucrats to reduce the number of public employees among whom a fixed quantity of pay and benefits is shared out. The incentive for interest groups to demand a reduction in the size of government will increase, in so far as the growth of government tends to produce more problems than benefits for those affected — for example, an increase in the regulation of businesses and unions, or in the costs levied in return for the benefits of public policy.

By contrast, theories that explain the growth of government by the inertia of political compounding start from the assumption that the present size of government does not reflect a conscious choice by any group in society; rather, it is a byproduct of past decisions. To suggest this is not to argue that government is

purposeless, for each of the particular decisions that collectively
create big government can have a distinctive historical rationale.
Yet the whole is greater than the sum of its parts. Decisions made
about government in the more or less distant past have
consequences additional to (and sometimes contrary to) the wants
of persons who took them originally, and the importance of this
proposition compounds through time.

The inertia of established commitments

The established commitments of government at any one point in
time do not necessarily reflect the choices or interests of today's
governors; instead, they reflect past decisions taken in the light of
past circumstances that may not remain relevant. Any newly
elected government finds that it must uphold the law of the land.
The commitments that politicians accept with their oath of office
are vast. Even when a country loses a war and its regime is
overthrown, the new regime continues most established
programmes without change. For example, when France moved
from the Fourth to the Fifth Republic in 1958, General de Gaulle
produced a new constitution, but he did not repudiate all the
commitments of previous French regimes.

The major elements of government are persisting commitments.
Laws are not enacted for a day or a year; they are usually enacted
without any limit on their duration. Taxes are not newly enacted
each year; to raise large sums of revenue a government simply
enforces tax laws already on the statute book. The bulk of public
employees do not have to worry about whether their jobs will
continue from year to year or after a general election, for tenure
regulations give them a permanent job. Organizations are
established to persist. A freshly elected government can appoint
new heads to established organizations, but it does not have a free
choice about the organizations its appointees are to direct; these
are laid down in statutes. The bigger government becomes, the
harder it is to reorganize it; continuity of institutions assures
continuity of programmes. Programmes are not altered as easily
as the intentions of politicians, or the verbal gloss given to policies.
The programmes that collectively constitute what government
does are determined by laws, revenues, personnel and

organizations that have far greater persistence than politicians holding office at the will of the electorate.

The modern welfare state is constrained by a fine mesh of commitments spun around it through the years. In theory, a new government could seek to repeal or alter the established commitments of government. But in practice there is little political incentive, for most established programmes create clients who expect these programmes to continue. Even if an election produces a change of the party or coalition in office, it does not mean that most voters want compulsory education abandoned, pension rights repudiated, or the health service returned to the market. The expectations of voters are institutionalized within government by politicians, bureaucrats and ministries responsible for these programmes.

So strong are the established commitments of government that government budgets start from the premise that most revenue is committed to 'uncontrollable' public expenditure, that is, to finance established commitments that must be met unless there is a wholesale repeal of laws on the statute books. In any given year, 75 percent or more of public expenditure will go by on the nod, because there is neither time nor will to challenge these programmes (cf. US Budget, 1982: part 3; ACIR, 1981: 218; Kamlett and Mowery, 1980). France has given official recognition to established commitments, dividing its budget into two parts: the *services votes*, which endorse established commitments in a single parliamentary motion, and the *mesures nouvelles*, a limited number of appropriations requiring scrutiny because of their novelty.

The commitments of government are dynamic. In politics inertia refers to the tendency of a body in motion to continue in motion. A newly elected government is not the custodian of an inert constitution, but jumps on board a set of organizations in motion. Established commitments not only secure the persistence of many elements of government but also provide forward momentum. The question thus becomes: In what direction does inertia lead?

The upward bias of political inertia. The influences on the size of government are not neutral. A bias towards growth in government can be hypothesized as the combined effect of economic and social changes, political values and political wants, as well as the specific consequences of established programme commitments. In the pithy phrase of Aaron Wildavsky (1979), 'Political addition is easier than political subtraction'.

Government as a dissatisfied institution. Whether an organization persists or alters its behaviour depends upon whether it is satisfied with its activities. In a satisficing model, an organization will change to the extent necessary to remove the cause of dissatisfaction (March and Simon, 1958). In addition to demands upon government to grow from those who want more programme outputs, the activities of government can themselves generate dissatisfaction, thus prompting further growth. Scharpf (1981: 14) argues that the unexpected economic challenges facing contemporary Western governments have increased dissatisfaction, as tried and true solutions no longer work in difficult economic circumstances, and governments are forced to search for new programmes.

'Policy as its own cause'. The more programmes that government adopts, the greater the probability that one programme will affect another (Wildavsky, 1979: 65). Interdependence among policies increases faster than knowledge grows. With any new or modified programme there is a high probability that its direct or indirect consequences will cause dissatisfaction as well as satisfaction. The media can publicize dissatisfactions, and excite a clamour for further action to remove the cause of dissatisfaction. Wildavsky argues there is a continuing expansion of programmes in an infinite regression of efforts intended to find the first cause of difficulty, and thus make possible a final solution.

Political imitation or diffusion. In a world with a high degree of political and economic interdependence, no government lives in isolation from its neighbours. The mass media and foreign travel diffuse knowledge of what governments in other countries do. If one country adopts a new welfare programme, there are pressures in countries at similar levels of social and economic development to emulate the programme (cf. Collier and Messick, 1975; Kuhnle, 1981: 127). At the policy making level, institutions such as OECD disseminate among dozens of Western industrial nations information about innovations and the best practices. In the expansive post-1945 world, the standard is not set by the median nation, but by the country that does most in a given field.

Political compounding. Seemingly small changes can have big consequences by compounding through the years. Although the annual rates of change in public revenues and expenditure appear small, the cumulative consequences are big. For example, in the century from 1876 to 1976 public spending in the United Kingdom increased from 3 percent to more than 40 percent of the gross national product, and in the United States from 13 to more than 30 percent. In Sweden, compounding has had an even bigger cumulative effect, increasing public spending from 6 percent of the national product in 1876 to more than 50 percent.

To focus upon the long-term cumulative consequences of seemingly small commitments is a very different perspective from that of politicians, whose time horizon is likely to extend no further than the next general election or the next major controversy in Parliament or Cabinet. It is also a very different perspective from that of many social scientists. The incrementalist model of politics does not consider the long-term impact of the cumulation of short-term incremental changes. Yet ignoring the long-term consequences of inertia is valid only if increases are evenly balanced by decreases, thus generating a cyclical pattern of change. To be concerned with the long term is to look further than the immediate interests of individuals. It is to reject the individualist and hedonistic perspective of J.M. Keynes, exemplified by his epigram, 'In the long run we are all dead.' Government has no biological limit to its life; it goes on and on and on.

In the long run a series of short-term commitments can cumulatively compound into very big commitments. As Aristotle noted, two millennia before free elections were mooted:

The expense is not noticed because it does not come all at once, for the mind is led astray by the repeated small outlays, just like the sophistic puzzle, 'If each is little, then all are a little.' This is true in one way, but in another it is not; for the whole total is not little, but made up of little parts. [Quoted in Larkey et al., 1981: 193]

The long-term consequences of compounding changes for many years can produce a scale of growth very different from what was intended. Social security pensions, which Braybrooke and Lindblom (1964: 72f.) cite as an incremental programme expanded by a series of piecemeal legislative amendments, has had a cumulative effect very different from what was intended by the initial sponsors of social security legislation. When pension programmes were first adopted around the beginning of the twentieth century, the benefit level was intentionally set low, confined to persons of limited means, and the age for claiming a pension was higher than the life expectancy of most manual workers. For example, when pensions were introduced in Britain in 1908, they were for needy persons aged 70 or above, but the average life expectancy of men was only 52 years. A process of lowering standards for entitlement and raising the level of benefits, combined with a dramatic increase in life expectancy, has resulted in old age pensions now being one of the biggest programmes of government, whether size is measured in money spent or in the number of people benefiting.

Shock political events. Any theory of the growth of government must accommodate one-off political events, that is, influences that are neither persisting nor recur regularly, such as the two world wars of this century. Shock events may introduce discontinuities, as in the repudiation of one regime and its replacement by another; or they may distort established programmes, as the absolute priority of military demands in wartime distorts public spending. Peacock and Wiseman (1961: 26ff.) have argued that world wars tend to encourage the growth of government after each war because of their displacement effect. In wartime a government will increase revenue greatly to achieve immediate objectives. Once the war is over, the resources claimed will be displaced in other programmes as the supply of revenue sustains a level of programmes far above what would have been possible in the absence of war.

The weakness of the displacement hypothesis is that it cannot be used to predict system shocks; its strength is that after the event it can explain (or at least accommodate) one-off events that have an impact too big to be ignored. The United States is the major Western nation where the theory has had most relevance since 1945, because America has been involved in major wars in Korea and Vietnam. The displacement theory is of limited help in understanding the growth of Western European governments in the long era of peace since 1945.

A theory that accounts for the size of government as a function of the inertia of established commitments can integrate a variety of social, economic and political influences. The economy grows slowly, but its compound effect upon public revenue is big. In any one year the extent of demographic change in society will be limited; but the impact of population change upon major welfare state programmes cumulatively can be big. In so far as political values and wants are strongly held, they are unlikely to be volatile, but changes in election outcomes show that popular preferences are in no sense fixed. The extent of change induced in any one year by pressure groups is likely to be little, but the cumulative effect can be big.

The best way to estimate the size of government tomorrow is to see how big it was yesterday, how big it is today — and then add a little. To say this is not to argue deterministically. The longer the time span ahead, the more open is the future. Past commitments can lose their force, but their effects decay gradually. Just as an individual's health is influenced more by all the measures taken in the past than by what he or she does today, so the size of government is more a reflection of past causes than contemporary choice.

Consequences of big government

Far more attention has been concentrated upon the causes of government growth than upon the consequences of big government. We know (or think we know) more about why government is big than about the consequences of size. The commonest evaluations are based upon a priori values. People who think government is good in principle believe that bigger government is better government. People who think its actions are harmful believe that bigger government is worse government. The principal studies of the optimum size of government in population terms are inconclusive. After asking, 'Can we say, then, that there is any optimum size for a political system?' Dahl and Tufte (1974: 135) reply, 'Clearly no'.

Because the constituent elements of government are interdependent, the most immediate consequences of any change in one element of government are registered in other elements of government. A large proportion of all activities of government involve relations *within* government, for example, between different ministries, between different bureaus within a government ministry, between politicians and civil servants within a ministry, and between central and local levels of government. Public officials spend a large portion of every day dealing with other public officials. One study of the policy process in Washington found that 70 percent of all actions were initially intended to influence another institution within government. Government actions ultimately influence society, but to do this requires much prior activity within government (Rose, 1976b: 69, 92, 125).

Potentially the most important consequence of big government is the effect of bigness upon political authority. The anxiety found in many discussions of big government arises from the belief that a government that is too big undermines its own authority. In so far as this is true, then a government that is growing of its own internal dynamic is threatened from within, rather than by revolutionaries or alien armies outside its gates. Neo-Marxists agree with monetarists that the growth of government threatens to undermine the authority of government. Instead of the programme outputs of government reinforcing popular support, the growth of government programmes is seen as progressively undermining its authority.

Political authority — the terms of relations between governors and governed — is central to government. Authority has two distinct elements: effectiveness and consent (Rose, 1979). An organization that cannot effectively influence the society around it is not a government. A government that acts without the consent of the governed is not government as we like to think of it in the Western world today. Political authority requires qualitative assessment, not quantitative measurement. We do not say that one regime has greater authority than another: we distinguish between regimes with legitimate or coercive authority.

Effectiveness is the first concern of government. Government is not only about good intentions; it is also about getting things done. Effectiveness is particularly important in big government, for the bigger a government is, the greater the impact of its programmes upon society, whether effective or ineffective. To be effective, a government must be able to mobilize resources, to allocate these resources within its own complex of organizations, and to distribute these resources to further public policies.

In Western nations today, individuals cannot be coerced to do automatically whatever government commands. Consent must be given. When government provides benefits to individuals, co-operation is likely. But government also requires consent for measures that take things from people, for example taxes. In the absence of consent, a government's effectiveness is likely to be reduced. Indifferent citizens may simply ignore government, evading taxes. In the extreme, citizens may actively dissent by demonstrations, illegal protests or armed violence intended to overthrow a regime. Within Western nations armed opposition to authority is rare and support for protest limited (see Table 8.4). But civic indifference, which is far less risky to individual citizens, can be debilitating for governmental effectiveness.

Consent and effectiveness are interrelated. The success of any public programme requires the more or less voluntary co-operation of citizens. A fully legitimate government must have both the consent of citizens, and demonstrate effectiveness in action. A government that lacks both effectiveness and consent has ceased to exist: it can be assigned to the dustbin of history. A regime that loses popular consent but still retains effectiveness may continue to govern — but not in a manner acceptable in Western Europe today. It must govern by coercion, as in Poland. In centuries past a regime that enjoyed popular consent but was ineffective may have survived indefinitely, but such are the demands upon contemporary government that it is unlikely to do so in the Western world today.

The postwar era has shown that big government is compatible with legitimate political authority. Problems of becoming big and remaining effective have been overcome. Even more important, in countries such as Germany, Italy and France, where the legitimacy of authority was uncertain, political consent has been secured. If government does no more than persist in doing what it has been doing before, there is a presumption that its authority will be unaffected. But we cannot assume that what was successful in the past will necessarily be successful in future. Here the question is: What are the consequences for government's effectiveness and consent if a big government grows bigger still?

When a big government grows bigger still, this is immediately likely to effect efficiency, not effectiveness. If organizational growth is subject to diseconomies of scale, then as government organizations grow bigger, more resources will be required to produce the same volume of public goods and services. Equally, if there are economies of scale, growth can lead to increased efficiency. Either way, government remains effective; only its costs are altered.

Loss of effectiveness

It is not the manager's concern with marginal efficiency that disturbs critics of big government: it is the fear that loss of efficiency can gradually lead to a loss in the effectiveness of government. As a big government grows bigger, a number of factors may contribute to its loss of effectiveness.

Limitations upon mobilizing resources. Money is the major resource constraint upon government. The size of the national product sets a limit to taxation. The growth of big government has shown that there is no particular ceiling on taxation. But few politicians would argue that doubling taxes would today double the amount of revenue collected. A buoyant economy is a surer way to increase public revenue by the expansion of the tax base. In so far as the high levels of taxation that accompany big government cause a slowing down in the rate of economic growth — a hypothesis about which there are differences among economists — then a growing government is subject to a tighter and tighter revenue constraint.

Of the three principal resources of government, laws are unique in being free; government has the capacity to enact all the laws it wishes. Moreover, since laws can be drafted and enacted at a relatively low cost, there is no theoretical limit to the amount of additional legislation that a big government could enact. The practical limits are imposed by the clock, the calendar and politics; there is a limit to the time and number of days that a Parliament can devote to discussing and voting upon bills each year. A second major constraint upon legislation is the need for political support to secure enactment.

In times of full employment, government will compete with private sector employers for scarce workers, thus limiting the proportion working for government. This is most true in tasks where the skills of workers are easily transferred, such as secretaries and manual labourers; it is less the case in such programmes as education, where government has a virtual monopoly in the employment of teachers. Labour shortages did not prevent the growth of government in times of full employment; in an era of unemployment, government's expansion is not limited by labour shortages, and many people would regard the expansion of public employment as a positive good.

Increasing organizational complexity. Large-scale organizations are pervasive in modern society. The modern state and the modern corporation, whether national or multi-national, reflect the ability of individuals to work effectively within highly specialized, impersonal bureaucratic frameworks, and big trade unions demonstrate the capacity for effective organization by employees. The effectiveness of organization is not, however, absolute. Hood (1976) has shown the limits to the effectiveness of any organization. Yet to say that an organization will be less than 100 percent effective is not to prove that its effectiveness will decline if it grows bigger still.

As government becomes bigger, its leaders may respond by further and further subdivision and specialization within a large organization, such as a Ministry of Defence, or by dividing tasks among a number of organizations, some new and some well established. The aim is the same: to limit the size of any one organization to what is 'manageable' or 'effective'. It is not so much the total size of government that creates organizational difficulties as the size of any one governmental organization. By creating new subdivisions within existing organizations and new organizations, government limits the size of any one organization, but no limit is placed upon the overall size of government.

Creating more organizations — or what comes to the same thing, more separately identified bureaus and agencies within an increasingly complex ministry — threatens to reduce government's effectiveness by increasing the probability of inter-organizational conflict. The subdivision of labour does not remove the interdependence of organizations with related tasks. What it does is to create agencies that have narrowly defined interests, and political resources to advance these interests. The resulting boundary disputes may be resolved, but the lengthy process of inter-organizational bargaining can reduce the effectiveness of existing programmes, and increase the difficulties of implementing new programmes (Hanf and Scharpf, 1978; Pressman and Wildavsky, 1973).

An increasing reliance upon 'soft' technologies. Whether a given programme is effective depends upon the relationship between its objectives and the means it has at hand. The means-ends technologies available to government agencies vary greatly from programme to programme. At one extreme, there are well tested 'hard' technologies, such as civil engineering, which since the days of the Roman Empire has given government the means to build roads, bridges and aqueducts. At the other extreme are social programmes intended to abolish poverty or crime — but lacking an effective means of doing so. In between are a number of relatively effective social technologies for such ends as teaching reading, writing and arithmetic.

Government will not lose effectiveness as long as the growth of government is confined to programmes with well tested means-ends technologies. For example, there is no reason to anticipate a decline in government's effectiveness if it doubles the number of infant schools to meet an increase in young children in the population, or increases the number of pensions paid to meet an increase in the number of elderly people. In so far as government introduces new programmes, then it is attempting to do things that it has not done before. By definition, the effectiveness of new measures is untested; new programmes are thus likely to have a higher failure rate than established programmes. Government's already established programmes are easier to accomplish, because government has tended to undertake, first, programmes where its technology is 'harder', leaving more difficult tasks for later.

An increase in contradictions between programmes. When government was relatively small, programmes were few in number and government sought to influence only a limited number of social activities. The probability of one programme affecting another was thereby limited. The growth of government has been intensive as well as extensive. In addition to attempting things not done before, government also adopts new programmes in areas that are already the subject of intensive government action. Increasing the number of programmes directed at a given problem — say, the economy — disproportionately increases the probability that new programmes will affect already established programmes. Whereas a century ago governments tended to confine their economic concern to worrying about a budget deficit, today governments also worry about unemployment, economic growth, international trade, industrial re-structuring, and inflation.

The more programmes become interdependent, the greater the probability of contradictions between programmes. Politics involves the articulation of conflicting views about what government ought to do, and about which programmes should have priority. In so far as more of society's activities become the object of government programmes, then more conflicts are internalized within government. Government programmes do not cause social conflict; they reveal existing differences of opinion about social priorities and goals. For example, the conflict between inflation and unemployment antedates the creation of the mixed economy welfare state. The creation of the welfare state changes what was formerly a contradiction within society to a contradiction between goals of government.

Reduction of popular consent
The impact of big government upon political consent is arguable. In so far as the most important areas of politics concern priceless values, these need not be affected by changes in the size of government. It is the structure of values that is of first importance. The existence of zero-sum conflicts, in which victory for one group means an unacceptable loss for the other, is the most likely cause of a regime losing full consent. This is more likely to arise from conflicts about national identity, religion or language, than from class differences. The latter can be resolved by bargaining about economic relationships, whereas religious and nationalist values do not admit of bargaining (Rose, 1971: Chapter 14). Northern Ireland illustrates the irrelevance of government's size to conflicts about political consent. By most measures, this 1.5 million people subsystem of the United Kingdom is small — except by the measure of numbers killed in political violence since 1971.

To argue that bigger government makes for greater consent is to make two assumptions for which evidence is lacking. The first is that popular consent rests upon government providing material benefits. This is palpably false. Whereas the welfare state is a relatively recent creation, usually dating only from the post-1945 era, many Western governments enjoyed popular consent for generations before. It is also incorrect to assume that the benefits provided by government programmes are cost-free. Critics of big government argue that it is the cost of welfare state programmes that is the biggest threat to popular consent to government.

Political consent cannot be taken for granted, for no regime is completely invulnerable to challenges to its authority. The question is: Under what circumstances can the growth of big government reduce popular consent? As big government grows bigger, a number of factors may reduce popular consent.

Excessive claims upon resources. Although laws are cheap to enact, they can be costly to implement. In so far as the growth of government involves more and more legal regulation of social affairs (as distinct from providing material benefits), the compliance costs falling upon citizens will increase. By definition, a new law to affect social behaviour seeks to make people forgo customary activities because of their loyalty to government. But the stock of civic loyalty is not unlimited. The more citizens are asked to accept government regulation of behaviour, the greater the probability that occasions may arise in which citizens decide to act outside the law. If the propensity to ignore a law is a constant among citizens, then doubling laws will also double the number of law violations. If the propensity to ignore laws increases with their quantity, then law-breaking will increase disproportionately.

If the growth of government increases claims for tax revenues, this will risk popular consent, in so far as increased tax demands reduce the readiness of the population to pay taxes. To a substantial extent, the payment of taxes depends upon voluntary co-operation between tax collectors and taxpayers. Without co-operation, government must accept a high degree of tax evasion and must rely upon taxes that are hard to evade; this is the case in France and Italy. In so far as government claims on revenue grow faster than individual earnings, take-home pay will decrease as a function of government's income rising. If this happens, a decline in popular consent need not be carried to popular rebellion. Instead, it can lead to civic indifference; rather than voluntarily co-operating with government's revenue demands, citizens may put their own economic interest first, avoiding and evading taxes (see Rose and Peters, 1978a; Rose, 1983a).

If the growth of government increases the number of public employees, this too can threaten popular consent, if public employees use their number and political skills to further their own ends. This could happen from good intentions, for example, because teachers believe that they know best what pupils and parents should do. In so far as the professional standards of public employees effectively govern what public employees do, ordinary citizens, as non-professionals, will have increasing cause to resent public servants acting as elitist guardians, and may react by withdrawing consent to the authority of experts.

The loss of responsiveness in organizations. 'The client is part of the organization' is a maxim that is even more apt in politics than in business (Barnard, 1938). In democratic systems of government the wishes of citizens are meant to determine the goods and services of government, as well as election outcomes. Yet the growth of government greatly attenuates the lines of communication between politicians elected to head a government department, and individuals who actually deliver its services to citizens. The base of the organizational pyramid becomes further from the minister on top, and more layers of officials intervene between the teacher, the policeman or the social worker, and the elected politician meant to direct these officials.

Instead of responding to directions from elected but distant officeholders, officials may increasingly follow professional norms, or personal convenience. Concurrently, the impersonality necessary in any large bureaucracy can appear as unresponsive or uncaring behaviour, making bureaucrats appear indifferent to popular wishes, thus causing citizens to feel less positive loyalty to the organizations of government.

The growth of 'improper' programmes. In so far as Western nations are mixed societies as well as mixed economies, distinctions exist between what it is proper for government to do (e.g., regulating public health) and what is an improper subject of government regulation (e.g., regulating population by compulsory sterilization). The range of activities deemed unsuited for government action has been contracting with the growth of government. Differences between Western and Eastern Europe illustrate that it is possible for government to do too much — at least by the standards of Western democracies. When big government grows bigger still, the greater is the probability that, accidentally or by intent, it will adopt programmes that a large fraction of the population regard as improper, thus weakening popular consent.

Assessing the consequences of big government for political authority involves two very different types of judgements, quantitative and qualitative. Judgements about the impact of size upon government's effectiveness are to some extent amenable to quantification, especially if losing effectiveness is defined as an increase in inefficiency beyond a certain threshold. Yet even if government lost much of its effectiveness, it would still be able to do a lot. Moreover, programmes that appear to be of doubtful effectiveness from one perspective (e.g., industrial subsidies to declining industries) might appear positively effective from another (e.g., from the viewpoint of the workers and firms receiving the benefits).

Political consent involves qualitative values first and foremost. Government's size is not a determinant of basic value conflicts within society; in Western nations revolutionary conflicts occurred before government became big. A Western government that grew too big would not necessarily meet with popular revolt, but the process of growth could unintentionally increase citizen indifference. In such circumstances government could still continue, but it would not go on as before.

3 THE USE OF LAWS AS A POLICY RESOURCE

Laws are a unique resource of government. Whereas any organization can raise and spend money and employ people to produce goods and services, only a government can enact laws,which tell people what they can and cannot do, and regulate social life. Whereas government usually claims less than half a country's gross national product as taxes and less than one-third of the labour force as public employees, it enacts 100 percent of the laws of a society. Because statutory authority is required for government action, laws are a necessary part of any public policy.

Laws tend to determine the scope of government, establishing the variety of things that government can and cannot do and the circumstances in which public agencies may act. Laws do not determine every action of government; instead, they set out more or less tightly defined guidelines for action. The ambiguities of language and of life inevitably leave much discretion in the interpretation of statutes (Hood, 1976: 59ff.). Furthermore, many laws are permissive rather than directive: they state what policymakers or citizens may do, not what they must do.

Laws are a resource of government that can be used in many different ways. In the first place, laws differ in whom they affect. Laws may regulate the behaviour of government itself; a substantial portion of every statute book lays down procedures that public officials must follow. Laws may regulate relations between individual citizens and government, or they may regulate relations between citizens. Second, laws differ in how they regulate actions. Laws may mandate behaviour, either prohibiting or compelling specified actions, or they may be permissive. Some laws compel individuals to do what they would not wish to do voluntarily (e.g. pay taxes or serve a term in the army) or forbid their doing what they might wish to do (e.g. drive at very high speed). In every Western nation, one set of laws compels children to be educated for a minimum number of years, whereas another simply states conditions for continuing education beyond the legal minimum. Third, programme objects differ; the typical welfare state law confers material benefits on individuals, just as nineteenth-century liberal legislation conferred political rights.

63

Finally, laws vary greatly in their impact upon other resources of government. Some laws, such as statutes concerning marriage and divorce, involve little public money or personnel. Others, concerning education and health services, require lots of money and employees to be effective. A third type of law makes a big claim upon public revenue but not upon public personnel, for example, entitling the elderly to a pension. Laws can be a necessary but not a sufficient condition of government action. One Act of Parliament can authorize a programme, but another is needed to determine how much money can be spent to implement the first Act's intentions.

The statutes in force at any given time reflect a great variety of political, social and economic influences. Custom and tradition were once more or less adequate to regulate society's affairs. The church, landowners and their associates set community norms. An illiterate agricultural worker without a vote, living in a tied cottage from which he could be dismissed by the landlord without notice, was subject to many forms of social regulation independent of Acts of Parliament. The rise of the modern state has substituted public law-making for private regulation. Whereas all laws need voluntary acceptance to be fully effective, a characteristic of modern representative government is the requirement that laws be endorsed by an elected Parliament. Political consent has replaced custom as the chief authority for laws.

The growth in government's activities, however, makes it very difficult for any Parliament to debate all the regulations of government. Whereas questions of principle, such as universal suffrage, could be and were debated by MPs, questions about chemical pollution or aircraft safety involve technical judgements about which elected representatives are usually not expert (cf. Dahl, 1970). Nor do elected politicians have the time to consider every clause of a law. Bureaucrats, by virtue of their expertise and strategic involvement in implementing programmes, fill the gap left by default of elected legislators. Today, bureaucrats are bound not only by rules but also by de facto rule-makers.

Members of Parliament today show limited concern with their role as lawmakers. They are partisans first and foremost, with a healthy interest in advancing their careers by articulating views about issues. Concern can be shown by an adroit parliamentary question, by a clever intervention in debate or committee, or by speeches outside Parliament that catch the attention of the media. Influencing the administration of existing laws to the benefit of constituents is another activity of MPs. In the British House of Commons, less than half the time is nominally devoted to the discussion of bills; of this a substantial amount is in fact used to make partisan and constituency points unrelated to the legislative task at hand (Borthwick, 1981: 66; Drewry, 1972). The lack of interest in legislation by nominal lawmakers is particularly striking, given that a disproportionate number of legislators in Western parliaments are lawyers by training (Blondel, 1973: 160).

Legal anthropologists have shown that every society has some fundamental legal problems in common, even though they respond in very different ways (Hoebel, 1954). Legal scholars conventionally distinguish between two major families of law in Western nations: the Roman or civil law tradition, dating back more than two thousand years, and the common law tradition, dating back nearly a millennium in England. The civil law tradition is the more widespread; only countries once subject to British rule, including the United States, have a common law base. There are major differences within each tradition. The activism of the American courts in interpreting the common law contrasts with the passive role of English judges. The rationalistic approach of the French Code Napoleon of 1804 differs from the historical jurisprudence reflected in the 1896 German codification of law. There are also similarities: common law judges consider legislative statutes as well as historical cases, and Roman law judges often have to examine past cases to discover how abstract and general codes can fit the facts of particular cases.

The comparative analysis of laws as a resource of government is doubly difficult. Laws are pre-eminently verbal instruments; their meaning is embedded in a nation's language and political culture. Laws are written in eight different languages for the ten nations of the European Community. The law is notorious for the use of distinctive phraseology. Lawyers hold that legal documents lose meaning when translated from their distinctive form to everyday language. In so far as this is true, translation of laws from one language to another will lose even more nuance.

A systematic comparative analysis of the use of law as a policy resource of big government cannot be undertaken with the precision accorded to an analysis of taxation or public employment, for laws are not readily amenable to quantitative measurement. None the less, it is possible to marshall some quantitative measures to test comparatively whether or not the growth of government is matched by the growth in legislation.

In this chapter the first section addresses the problem of measuring the scale of laws, a necessary step in determining whether the annual volume of legislation is growing or contracting. The quantity of laws looks very different depending upon whether one looks at the number of laws enacted in a single session of Parliament, or the total number of laws in force. Statute books may appear bulky because of the contemporary actions of big government, or because of the inertia accumulation of laws enacted by past Parliaments. The second section evaluates the relative importance of pressure group and partisan influences for the enactment of legislation. The third section considers major effects of laws: whether the persistence of past laws makes the statute book increasingly obsolete as society changes; whether laws usually establish norms for behaviour or authorize the allocation of public money and employees; and to what extent lawmaking by elected parliaments is being superseded by the promulgation of regulations by non-elected bureaucrats.

The inertia accumulation of laws

In theory, government grows without any change in the number of laws on the statute books. When more people live longer, no new law is required to increase the total money to which pensioners are entitled; nor is legislation required to increase the pension, if an automatic cost-of-living increase is written into an existing pensions act. Expenditure on such 'uncontrollable' programmes could be limited only by amending or repealing laws entitling people to costly benefits. Nor is new legislation required to increase the number of public employees, given a large body of existing laws about the recruitment and tenure of public officials. If the growth of government were completely independent of legislation, then measures of government revenue and public employment would be sufficient. In fact, new laws are annually added to the statute book.

If each Act of Parliament made an identical claim for money and employees, there would be no need to analyse laws as a separate policy resource. Readily quantified measures of money and manpower would be precise and sufficient indicators of the scale of legislation. In fact, laws differ greatly in the extent to which they imply the need for government to mobilize money or manpower.

Some laws, for example, company law or the law of probate, make virtually no claim upon government resources; they simply regulate social activities of individuals and organizations. The resources relevant to put a law into effect are variable, not constant.

The need to study the use of laws as a policy resource is particularly pressing, since laws have tended to be ignored by money-oriented policy analysis. The assertion that laws are of no consequence, and provide no knowledge additional to that obtained from the fiscal system and public employment, can be justified only by a careful and thorough analysis of law as a policy resource. The evidence in this chapter and in Chapter 7 shows that laws differ from taxes and employees as a policy resource in ways significantly related to the size of government.

Laws are far less amenable to quantitative measurement than are other major resources of government. Whereas one hundred units of revenue can be much the same as another hundred, one law will not be the same as another law. There is no standard international (or national) measure of laws, as there is a metric system for measuring length, or international currencies like the dollar and the Deutsche Mark. Each statute is unique in its specific content. The specific qualities of each law are at least as important as the generic characteristics basic to quantification. To attempt to measure the volume of laws is to go against the grain of conventional legal scholarship.

Legal scholarship has generally been non-quantitative in nature, limited to the sorts of questions and to the kinds of research that lend themselves to the interpretation of prescriptions, . . . addressed to interests more like those of the philosopher or the historian of ideas than those of the social scientist. [Merryman et al., 1971: 14]

The fact that lawyers generally think about single statutes, court cases or specific historical circumstances does not mean that the law is without regularities. Only the existence of regularities allows a lawyer or a judge to advise what is or is not a legally correct way to behave. Without predictable patterns in the law, neither lawyers nor laypersons could expect to know what the law is. The existence of patterns assists measurement, for it implies a persistence or constancy through time, making it possible to devise legal indicators to measure changes in laws through time.

An indicator such as the number of laws passed in a single session of Parliament does not tell us everything we want to know, but it can offer evidence relevant to questions of special concern here. No indicator can tell us everything we want to know about a government programme. The fact that a pound or a dollar spent on bombs purchases a very different product from money spent in education does not negate the use of money as a measuring rod of public policy. Because laws about marriage and divorce differ from laws about pensions, this does not mean that no generalizations are possible about law as a policy resource. The heterogeneity of laws is no greater than the heterogeneity of the objects of public expenditure.

The simplest measure is a count of the number of laws that a national parliament enacts each year. The quantity of legislation cannot measure the quality of laws, but it can identify countries where legislators do a lot or a little lawmaking and indicate the annual rate of legislation. One can thus test whether there are systematic differences between Roman law and common law countries in the rate of legislation. It could be hypothesized that Roman law countries enact more laws in order to provide a more comprehensive code of regulation, whereas common law countries enact fewer laws, because of a preference for judicial interpretation.

The annual amount of legislation varies substantially from country to country, but differences occur among common law countries, and among Roman law countries (Table 3.1). In 13 Western nations covered by an Inter-Parliamentary Union survey, the most laws were enacted in Italy (588) and America (452), and the least in Canada (53) and Switzerland (21). The average number of laws enacted annually in common law countries is nearly the same (192) as the figure for Roman law countries (200).

One test of the importance of a law is whether or not it is a government bill. Nearly every parliament makes separate provision for bills introduced by the government of the day as distinct from bills introduced by MPs acting as private members. When government legislation is examined, the annual rate of legislation is substantially decreased (Table 3.1). On average, a government puts forward 138 bills to Parliament each year, and 113 are enacted. Government bills have a success rate of 82 percent. The fact that more government bills are enacted in Roman law than in common law countries probably reflects differences in partisan and parliamentary traditions. For example, the American President is uniquely weak, for he is the only government leader likely to have more than half his proposals rejected. A government with a parliamentary system is virtually certain of having at least two-thirds of all government proposals enacted as law. Excluding the very atypical cases of the United States and Italy, 87 percent of all laws enacted by a Parliament in a given year are government measures.

TABLE 3.1
National variations in laws enacted annually

	All Acts (annual total)	Gov't-sponsored
Common law countries		
United States	452	47
New Zealand	162	143
Britain	148	69
Australia	145	145
Canada	53	44
Average	192	90
(Range)	(53-452)	(44-145)
Roman law countries		
Italy	588	103
Netherlands	271	270
Denmark	178	177
Austria	170	143
Belgium	163	150
Germany	111	90
France	93	67
Switzerland	29	27
Average	200	128
(Range)	(29-588)	(27-270)

Sources: Principally calculated from Inter-Parliamentary Union (1976: Table 49); US Presidential figures, annual average, 1970-75, calculated from Wayne (1978: Table 5.2); Italy: calculated from Merryman et al. (1971: Chapter 5), annual average for 1968-70.

In the great majority of Western nations today the executive branch of government, not the nominal legislature, is the chief initiator of laws. Parliament's role is to endorse the legislative proposals of the government rather than to scrutinize, amend or defeat government proposals (Griffith, 1974). The readiness of parliament to endorse government measures is particularly striking, for most of the countries reviewed here have coalition governments. Coalition governments in the Netherlands, Belgium and Switzerland are even more likely to have their bills endorsed by parliament than a single-party government in Britain.

When the text of laws is examined, there are very striking differences between countries in the extent to which a government spells out the details of a measure in its statutes. This is shown by the great variation in the average length of a law between Britain, France, Ireland and Sweden (Blondel et al., 1969: 75). In France and Sweden there is a tendency to enact relatively short laws; the average French statute in the sample is 600 words long, and the average Swedish statute 1,600 words. By contrast, the average Irish statute is 2,800 words long and the British, 7,500 words. Stylistic differences in legislation also lead to big differences in the average number of clauses contained in each Act. French acts are succinct, averaging only seven clauses, whereas Swedish and British acts average 16 and 19 clauses respectively. Irish laws are the most comprehensive, with 35 clauses.

The result of different national styles in writing Acts of Parliament is that the French produce short laws that briefly cover a few points; the Swedes, medium-length laws that briefly cover a variety of points; the Irish, laws that treat a large number of points but do so even more briefly than the French; and the British, long Acts that treat a variety of points at relatively great length.

Britain and Italy illustrate two extremes in the amount and significance of legislation. The British government puts relatively few laws to Parliament each year and the measures that it does put forward are meant to be big in a political as well as a verbal sense. Before a government bill even goes to Parliament, it must survive scrutiny by civil servants and parliamentary draughtsmen who write the laws; by pressure groups likely to be affected by the bill; and by the Cabinet that will be held responsible for the bill. The scrutiny given means that it usually takes two or more years from government approval of the principle of a law to parliamentary enactment. The government of the day proceeds cautiously in using its disciplined parliamentary majority, seeking extra-parliamentary support, in order to avoid mistakes or unpopularity when introducing a bill that is a major commitment of government policy.

By contrast, in Italy the Parliament passes lots of little laws (*leggine*). Notwithstanding the instability and apparent weakness of the Italian government, each year the Italian Parliament passes hundreds of laws. In 1970, for example, the Parliament approved 518 laws; of this total 77 percent were little laws approved by committees of the Parliament, as against 23 percent that were laws examined by the Parliament as a whole (Merryman et al., 1971: Table 5.05). In spite of intense inter-party and factional rivalry, the Italian Parliament is ready to pass hundreds of little laws because they provide small benefits of interest to particular groups of legislators (di Palma, 1977). The Italian Parliament finds it difficult to approve laws that are likely to have a big impact upon society, because these emphasize divisions within the governing coalition. In order to maintain a coalition's temporary unity, there is a tendency to avoid proposing major bills, or else to legislate by *decreti leggi* (decree laws), which were initially meant only for emergency use, but are now being issued on the assumption that nearly every week there is an emergency (Hine, 1981; 72). Similarly, the United States Congress enacts more bills put forward by individual congressmen representing specialized interests than bills put forward by the President in the national interest (cf. Wayne, 1978: Table 7.2; Bibby et al., 1980: Table 7.4).

Given knowledge of the annual quantity of legislation, the next question to ask is whether the annual rate of legislation is rising or falling. Even if we do not know how many laws constitute a large number, it is possible to measure trends within a nation and to compare trends cross-nationally. Is the annual volume of legislation increasing, as growth-of-government theories imply, remaining constant or contracting?

The annual volume of new legislation has been contracting in Britain in the twentieth century (Table 3.2). From 1901 to 1939, each Parliament enacted an average of more than 100 laws in each full session, notwithstanding periods of minority and coalition government. The total volume of laws averaged 116 per session for the first 38 years of the twentieth century. Even though British government has grown substantially since 1939 by every other measure, the annual rate of legislation has actually declined. In no Parliament since 1939 has there been an average of 100 laws a year, as was always the case earlier. In the postwar period Parliament has on average enacted 86 laws annually with very little variation from Parliament to Parliament. The number of bills becoming laws dropped as low as 56 in the 1976-77 session of Parliament. The steadiness in the volume of legislation is particularly striking in view of the frequent changes of party control of Parliament in the period, and in prime ministers.

TABLE 3.2
The declining rate of legislation in Britain, 1901-1979

Period	Number of full sessions	Number of laws	Average per full session
1901-14	14	1,671	119
1914-18	4	434	108
1919-39	20	2,203	110
1939-45	6	331	55
1945-51	6	527	88
1951-64	12	1,040	87[a]
1964-70	4	451	92[a]
1970-74	3	294	92[a]
1974-79	4	415	79[a]

a. Incomplete sessions of Parliament caused by general elections are omitted in calculating annual average.
Source: Calculated from Butler and Sloman (1980: 169-172).

In the United States too there has been a decline in the past 50 years in the annual amount of new legislation (Table 3.3). The peak session for the enactment of public bills occurred in the 70th Congress of 1927-29, when 1,037 public laws were enacted. This represents a tenfold increase from the 1st Congress of 1789-91. Since the 1920s, however, the annual rate of legislation has declined, falling to 633 Acts in the 95th Congress of 1977-78. The decline appears to be a phenomenon of the postwar era, for both the 80th Congress, which President Truman railed against as a do-nothing Congress because it would not pass his recommendations, and the 85th Congress, in President Eisenhower's second term, approved public laws on a scale approaching the record of the 70th Congress.

The decline in the number of public laws has also been matched by the decline in the number of public laws introduced by congressmen, from a high of 43,921 in the 61st Congress of

1909-11 to 16,627 in the 95th Congress of 1977-78. This is particularly striking evidence of a decline in congressmen's interest in legislation. There are no restrictions upon the number of bills that can be introduced by congressmen; there is ample staff assistance to draft bills, and there are many political incentives for congressmen to seek favour with their constituents by introducing bills that they know will be popular, even if lacking any chance of passage (cf. Mayhew, 1974).

TABLE 3.3
The rise and decline in the rate of legislation in the United States Congress, 1789-1978

Congress (2-year session)	Public bills Introduced	Enacted	% Enacted
1st (1789-91)	144	94	65.3
25th (1837-39)	1,566	138	8.8
50th (1887-89)	16,664	508	3.0
60th (1907-09)	37,981	350	0.9
70th (1927-29)	23,238	1,637	7.0
75th (1937-38)	15,120	788	5.2
80th (1947-48)	10,108	906	9.0
85th (1957-58)	18,205	936	5.1
90th (1967-68)	24,786	640	2.6
95th (1977-78)	16,627	633	3.8

Sources: Bureau of the Census, Historical Statistics of the United States: Colonial Times to 1957, Washington, DC, Government Printing Office, 1960, Series Y 129-138; Bureau of the Census, Statistical Abstract of the United States: 1979, Washington, DC: Government Printing Office, 1979, Table 823.

The decline in the use of laws as a resource of government is also evident in presidential programmes. Although presidential proposals are a small fraction of all public bills, they are usually the most important part. In the Eisenhower presidency, an annual average of 216 proposals was put forward from the White House, and 45 percent were approved. Under President Kennedy the average number of legislative proposals rose to 351 a year, but the success rate fell to 39 percent. Under President Johnson the number of proposals rose to a high of 469 in 1965 and averaged 380; the success rate rose to 57 percent. In the Nixon-Ford presidency, the number of presidential legislative proposals fell to an annual average of 165 a year, and the success rate dropped to 21 percent (Wayne, 1978: Table 5.2, 170).

In Germany too there has been a tendency for the number of laws passed by Parliament to decline. The number enacted by the Parliament of the Federal Republic is lower on average than the number enacted in the interwar Weimar Republic. It is, however, substantially greater than laws enacted prior to 1914 under the Kaiser, which belonged to an era of confederal and less represent-ative as well as smaller government (Table 3.4). From 1949 to 1980 the German Parliament passed an average of 115 laws a year. The highest rate was in the first Parliament of 1949-53, which was faced with the need to reconstruct a new system of government. Since then there has been a decline in the total number of bills put forward and enacted; the low point was reached in the 1976-80 Parliament, which considered an average of 121 bills each year and approved 88.

TABLE 3.4
The decline in the rate of legislation in Germany, 1903-1980

Period	Regime	Bills introduced		Laws enacted	
		Total	Annual average	Total	Annual average
1903-06	Kaiser Wilhelm II	not available		81	27
1924-28	Weimar Republic	not available		390	118
1949-53	Federal Republic	805	201	545	136
1953-57	Federal Republic	877	219	507	128
1957-61	Federal Republic	613	153	424	106
1961-65	Federal Republic	635	159	427	107
1965-69	Federal Republic	665	131	453	113
1969-72	Federal Republic	577	192	335	112
1972-76	Federal Republic	670	167	516	129
1976-80	Federal Republic	485	121	354	88
Totals, 1949-80		5,327	172	3,561	115

Sources: 1903-06 and 1924-28: Gerhard Loewenberg, *Parliament in the German Political System*, Ithaca, NY, Cornell University Press, 1967, p. 279; 1949-1980: Schindler (1981: 12).

The pattern of decline in the annual enactment of laws can be found in other countries too. In Norway the annual number of laws passed by the Storting has fallen from 102 in the 1958-61 session to 86 in the 1977-81 session, averaging 89 laws a year for the 24-year period (Laegereid and Olsen, 1981: Table 1). In Japan the number of bills passed by the Diet has declined from 331 a year on average from 1947 to 1952, when Japan was constructing a new regime, to 89 a year from 1975 to 1980 (Pempel, 1981: Table 4). In France the volume of legislation proposed and enacted in the Fifth Republic has declined in comparison with the Fourth Republic, when, as in Italy, French deputies were in a strong position to promote 'little laws' (*propositions de lois*) favouring constituency or personal concerns. The more centralized system of presidential government in the Fifth Republic has brought with it a reduction in the number of little laws, and a gradual reduction in the number of public acts (*projets de lois*) as well (cf. Williams, 1958: 202f.; Frears, 1981; Quermonne, 1980: 302).

While the legal systems of Britain, France, Germany, Norway, the United States and Japan are very different from each other, each country shows a consistent trend: a decline in the number of laws enacted annually in the post-1945 era. The extent and the timing of decline vary from country to country. In the countries for which there is the best long-term data — Britain, Germany and the United States — the decline in the rate of legislation dates from peaks before the Second World War. The number of government laws enacted each year was higher when government was smaller.

In a single year the average government of a Western nation does not flood its citizens with lots of laws. On average, 196 laws are enacted each year, less than four a week. Moreover, the number of important (that is, government) measures enacted into law is much less, averaging little more than two new laws a week. In a government with 20 or more Cabinet ministers, the average minister can expect to see five laws enacted on his department's recommendation each year. Even when allowance is made for the fact that Parliament is not in session every week of the year, the total number of new laws enacted each year is low in comparison with the potential for government action.

Causes of change in the statute book

The inertia of established commitments is the principal cause of the quantity of legislation on the statute books in every Western nation today. Once enacted, a law remains in force indefinitely. Laws have an inertia momentum, accumulating on the statute book from year to year. By contrast, public revenues are collected and spent within the space of a year. While the number of public employees changes more slowly because of tenure rules, a fraction retire each year and in the course of a decade a third to one-half of public employees will resign or retire. Very few laws are subject to sunset provisions, expiring on a fixed date (March, 1982).

Legislative inertia has a bias towards growth. It is far more common for a Parliament to enact a new law or amend an established law than to repeal a law in its entirety. Once enacted, every law has defenders within government and beneficiaries outside government. To propose the repeal of a law is to mobilize an opposition that is strategically placed within government, and clear about its own self-interest. The laws enacted each year are added to a large number of statutes from previous years and centuries. Even though the number of laws enacted in any one year is relatively small, the cumulative total is big.

Particularly striking evidence of the inertia persistence of laws is found in countries where regimes have been interrupted by war and internal coups. In France the Code Napoleon of 1804 is still in force in much amended form, even though there have been nearly a dozen regimes since. In Italy a few laws are still in force from before the creation of a nation-state in 1861, and in Germany a substantial number of laws have survived numerous changes of regime since the creation of a modern German state in 1871.

The British statute books are particularly suited to demonstrate the cumulative effect of the inertia of established commitments, for Parliament has been enacting laws since the thirteenth century, and there is an unbroken history of legislation since. The hand of the past lies heavy upon the statute book; the oldest law in force dates from 1267. Of all Acts approved by Parliament, one-sixth date from before the accession of Queen Victoria in 1837 and nearly one-third from at least a century ago. The median statute in force was enacted in 1940 (Table 3.5).

Theories of choice cannot explain the amount of legislation in force in a Western nation. The laws in force at any given time are not what the governing party has chosen, but what that party has inherited. When a new government takes office, it swears to uphold the laws of the land. The laws that each government

inherits from its predecessors are not determined by its own hand.
The median statute in force in Britain today was enacted before
the Prime Minister or the great majority of MPs entered
Parliament. Tacit acceptance of past laws as faits accomplis
cannot be taken as a positive endorsement of established statutes:
it is no more and no less than an acceptance of pre-existing
obligations.

TABLE 3.5
The inertia accumulation of laws in force in
the United Kingdom, 1980

Enacted	As % all laws in force	Cumulative %
1267-1837	17	17
1837-1901	19	36
1901-1939	13	50
1939-1951	7	57
1951-1964	12	69
1964-1979	31	100

Source: Compiled from *Index to the Statutes*, London, HMSO, 1981: i-clvii.

Paradoxically, the inertia of established legislative
commitments results in annual growth occurring at a decelerating
rate. To add 100 laws to a statute book that already has 2,000 laws
is to increase the total number of laws by 5 percent. If legislation
were enacted at the same rate for another 20 years, the addition of
another 100 laws would only add 2 percent to a total of 4,000
statutes. A constant rate of increase in the number of laws enacted
each year will represent a slowing down in the percentage rate of
growth, and deceleration will be proportionally greater as the
annual rate of legislation contracts (see Tables 3.2-3.4).

The causes of the enactment of particular laws can differ from
the policy intentions to which laws can give expression. Policies
are typically conceived in terms of broad social, economic and
political purposes, such as the promotion of education or income
security. From this perspective, laws are but a means to authorize
programmes to realize broad policy goals. The object is not to add
one more law to the statute book but to achieve a policy objective.

If this can be done without legislation, for example by increasing public spending or altering administration under existing law, so much the better.

But law is a resource of government in its own right, and it is a distinctive resource. Laws convert the preferences of a transient government of the day into binding commitments upon future governments. Moreover, the procedures and practices of lawmaking influence how easily programmes can be enacted, amended or abandoned. Hence, it is important to explore distinctive determinants of the addition or subtraction of laws from the statute books, as a prelude to the consideration in Chapter 7 of the forces determining programme goals.

The constitution of a country is an important determinant of lawmaking, for it establishes the basic framework of legislation, and the institutions empowered to enact statutes. In every Western nation except France and the United States, parliamentary institutions link the executive and the legislature, making it easier for parliamentary governments to enact more laws each year. Among the 13 countries reviewed in Table 3.1, France and the United States rank tenth and eleventh respectively in the number of laws their government annually enacts, averaging 57 laws enacted a year, as against 123 laws in parliamentary systems.

Federal systems of government differ from unitary systems in that the constitution of a federal country usually gives lawmaking powers to the partners of the federal compact. Equally important, a federal constitution is likely to restrict the lawmaking powers of the national government. The extent to which this is the case is again demonstrated by Table 3.1, which shows that the national legislatures of federal systems enact nearly one-third fewer laws (160 on average) than the national parliaments of unitary states (229). Moreover, fewer government bills (83) are enacted on average in federal countries than in unitary systems (140), and this difference holds true among Roman law countries, differentiating Austria, Germany and Switzerland from unitary states, as well as among common law countries, differentiating the United States, Australia and Canada from Britain and New Zealand.

Within a federal system of government, the existence of lawmaking authorities below the national level creates the potential for variations in statutes. With 50 states, America offers great scope for variations in state laws; Switzerland, with its longer tradition of cantonal autonomy and diversity, and Canada, with a bi-cultural tradition reinforced by provincial legislatures, also have substantial scope for diversity in laws.

The federal constitution grants the same lawmaking powers to all 50 American state legislatures, but the 50 states vary substantially in the way in which they organize to legislate, and in the amount and substance of their legislation (Table 3.6). The legislature of an American state will meet annually for anything between 30 and 120 formal sessions. The volume of bills introduced annually varies by a factor of 25 between the states, and the percentage of bills enacted varies greatly too. The New York state legislature receives the most legislative proposals a year (10,841) and enacts the lowest proportion into law (7 percent). On average, an American state legislature will enact 479 laws annually, but the range is great, from 1,294 in California to 102 in

TABLE 3.6
Variations in lawmaking among the American states

	Average	High/low		Stand dev.	Coeff't var'n
Number of bills:					
Introduced	1,935	10,841	New York	2,030	1.05
		424	Wyoming		
Enacted	479	1,294	California	264	0.55
		102	Vermont		
% bills enacted	30	59	South Dakota	15	0.50
		7	New York		
Uniform Acts					
No. states enacting a uniform Act	21	50	(2 Acts)	17	0.79
		1	(2 Acts)		
No. uniform Acts adopted by a state	30	50	Minnesota	7	0.23
		15	Louisiana		

Source: Calculated from Council of State Governments (1982: 86-89; 206-207). Numbers of bills are averages for the 1979 and 1980 sessions. The total number of proposed uniform Acts is 72.

Vermont. Average figures for legislation are not good guides to the use of law in any particular state, since the standard deviation and coefficient of variation reflect very substantial departures by individual states from the national average.

Federal systems show substantial interstate differences in legislation on the same topic. The National Conference of Commissioners on Uniform State Laws regularly recommends the adoption of uniform acts by state legislatures in order to reduce interstate differences in laws concerning procedural matters such as juries and criminal extradition, as well as such matters as marriage, divorce and the division of income for tax purposes. Of the 72 uniform laws recommended, only 26 have been adopted by as many as half the states. On average, 30 states have adopted a proposed uniform law. Only two uniform laws have been enacted by all the states, concerning Anatomical Gifts and Reciprocal Enforcement of Family Support Orders; and two uniform measures, concerning audio-visual depositions and corporative fault, have been adopted by only one state.

The net consequence is that in a federal system citizens in different states are subject to statutes that differ in both quality and quantity. If a recommended uniform act is taken as the national model, then most states depart from this standard. Only 21 of 50 American states on average have enacted a uniform law. Minnesota, which comes closest to supporting the idea of uniform legislation, has yet to adopt nearly one-third of the proposed standard laws, and 13 other states share with Louisiana the distinction of having adopted less than one-third of uniform laws. Most of the variation in laws between states reflects political differences; only two-fifths of the variation can be explained by differences between the states in population, urbanization and industrialization (Rosenthal and Forth, 1978).

Procedural and technical features of lawmaking are a second important influence consistently limiting the number of laws likely to be enacted by a government in any one year. In theory, the number of laws a government could enact is virtually limitless; an absolute dictatorship might enact laws as fast as it could print them. In practice, the preparation of legislation is a highly complicated and time-consuming matter. Laws take time to draft. Because of the unique character of their binding authority, a government will not casually mandate or prohibit activities, nor does it wish to confront lawyers or judges with an act so vaguely or ambiguously written that interpretation is effectively in the hands of the courts. Old laws must be borne in mind when writing new laws; a government does not wish to enact a new statute that will contradict or disturb existing statutes. The timetable of a national parliament is a restriction too; it is likely to meet for about 10 or 12 hours a week on average to conduct its business, or even less (cf. Inter-Parliamentary Union, 1976: Table 24). It takes months for a proposed law to be scrutinized by a national parliament, and parliaments have limited time for scrutinizing legislation.

The very persistence of laws from decade to decade gradually creates pressures to change in response to changing circumstances. The world changes, but laws remain. A law normally reflects specific circumstances of a given time and place. The remedies it proposes will have some generality, but its diagnosis of the problem and prescriptions are rooted in a particular conjunction of political and social circumstances. The circumstances of the 1980s are not the same as the 1950s or the 1920s. The longer a law stays on the statute books, the more likely it is that the circumstances giving rise to it will change. Since the impact of a law is the joint product of fixed characteristics of a law and changing characteristics of society, the older a law, the greater the risk of obsolescence.

Old laws need not become obsolete, if explicitness and certainty of detail, which in the course of time can cause rigidity and inflexibility, are exchanged for generality, which makes it possible to adapt old laws to meet new circumstances. Constitutions provide the best example of laws that are durable because general, being most specific about procedures and least specific about substantive goals. Flexibility is particularly important, given the difficulty of amending a constitution, and the desire of the authors of a constitution that their work should long endure. The American Constitution, written in 1787, is a particularly good illustration of flexibility in interpretation being a necessary price for centuries of endurance. American judges can so interpret the Constitution in the light of changing circumstances that racial segregation was ruled constitutional in 1896 and unconstitutional in 1954.

In a Darwinian sense, laws that remain on the statute books for many generations may be reckoned to survive because they are fit; if they were not, they would be repealed. A scanning of British statutes indicates that laws persisting from Victorian times and even earlier do so because of their very general phrasing. For example, the 1835 Highway Act is not concerned with regulating the speed or safety of horses. It gives government broad powers to regulate the conduct of users of the Queen's Highways, powers stated broadly enough to suit not only the era of horse-drawn wagons but also that of today's fast-moving motor transport.

The complement of the survival of the fittest is the cutting back or pruning of unfit or obsolete legislation. The gardening metaphor is apt, for if the statute book is left unattended the slow but steady addition of new legislation is likely to compound problems, with new and obsolescent laws conflicting with each other. Just as cutting the grass does not reduce a lawn but maintains it at a constant height, so pruning back old laws, planting new laws, and grafting new clauses in place of old need not increase the total amount of legislation. Moreover, old legislation is usually not dealt with by uprooting (that is, repeal), but by a process of piecemeal amendment.

The need to prune and renew legislation means that a substantial amount of nominally new laws in fact are no more than the consolidation of a number of established Acts of Parliament into a single more coherent statute. In the British Parliament, 15 percent of all government measures are consolidation Acts. Even more important, consolidation Acts are disproportionately long; 32 percent of legislative bulk, as measured by the number of sections in all laws, is in consolidation Acts for existing legislation (Burton and Drewry, 1981: 206ff.).

A pilot examination of legislation enacted by the British Parliament in the early 1950s found that only one-eighth of laws were still unchanged by 1981, nearly half had been amended, and the remainder repealed in order to be replaced as part of a process of the renewal of legislation (Rose and Van Mechelen, forthcoming).

The pressure to consolidate older Acts means that the British Parliament is continually altering statutes. Even though Parliament enacts upwards of 100 Acts each year, so many involve amendment and repeal of existing Acts as part of the consolidation process that the statute book can still contract in total bulk. While there were 3,680 public general Acts on the statute book at the date of the election of a Labour government in Britain in 1964, there were 36 fewer Acts by the time Labour left office in 1970. By early 1974 the total number of public general Acts in effect in Britain had fallen by an additional 164 to 3,480. In a decade, a gross increase of 20 percent in statutes became a net reduction because of consolidation Acts replacing a congeries of older acts (Burton and Drewry, 1981: 206f.).

The extent of continuous cultivation and renewal of legislation can also be shown by examining a particular subject area. In the case of income tax, continuously in force in Britain since 1842, only three of the 43 income tax laws now in force date from earlier than 1965, and the median Act dates from 1974. Even a relatively new law, like the 1973 Value Added Tax, has been subject to alteration by 17 measures since. The typical subject of legislation by the British Parliament is regulated by about two dozen Acts. Of these, at least one was enacted prior to 1900, and at least one in the past 12 months. The median Act in a subject area is usually 15 to 20 years old (Rose and Van Mechelen, forthcoming).

Lawmaking is influenced by politics as well as by technical and institutional pressures. Parties and pressure groups often advance demands for distinctive legislation. A conventional party government model of lawmaking assumes that the entry of a party into government initiates a cycle of legislation based upon the new government's ideology, long-term programme and immediate election pledges. A socialist government would be expected to enact laws intended to benefit persons with below-average incomes and regulate the private sector of the economy, and a conservative government to enact laws benefiting the private sector of the economy and well-to-do people. The party government model is a conflict model; legislation reflects policy differences between political adversaries.

By contrast, a pressure group model of lawmaking implies a high degree of consensus. It hypothesizes that laws emerge from a lengthy process of negotiation between affected groups, including party politicians and civil servants, as well as business firms, trade unions, and other interests. A newly elected government may wish to press divisive partisan policies, but it soon finds that there is 'something stronger than parties' (Rose, 1980a: Chapter 8), namely, the interests of pressure groups, reinforced by established statutory commitments.

A distinctive feature of the pressure group model of legislation is that no law is likely to be proposed until there is more-than-majority support. The adoption of many complex policies involves bargaining between opposing interests willing to accept the necessity of compromise. A law that is enacted against strong opposition in Parliament is less likely to be successful than a bill agreed as the result of bargain between all affected groups. When successful, government negotiation with pressure groups can lead to a law being enacted that no party will oppose in

Parliament, because the interests supporting it are found in both government and opposition parties, and cut across party lines. In the absence of agreement, a government can delay rather than bring forward a divisive bill.

The procedures of Parliament, as well as the informal norms of preparing legislation within government, encourage widespread consultation with affected interests and MPs of all parties. A survey by the Inter-Parliamentary Union found that virtually all Western nations have procedures for consultations with extra-parliamentary interests before a bill is presented to Parliament. Consultation procedures are particularly clear, because formalized, in Sweden.

> Government bills are based on reports by committees of inquiry. These reports are, as a rule, submitted to state agencies, local government authorities and private organisations, before a draft of a bill is prepared and introduced into the Riksdag. [Inter-Parliamentary Union, 1976: 627]

In Switzerland there is no formal legal requirement for consultation, but the country's government by permanent coalition is an effective political guarantee of consultation: 'The government consults the cantons, political parties and interested organisations before it submits a bill to Parliament' (Inter-Parliamentary Union, 1976: 628).

A review of evidence from a variety of Western parliaments consistently supports the pressure group model of lawmaking. Government bills are usually not opposed in Parliament. Parties do not clash when interests are agreed. In Britain every bill introduced in the Commons can be made the subject of a division — if the opposition party wishes to oppose it. The conventions of British parliamentary practice and the adversary model of party government emphasize that the Opposition should oppose most government bills on the second reading vote of principle. But the pressure group model implies the opposite. In fact, the evidence supports the pressure group model; most laws in Britain are consensual measures. In the 1970-74 Parliament, 80 percent of all Conservative government bills were approved without a vote against by the Opposition on second reading, and in the 1974-79 Parliament, when a Labour government faced a Conservative Opposition, the figure was 77 percent. Less than one-fifth of the hundreds of government bills put forward during the decade could be considered the cause of major inter-party conflict in the Commons (Rose, 1980a: 80).

In the United States Congress, representatives see their role as promoting bills for which everybody can vote rather than advancing legislation that will maximize inter-party divisions. Hence, many votes are voice votes, so that there is no record of differences. In record votes since 1970, a majority of the congressmen in one party have voted against a majority of congressmen in the other party in only 37 percent of all votes (Bibby et al., 1980: 103). If a strict construction is given to party conflict, requiring 90 percent of each party to vote against the other party, this is found in less than 10 percent of roll call votes since 1945. In the 89th Congress of 1965-67, which endorsed much of President Johnson's Great Society legislation, the two parties were strictly in opposition to each other on only 2 percent of all recorded votes (Cooper et al., 1977: 139).

Continental parliaments, too, follow a consensual pattern in lawmaking. In Germany less than 10 percent of legislation in the Bundestag is the subject of partisan controversy (Schindler, 1981: 12). The German process of lawmaking is pre-eminently a process of consultation and bargaining, reinforced by the fact that the second chamber, the Bundesrat, must approve most legislation endorsed by the Bundestag, and the Bundesrat can be controlled by a party opposed to the government. In the Italian Parliament committee hearings are used to prepare legislation that can be endorsed by the full Parliament without the necessity of a recorded vote along party lines (di Palma, 1977: 58). Where coalition governments are found, this strengthens the tendency for government to propose laws that reflect the lowest common denominator of interests across party lines.

The process of lawmaking is pre-eminently a political process. Social, economic and demographic influences may provide a stimulus to legislation. None the less, the framers of legislation are in government, and no social or economic influence can be registered except in so far as it is meditated in the policy process. Only after a law is enacted, especially if it establishes entitlements to welfare benefits, can social, economic and demographic factors influence its claim on resources.

Consequences of legislation

The consequences of laws affect government as well as society. Laws regulate the procedures by which public policies are carried out. Laws also give persisting programmatic substance to vague statements of political intentions. Laws can affect the resources of government, authorizing the recruitment of public employees and raising large sums of tax revenue. Laws can also be a resource in themselves, establishing norms for social conduct and giving legal recognition to rights and obligations. Not least, laws can reinforce popular consent, because they embody popular expectations of legitimate government; or erode consent, if citizens perceive a conflict between what government declares is legal and what is popularly believed to be fair or right.

The extent to which laws are concerned primarily with regulating the administrative procedures of government should never be underestimated. When government is big, the need for impersonal bureaucratic rules is particularly great, for informal subjective judgements cannot be applied reliably or acceptably by millions of public employees. Nor would citizens endorse public officials acting lawlessly. The civic ideal of equality before the law requires a large number of procedural rules to ensure that different citizens are treated alike in like circumstances. In Britain 35 percent of statutes concern administration and another 15 percent are consolidation acts. Laws concerning administration are more numerous than laws concerned with programmes and finance (Burton and Drewry, 1981: 112).

In so far as government is concerned primarily with raising money, the effectiveness of laws is of particular concern; ineffective tax laws will reduce government's tax revenue. The creation of the modern state has depended upon government developing effective means to raise more and more revenue. Countries vary in the means used to collect taxes, and in the effectiveness of particular taxes. None the less, even where some types of taxes are notoriously difficult to collect (for example, income tax in France) the French government collects a larger proportion of the national product in tax than does the United States, by relying on social security and sales taxes.

In so far as government is concerned primarily with distributing material benefits to individuals, legislation is a necessary but relatively unimportant step in the process of providing programme outputs. Legislation will authorize government to spend money and to employ officials, but it will be only an incidental means for providing the programme benefits of the contemporary welfare state.

In so far as laws are concerned primarily with norms regulating social life, they are a unique resource of government. This is true whether laws regulate procedures within government, relations between citizens and government, or relations between individuals and organizations in the economy and society. Laws that lay down conditions for holding elections, forming a limited liability company or adopting a child do not depend for their effect upon money or manpower. They are a unique resource affecting society without invoking the measuring rod of money. The fact that we take for granted the advantages of the rule of law does not make it less important. Its influence is fundamental, because it is a priceless as well as costless precondition of life as we know it in Western nations today.

Laws tend to be norm-intensive rather than money-intensive. A comparative study of legislation in four Western nations found that two-thirds to three-quarters of laws examined regulate the affairs of government, of individual citizens, and of groups (Table 3.7). Less than one-third of laws are concerned with the distribution or redistribution of costly benefits, whether in the form of cash transfer payments or welfare goods and services. The evidence is illustrative rather than conclusive, for it concerns only one year's legislation. But the findings are consistent, notwithstanding the different political circumstances of the governments of Ireland, Sweden, France and Britain — and not to mention differences in legal systems between the four countries.

When the claims of government departments upon legislation and public revenues are compared, there are very striking contrasts between the claims of different government departments upon these resources. A pilot study of Britain found that four traditional government ministries — the Treasury, the Foreign Office, the Law Offices and the Home Office — have accounted for nearly half of all legislation, whereas they account for about one-twentieth of public expenditure. Trade and Industry and Local Government and Housing are also fields where government departments rely more upon law than money to advance their policy aims. By contrast, the major departments of the welfare state — Education, Health and Social Security — account for about half of all public expenditure, but for only one-tenth of legislation. A similar discrepancy between the use of money and the use of legislation is found in Washington (Rose, 1976b; Table 2.1).

TABLE 3.7
Laws more often norm-intensive than money-intensive

Type of law	Britain	France	Sweden	Ireland
	%	%	%	%
Norm-intensive				
Constitutional	16	22	18	11
Citizen regulation	24	18	21	39
Group, self-regulation	29	27	36	25
	—	—	—	—
Total	69	67	75	75
Money-intensive				
Distributive	27	25	14	25
Redistributive	4	8	11	0
	—	—	—	—
Total	31	33	25	25

Source: Adapted from Blondel et al. (1969: Table 2).

Laws can also be effective in controlling resources outside the Budget. Private as well as public expenditure is affected by laws that confer such benefits as tax expenditures (that is, granting groups and organizations conditional exemption from tax levies). Leaving a pound or a dollar in a citizen's pocket is a less obvious benefit than placing it there by a combined taxing and spending operation, but it is a benefit none the less. In a complementary fashion, government can affect the private sector's spending or employment policies by passing regulations that compel firms to spend money for specified purposes (for example, to reduce air pollution or increase factory safety), or that require employers to demonstrate that they do not discriminate on grounds of race or sex by hiring a more or less clearly established quota of employees of a given race or sex.

When government passes laws that impose costs upon private sector or other public sector organizations, it is externalizing on to these agencies the burden of carrying out public policies. The government's role in regulating industry and commerce by law dates back to the mid-nineteenth century Nightwatchman state and before. What is new today is the scale of externalized costs. Whereas requirements to register births, deaths and marriage impose trivial costs, requirements to install and maintain expensive anti-pollution equipment or safety devices to guard against remote risks can be very expensive.

In the United States the use of regulation to mandate costly actions has been fully developed, as have estimates of the cost of regulation. A study by the Joint Economic Committee of Congress estimated that the federal administrative costs of regulation were $4.8 billion in 1979, and rising. The compliance costs for the organizations required to meet the safety, health and other standards laid down by the regulations were 20 times greater, $98 billion, and rising (ACIR, 1980: 145). Moreover, federal regulations affect state and local government, offsetting to a significant extent the benefits gained from federal grants. For example, the Clean Water Act mandates American cities to spend nearly $120 billion to improve sewage treatment plants. Laws and regulations increase the impact of government upon the economy by a sum equivalent to about one-sixth of total federal expenditure.

Tax laws can be written to confer money benefits on individuals and institutions, as well as to take money from them. Tax expenditures (Surrey, 1973) occur when a government exempts from taxation certain types of income (e.g., interest on government bonds or investments in oil), or allows deductions from gross income for specified types of expenditure (e.g., interest payments on home mortgages or on energy-saving goods). Just as costly regulations reduce net income, exemptions from taxation effectively leave more money in the hands of individuals and corporations than they would otherwise have. The principal tax allowances are deductions by individuals and families to meet their minimum living costs, interest on loans for house purchase, exemption from capital gains tax on the sale of a person's home and corporation tax relief.

The effectiveness of laws is influenced by the extent to which there is consent to particular laws, as well as to government in general. Laws are meant to regulate social behaviour, but they also reflect social norms prevalent within society. As long as there is little discrepancy between the two, laws will be effective without recourse to coercion. For example, the criminal prohibitions of murder and incest are upheld by social taboos as much as or even more than by coercion. In so far as discrepancies exist, for example in the regulation of drinking habits or sexual mores, then police powers will be needed to bridge the gap. The greater the discrepancy between social and governmental norms, the less the effect of laws; there is a ceiling upon the extent to which laws can be made effective by force alone; as prison wardens and occupation armies know, there are limits to effective authority.

Formally, consent is given to laws by the approval of Parliament. In contemporary democracies, approval by Parliament is meant to indicate popular consent, because MPs are popularly elected. But approval by Parliament is a very imperfect indicator of popular consent. Members of Parliament do not draft government bills, nor are they normally able to make substantial amendments; this is done in ministries. The time available for individual MPs to spend in discussing a bill is very limited (cf. Inter-Parliamentary Union, 1976: Table 24). Not least in significance, party discipline guarantees a government approval for the great majority of the bills that it puts to Parliament. Parliamentary endorsement is a necessary condition of laws taking effect, but the consent obtained does not reflect the deliberate and personal commitment of all legislators.

A potential challenge to popular consent arises from government's growing practice of making binding rules without positive parliamentary approval. The executive branch of government usually has power to make and enforce secondary regulations in furtherance of programmes established by primary laws (that is, acts approved by Parliament). Parliament delegates to ministers and civil servants the power to make the many binding rules deemed necessary or desirable to achieve broadly defined programmatic ends. The conditions under which secondary regulations can be brought into force are laid down by Parliament, but usually do not require its positive vote of approval. Parliament retains the right to veto secondary regulations or to amend the Act authorizing regulations, but this power is rarely exercised. In so far as the amount of secondary regulation is large and growing, it is possible to scrutinize regulations only on a very selective basis.

Bureaucratic rule-making is greater than parliamentary law-making in Western nations today. In Britain, 79 percent of policy bills coming forward in Parliament make substantial provision for delegated secondary legislation through Statutory Instruments (Burton and Drewry, 1981: 130). The total number of Statutory Instruments issued each year is above 2,000, more than 20 times the total number of laws enacted each year (Butler and Sloman, 1980: 169-172, 190). In theory, each instrument is scrutinized by a committee of MPs and can be called to the attention of the Commons for full consideration; in practice, less than 1 percent are given attention in the House of Commons.

Since many more Statutory Instruments are enacted than Acts of Parliament in a given year, there is now more secondary legislation in force in Britain than primary Acts of Parliament, and the disparity is increasing annually. Because the use of Statutory Instruments is relatively new, these regulations are therefore less subject to obsolescence. Moreover, because it is relatively simple to change Statutory Instruments, ministries can avoid obsolescence by issuing new regulations more easily than can be done by enacting consolidation Acts in Parliament.

In the United States, regulations issued by the federal government have been increasing at a substantial rate in the 1960s and 1970s, more or less doubling from 1970 to 1975 (Lilley and Miller, 1977: Table 1), and the number if not the scope of such regulations appears to exceed that of public laws. In Japan too, the number of secondary ordinances is about four times as great as the number of laws approved by the Diet, and the use of ordinances is increasing relative to statute laws (Pempel, 1981: Figure 2).

The growth of secondary legislation is not to be interpreted as government rule-making heedless of popular wishes. One reason for using secondary legislation is that it improves the responsiveness of government. Officials can act promptly to change rules without the delays imposed by conventional parliamentary legislation. Secondary legislation may deal more adequately with technical matters, because it is formulated by experts rather than politicians in Parliament (Inter-Parliamentary Union, 1976: 694). In so far as the co-operation of affected groups is necessary or desirable, Statutory Instruments may be promulgated with the advice and consent of the affected interests. The shift from public lawmaking in Parliament to bureaucratic rule-making can be interpreted as evidence of the inadequacy of parliaments to deal promptly with many technical matters of narrow concern.

The increasing contact between individual citizens and government agencies arising from the expanding scope of laws and regulations involves two types of asymmetries. First, there is an asymmetry of power between a single individual and any large organization, public or private. Second, there is an incongruity of outlooks between individuals and agencies that must apply impersonal rules. An individual is concerned with his or her specific problem. By contrast, public officials are meant to be detached from individual problems, applying rules with procedural correctness and consistency, in order to maintain individual equality before the law. The procedural rationality of the bureaucrat can conflict with the substantive rationality of an individual seeking help from government. Whereas an elected representative must be responsive to individual concerns or risk an electoral penalty, a bureaucrat is duty-bound to respect the discipline of procedures.

As the number of contacts between individuals and government agencies increases, the frequency of misunderstandings, friction and conflict between individuals and government is likely to increase, and to increase at least in proportion to the frequency of interaction. Roman law and common law countries have different traditions for dealing with conflicts between the individual and the state (Ehrmann, 1976: 127ff.). Roman law countries have tended to follow the French example of establishing a separate system of administrative law, with a Conseil d'Etat making the final finding of law when disputes arise between individual citizens and public agencies. By contrast, common law countries start from the assumption that disputes between individuals and public agencies should be resolved in conventional courts of law.

The growing scope of government legislation has resulted in the growth of the number of cases involving citizens in legal or quasi-legal disputes involving their claims as citizens, as distinct from obligations under the criminal law. This is most evident in the growth of special administrative tribunals of a quasi-judicial kind in Britain and America, and in the establishment, in both Roman law and common law countries, of the office of Ombudsman to investigate complaints of public officials maltreating individuals. In Britain, tribunals deal with income tax and property tax, the payment of welfare benefits, mental health, immigration disputes, land use planning permissions and charges of racial discrimination. In the United States, the regulations complained of as costly by businessmen are typically enforced by an agency or board with some quasi-judicial powers. There are also special tribunals for disputes involving government agencies and individual citizens, such as the Federal Trade Commission and the Occupational Safety and Health Review Commission, and a very substantial increase in civil cases in the federal courts (cf. ACIR, 1980: Tables A-9, A-10; Lowi, 1969).

When a citizen enters into a conflict with government at an administrative tribunal, whatever the outcome, government is likely to lose popular favour. If the tribunal rules for the citizen, this is independent confirmation of the individual's assertion that government doesn't know or care what it is doing to people like him. If the tribunal rules against an aggrieved citizen, then he or she may continue to be aggrieved because of the denial of what was claimed as the individual citizen's right.

The increase in regulations does not necessarily mean that grievances have increased in society. For example, before the growth of cash transfer public assistance programmes, poor families were aggrieved because they lacked money for many necessities. The important point here is that the expansion of government's role has meant a redirection of popular concerns. Instead of blaming the market or local charities, an individual who believes his or her income is inadequate may blame government, if a tribunal rejects an appeal for a cash grant.

Laws and regulations are meant to confer increased benefits upon society. But laws and regulations have political costs as well as benefits. An increase in laws increases the opportunities for friction between citizens and the state, friction that is rule-induced because it involves more contacts between individual citizens and impersonal bureaucratic officials who, whatever their expertise and impartiality, cannot claim to be as immediately accountable to citizens as elected members of Parliament.

4 RAISING TAX REVENUES

Money is a sine qua non of government. This is true whether the amount of revenue required is that of a laissez-faire state or a contemporary welfare state. Without money to put the intentions of government into effect, many laws would remain a dead letter on the statute book.

'The history of the state is inseparable from the history of taxation' (Ardant, 1975: 102). In medieval times the limited capacity of the government to raise revenue was a major constraint upon the king's will, whether the reigning monarch wanted the money to finance wars, for conspicuous consumption or for charitable and religious works. The development of taxation was inextricably linked with the development of a money economy, capitalist institutions and industrialization. Finding methods to increase taxation was essential for the transition from a pre-modern state to the state as we know it today (Braun, 1975). Means had to be found to raise more money without triggering tax revolts that could lead to the breakdown of public order, or even the overthrow of a regime. To raise more money, monarchs had to share their power with parliaments.

Today, government is concerned with raising and spending vast sums of money. The two tasks are complementary: government cannot spend money that it cannot raise, and it must levy taxes to meet spending commitments. Even though taxes and expenditure are both expressed in money terms and must be made equal in bookkeeping, they are not identical. Taxation is first of all concerned with extracting money from the national economy. By contrast, public spending is a means of financing programme benefits. Officials in spending departments do not ask how money is to be raised to pay for their programmes; that is the concern of tax officials dealing with the other side of the fiscal system.

The contrast between raising and spending money is easily enough appreciated by glancing at the headings conventionally used to describe major sources of tax revenue: income tax, social security tax, customs and excise taxes, sales and value added taxes, corporation tax and property tax. By contrast, the headings describing public expenditure refer to programmes: pensions, education, health, defence and so forth. Contemporary political scientists have tended to concentrate attention upon only one side of the budget; government's allocation of expenditure. As Crecine (1969: 34) notes, 'Revenue is taken as given.' But the bigger the sums to be raised, the more likely revenue-raising is to be problematic.

From an individual citizen's perspective, taxes are tangible and substantial evidence of the *costs* of government. Taxes are paid not because citizens desire to give money to government, but because government demands money from citizens. By contrast, public expenditure is usually regarded as evidence of the *benefits* of government. The money that government spends on pensions, education and health care provides goods and services that citizens rely upon as part of their everyday life, and usually receive without charge. But welfare state benefits are not free; the costs must be met from public revenues. The contemporary welfare state's budget involves both big costs and big benefits (Rose and Peters, 1978a: Chapters 3-4).

Before we can understand why tax revenue grows, we must understand how government collects taxes. The first task of this chapter is to identify the variety of ways in which government raises money, to compare the relative contribution of different taxes to total tax revenues, and to test the extent to which there are cross-national similarities in patterns of taxation. Because government's revenue comes from a multiplicity of sources, it has a multiplicity of causes. The second section of this chapter concentrates attention upon causes of tax increases. It is particularly important to understand the extent to which tax revenues are outside the control of the government of the day, being determined by the inertia of established government commitments, and by the nation's economy. The consequences of taxation are multiple, and increasing taxes when government is already big can have a different impact than increasing taxes from a low level. The concluding section considers whether governments are likely to face a ceiling upon the amount of money that they can raise from taxes, and the consequences of political resistance to higher taxes.

The variety of taxes
From the perspective of the Budget as a whole, the sum total of tax revenues is of primary importance. It is the total amount of money

that government raises that constrains public spending, and it is the gap between total spending and total tax revenue that determines the size of the public deficit. Total tax revenue is important too in the government's management of the national economy. It is also important in electoral terms. Whereas a particular tax at a given level of government is likely to have only a marginal impact on total revenue, every household will feel the combined impact of taxes collected at all levels of government. If one tax is lowered only to have this offset by an increase in another tax, the aggregate effect remains the same.

There are great differences between nations in the share of the gross domestic product claimed as tax, ranging from 50 percent in Sweden and 47 percent in Norway to 24 percent in Spain and 19 percent in Turkey (OECD, 1981: Table 1). In the average OECD nation, taxes account for 37 percent of the national product.[1] Among European nations, Germany and Britain are average, whereas the United States ranks relatively low, sixteenth among 23 countries. Moreover, America's relative position has fallen since 1960, when the United States ranked eleventh, with taxes accounting for 27 percent of the national product.

Taxation is a singular noun, but taxes are plural. Government raises money in a multiplicity of ways; no government relies solely upon a single source of tax revenue. Government levies taxes upon many different types of economic transactions. It taxes directly the income of individuals, and it taxes the profits of corporations. It levies earmarked taxes upon employers and employees to finance social security programmes. Earnings are spent on goods and services subject to a host of sales, value-added, and customs and excise taxes which indirectly add to their cost. Government can also levy rates or property taxes upon homes, factories, shops and office buildings. Individuals who have amassed an above-average amount of personal wealth can be subject to an annual wealth tax while alive, and to an estate tax after death. Nor is this the end of government's revenue resources. When raising taxes appears difficult or undesirable, government can borrow money. It can also generate some revenue from fees, royalties and nationalized industries. OECD identifies 39 different categories of tax revenue; the median country levies taxes under 21 different principal headings.

No one agency within government is responsible for all the taxes of government. In every Western country central government is the principal revenue-raiser. But central government does not rely solely upon a Department of Inland Revenue. Tax collectors specialize, some collecting income tax and others customs and excise tax. Social security levies for pensions, unemployment and health care may be collected by administrative organizations separate from the principal body of Inland Revenue staff. Public enterprises usually have separate accounts, involving large sums of revenue and expenditure arising from their market trans- actions. Central banks finance the long-term debt of government, and borrow money to meet current deficits.

Local government (and intermediate tiers of government where they exist) also have revenue-raising powers. The proportion of taxes raised by local and provincial governments varies from 46 percent in Canada and 41 percent in Switzerland to 1 percent in the Netherlands and Italy. In federal systems in the OECD world, local and intermediate tiers of government raise an average of 32 percent of taxes, as against 68 percent raised by central government. In unitary systems local government raises only 14 percent of revenue. Among OECD nations there is nil correlation (0.004) between total tax as a share of the national product and the share of tax raised by state and local government (cf. OECD, 1981: Tables 1,11). Hence, there is no need to complicate this chapter by considering in detail differences in taxation between federal and unitary systems.

To think about tax revenue solely in terms of a single total figure is to confuse the whole and the parts. Within any country the taxes that collectively make up the total tax revenue are numerous, and differ in their characteristics. The institutions that levy taxes are also numerous and diverse. To generalize about taxation from total tax revenue is to assume what remains to be proven, namely, that within a given country different taxes are much the same in their revenue yield, in their causes and in their consequences. This assertion can be proven only by systematically disaggregating total tax revenue into its principal constituent parts, and comparing the results to see to what extent different taxes are in fact similar within a given nation. Subsequent pages will show that there are major differences between taxes. No one tax accounts for the great bulk of a nation's revenue, and there are substantial variations in the revenue raised by principal taxes. Moreover, changes in individual taxes are not identical with changes in the total tax revenue.[2] Total taxation is an aggregate figure masking movements by different taxes at contrasting rates and in opposite directions (Rose and Karran, 1983).

Measuring public revenues is relatively simple by comparison with measuring laws, for contemporary governments always collect taxes in money terms. (In medieval times taxes could be paid in goods, such as farm crops, or in services, such as labour on the roads or in the ruler's army.) Every modern government produces compendious reports of the money it collects in taxes each year. To determine how much money a government raises annually in revenue we can turn to official documents. Moreover, there is a ready source at hand for cross-national analysis, for OECD has invested two decades of effort in compiling data about taxation in member-nations according to cross-nationally comparable categories for each year from 1965; less detailed data are available for 1960 and 1955.[3] The analyses that follow concern taxation within and across 20 OECD nations.[4]

To establish the relative importance of particular taxes within a nation, it is necessary to think in terms of a *national tax system* (NTS) divided into constituent *tax components* (TCs). Each tax component can be measured as a percentage of the total national tax system. The idea of a national tax system reflects the fact that total revenue and individual components are interdependent; the amount of revenue raised by one tax affects other taxes. If, for example, a government collects a high rate of income tax, it may not need to collect a high rate of sales tax, whereas a government that levies a low rate of income tax may need to collect more money from other sources, say, levying high social security taxes. Tax components can be compared cross-nationally, whereas pounds, francs, Deutsche Marks and lira are not commensurable; nor is it possible, in an era of floating exchange rates, to convert national currencies into a common constant denominator, such as the US dollar.

Three propositions succinctly describe the great variety of taxes used within a national tax system, and variations within and between nations in tax components.

1. Every Western nation employs a wide variety of taxes to collect revenue

In order to concentrate attention upon the principal sources of tax revenue, the very detailed 39-category OECD classification must be aggregated into ten major components, each sufficiently significant and large to merit separate attention (Table 4.1). Of the ten different revenue components, five are used by every country: income tax, corporation tax, wealth and estate taxes, excise and goods taxes, and customs and exports taxes. Value added (VAT) and sales tax are used in 19 of the 20 countries; and social security taxes are levied separately in 18 countries. On average, a country makes use of 8.5 of the ten different sources of taxes, and four nations — Britain, France, Germany and Austria — make use of all ten sources. The minimum number of components in a national tax system is seven.

The best way to appreciate the number and variety of taxes in use in Western nations today is to review them one by one, noting particular features of each form of tax, and giving in brackets the average share of the national tax system contributed by each tax component.

TABLE 4.1
Cross-national variations in the use of tax components

Tax	National mean	Highest	Range	Lowest	Standard deviation
		(as % contributed to national tax system)			
Income	33	62	New Zealand	13 France	11
Social security	24	46	Spain	0 Australia, NZ	14
(a) Employer	15	36	Spain	0 Australia, NZ	10
(b) Employees	7	16	Netherlands	0 Australia, NZ, Norway, Sweden, Finland.	6
VAT and sales	13	22	Denmark	0 Japan	6
Excise and use	12	27	Ireland	1 Luxembourg	6
Corporation	8	17	Japan	2 Sweden	4
Property	3	11	UK	0 Belgium, Finland	4
Wealth and estate	3	7	Switzerland	0.9 Sweden	2
Customs	2	6	Luxembourg	0 Belgium	2
Payroll	1	7	Austria	0 11 countries	2
Unclassifiable	0.7	5	Japan	0 8 countries	1

Source: Calculated from OECD, *Revenue Statistics of OECD Member Countries, 1965-1981*, Paris, OECD, 1982; data for 1980.

Income tax (OECD average, 33 percent). For income tax to generate a large amount of public revenue, three conditions must be met. First, income must be received in money, and not in kind. Second, a portion of the population must have a surplus income, that is, earnings sufficiently above the subsistence level so that taxpayers can maintain their living standard after making a substantial contribution to the tax collector. A broad income tax base capable of generating a large total revenue arose in Europe only as a consequence of post-1945 affluence. High taxes on the income of a wealthy few (a feature of progressive income taxes) do not produce as much aggregate revenue as a standard rate tax on the income of the many. Third, government must have an effective means of collecting income tax. In most Western countries, the employer deducts income tax from wages at source, the pay-as-you-earn principle. But this method of collecting taxes came into widespread use only in the exigencies of the Second World War. It is still not systematically used in France or Italy, and income tax is a relatively small component of national revenue there.

Social security taxes (24 percent). Pensions and other social security benefits are usually financed on a quasi-insurance basis. Individuals make a regular payment to qualify for benefits, but the insurance principle is breached in several fundamental ways. The payments made to beneficiaries are not limited by their contributions, and government augments social security funds by contributions from general tax revenue. Moreover, contributions to social security funds are compulsory not voluntary, as is the case of conventionally purchased insurance. Receipts from social security taxes are often earmarked to finance specific social benefits, making social security contributions atypical taxes; they are unrequited payments into a general revenue fund. Because social security taxes assure earmarked benefits, countries that have trouble collecting income tax, such as Italy, France and Spain, rely particularly upon them.

The politics of social security taxation divides payments unequally between employers, who on average pay two-thirds of social security taxes, and employees, who pay about one-third. The reason for this is that far more voters are employees than employers; any levy on the many is electorally more sensitive than a levy on the few. A contribution by an employee is a deduction from his wage; a 12 percent tax would mean 12 percent less in wages at the end of a week. By contrast, a levy on an employer appears to an individual employee as a fringe benefit — even if the employer treats social security taxes as part of total wage cost, and therefore pays less in wages.

Value added (VAT) and sales taxes (13 percent). In addition to taxing individual earnings, every European government raises revenue by taxing expenditure. General sales taxes take a variety of forms: they may be levied on goods at one point only, as in the retail sales tax in the United States, or imposed upon each stage in the process of production and sale, as is the case with value added taxes. Because these taxes are levied on the current value of sales, they will yield more revenue when an economy is expanding, as in the 1960s, and when inflation increases the money price of goods, as in the 1970s and 1980s.

Excise and use taxes (12 percent). Excise taxes are levied at high rates on specific goods, especially tobacco, alcoholic drinks and petrol. Use taxes of less importance include motor vehicle licences, television licences, and licences to sell alcoholic drinks or tobacco. The reasons for levying a distinctive and high rate of tax on a particular product are varied: to tax purchasers of luxury goods; to restrict consumption of potentially damaging commodities (tobacco) or commodities potentially in short supply (petrol) and, not least, to raise money for government.

Corporation tax (8 percent). Taxes on corporation profits are relatively low by comparison with taxes on the gross trading activities of corporations. For a government to rely heavily upon a profits tax is to be at the mercy of the economy. When firms make money the revenue will rise, but tax revenue will fall with a decline in profits. Moreover, a high rate of corporation tax may discourage investment and industrial development. Taxing gross pre-tax revenues of firms by a variety of means — employer contributions to social security funds, value added tax, customs and excise taxes and property taxes — is a much surer and larger source of revenue.

Property tax (3 percent). Because property taxes vary substantially from country to country, an OECD average is misleading. In Anglo-American countries property taxes account for up to 11 percent of total tax revenue and an even larger share of local government revenue. By contrast, in continental Europe property taxes contribute nothing or virtually nothing to government revenue. Property taxes have provided the initial stimulus of the so-called tax revolt in the United States, heralded

by a 1978 California constitutional referendum placing a ceiling
on property tax increases, and by the attention given rates (that
is, property taxes) in debates on taxation in Britain. But the
political attention given property tax has been out of proportion
to its contribution to public revenue.

Wealth and estate taxes (3 percent). Inheritance taxes produce
a very small amount of revenue, because only a small proportion
of a country's taxpaying population dies each year, and most
people have little property to bequeath. To place an annual levy
on wealth is administratively difficult, for it assumes that
government can readily assess a person's total wealth, a much
harder task than assessing the value of a house. It is
administratively simpler to tax wealthy people in other ways —
by income, sales and excise, property, corporation and
inheritance taxes.

Customs and export taxes (2 percent). Long before the
industrial revolution, governments taxed imported goods to
encourage home manufacture and to prevent money leaving the
country. In so far as ports of entry can more easily be kept under
surveillance than domestic manufacturers, customs taxes also
provide a more effective tax handle than do taxes on retail sales.
Export taxes can be levied to prevent goods leaving a country, or
in oil-producing countries to pre-empt taxes that would otherwise
be collected by foreign governments. Whereas customs once
provided a substantial share of national tax revenue, the
promotion of free trade in the European Community and
worldwide through the General Agreement on Tariffs and Trade
(GATT) greatly limits the importance of customs duties in
Western nations.

Payroll taxes (1 percent). A tax on the total gross value of a
company's payroll or a per capita levy on the number of
employees is only found in five OECD nations, but where it
occurs it can be substantial. In Austria payroll taxes account
for 7 percent of national taxes and in Australia for 5 percent,
thus allowing a relatively low rate of income tax in Austria and
compensating in part for the absence of a social security tax in
Australia. In a period of full employment, payroll taxes can be
used to encourage a more efficient use of labour as well as to raise

government revenue. In a period of high unemployment, however, payroll taxes can be regarded as undesirable because of being a disincentive to employ workers. *Otherwise unclassifiable taxes (0.7 percent)*. While nearly every country has some distinctive or unique taxes, very little revenue is generated thus. There are no new taxes to be discovered, only variations on familiar themes. Politicians looking abroad in the hope of finding a new and painless way of augmenting revenue will find little or nothing. Variations between national tax systems arise from differences in rates of standard taxes rather than from the use of novel taxes in a national tax system.

2. Every tax component varies cross-nationally in the proportion of revenue it contributes to the national tax system
While every country draws some revenue from most of the taxes analysed here, there are big differences between countries in the proportion of revenue contributed by a particular tax. For example, income tax contributes 62 percent of total tax revenue in New Zealand, as against only 13 percent in France. Social security taxes contribute 46 percent of tax revenue in Spain, and nothing in Australia or New Zealand. Excise taxes contribute 27 percent of tax revenue in Ireland, and 1 percent in Luxembourg (Table 4.1).

A precise statistical way to measure the variation between nations in the use of a particular tax is to calculate the standard deviation from the cross-national mean. The larger the standard deviation, the greater the cross-national difference in the use of a particular tax (Table 4.1). The largest standard of deviation, 14 percent, is for social security taxes. Since two-thirds of all countries should fall within one standard deviation plus or minus of the average share of revenue raised by social security taxes, 24 percent, this means that social security taxes tend to raise anything from 10 to 38 percent of total revenue among OECD nations — and one-third of nations are outside even this wide range. The dispersion of income taxes is similarly high; the standard deviation of 11 percent means that for two-thirds of OECD nations income tax contributes from 22 to 44 percent of revenue, and one-third are outside this range.

The differences between countries in the use of particular taxes are great. The coefficient of variation (that is, the standard deviation divided by the mean) is above 0.50 for eight of the ten taxes examined in Table 4.1, and averages 0.98. Whatever the tax and whatever the country, there are very substantial differences between the average share of revenue the tax raises, and the share actually raised within a specific country.

3. Every country's national tax system differs substantially from a Standard Tax System

Combining the average share that each tax component contributes to national revenue produces a Standard Tax System, showing what taxation would be in a hypothetical country in which every tax yielded the average amount of revenue for that tax in OECD nations. The standard nation would raise 33 percent of its tax revenue from income tax, 24 percent from social security and so forth, down to 0.7 percent from unclassifiable other taxes (cf. Table 4.1).

In so far as OECD nations all have a comparatively high standard of economic development and are all open economies subject to the same international trends, the profile of taxes in any one nation would be expected to approximate to that of the Standard Tax System. The similarity of a country's national tax system to the Standard Tax System can be precisely measured by a Distance Index, calculated by subtracting the share of total tax raised by a particular component in a particular nation from the share raised in the Standard Tax System, ignoring the sign, and summing these differences. The Distance Index thus cumulates the difference of each of the ten tax components from the share of revenue raised by that tax in the Standard Tax System.

The hypothetical Standard Tax System is just that, an intellectual abstraction rather than a reflection of patterns of taxation common to many Western nations. On average, an OECD nation deviates 42 percent from the standard (see Table 4.2). The distance is greatest for New Zealand (66 percent) and

Australia (65 percent), which have no social security tax and unusually high levels of other taxes in compensation, and France (62 percent), which collects relatively little revenue from income tax, and therefore requires unusually high social security, VAT and sales taxes. Only five countries have a distance index of less than 30 percent. Belgium, the country that departs least, none the less differs by 25 percent from the Standard Tax System.

TABLE 4.2
The distance of national tax systems from a Standard Tax System

	Distance Index[a]		
Nation	1965	1980	Change 1965-80
	%	%	%
Belgium	47	25	−22
United Kingdom	35	27	−8
Germany	46	26	0
Sweden	44	29	−15
USA	37	30	−7
Norway	43	29	−14
Italy	52	33	−29
Ireland	64	34	−30
Canada	40	34	−6
Switzerland	41	35	−6
Netherlands	31	37	+6
Austria	40	40	0
Luxembourg	40	46	+6
Finland	34	49	+15
Japan	44	50	+6
Spain	44	58	+14
Denmark	54	60	+6
France	65	62	−3
Australia	50	64	+14
New Zealand	55	66	+11
Average	44	42	−2

a. The distance figure for each country is calculated by subtracting the share of revenue yielded by a given tax in a given country from the average OECD share of revenue raised by the tax, ignoring the sign and summing the results. Social security is reckoned as one tax here.

Source: As in Table 4.1.

Equally significant, there is no evidence of convergence among the national tax systems of OECD nations. In 1965 the average country deviated 44 percent from the Standard Tax System. Subsequently, the Standard System itself has changed in consequence of an increase in revenue from income tax, a fall in excise, use and customs taxes, and a host of minor changes. Notwithstanding a 21 percent shift in the Standard Tax System, national tax systems remained as far apart in 1980 as in 1965. Ten countries diverged further from the standard, and ten moved slightly closer (Table 4.2).

The substantial departure of every country from an international average is explained by the fact that OECD nations tend to fall into two distinct clusters. Anglo-American nations and Scandinavian countries tend to be relatively high in reliance upon income tax, and relatively low on social security taxes. Seven continental European countries tend to rank high on social security taxes and be relatively low in the use of income tax (Figure 4.1). There is a very strong negative correlation (−0.82) between the two principal direct taxes, income tax and social security taxes; furthermore, correlations between other taxes are statistically weak or non-existent. The more money a country raises in income tax, the less it raises in social security taxes and vice versa. These two taxes, which between them account for 57 percent of the standard nation's tax revenue, substitute for each other. The more one direct tax is used, the less the other tax is used. Generalizations about direct taxes can thus be misleading, given the great difference in the use of these two taxes in any one country.

Even though all Western nations raise large sums of money in taxes, the extent to which any one tax is relied upon varies greatly between nations. There is no single pattern to which most nations tend to conform. Total tax revenue is the sum of moneys collected under a great variety of tax laws. To understand how large sums of money are mobilized by government to meet the cost of the contemporary welfare state, we must examine differences within and between nations in the use of particular taxes.

How and why taxes grow

Before we can attempt to explain the causes of the growth of tax revenues, it is necessary to decide how to measure the extent of growth. The extent to which taxes have grown is, to a surprising

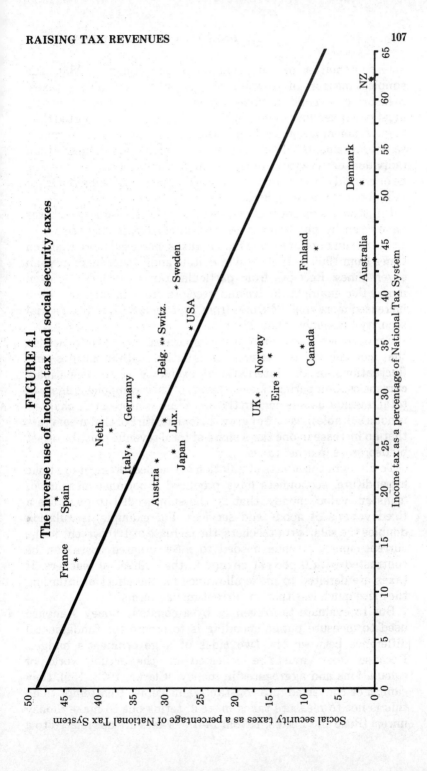

FIGURE 4.1

The inverse use of income tax and social security taxes

extent, a matter of definition (Rose and Karran, 1983). The simplest measure of growth is the current money value of taxes. Measuring revenue in current money is reasonable, for people must pay taxes with money in hand, and receipts are reported thus in government accounts. Moreover, it is consistent with common-sense statements about taxes being high, and rising. If an individual pays twice as much income tax or property tax today as he or she did a decade ago, it is hardly surprising if there is a lot of talk about taxes being high.

Inflation has meant that everywhere in the Western world taxes have risen by hundreds of percent in current money terms. In Italy, the amount of money paid in taxes increased more than ten times from 1965 to 1980, and in Britain and France by more than seven times. Receipts from particular taxes can increase even more. For example, in Ireland receipts from income tax have increased more than 24 times from 1965 to 1980, and from social security taxes more than 28 times.

For purposes of cross-national comparison, measures are needed that control for the effects of inflation within nations and fluctuations in the international exchange rates of national currencies. Comparing taxes in terms of their component share of total revenue, as was done in the preceding section of this chapter, is not a suitable measure of growth, for a feature of that measure is that an increase in one tax's share of total revenue must be offset by decreases in other taxes.

To discount the effects of inflation in the measurement of public expenditure, economists have produced a notional measure of 'constant-value' money, that is, the sum needed to purchase a fixed volume of goods and services. For example, if inflation doubles the salaries of teachers, the increase of 100 percent in the current-money revenue needed to meet inflated costs can be contrasted with 0 percent change in the number of teachers. If taxes are deflated to make allowance for the effect of inflation, they rise much less than in current-money terms.

But to evaluate tax revenues by a constant-money standard used to measure public spending is to ignore the fundamental difference between the two sides of a government's budget. Because taxes must be collected in 'the actual world of calculations and aggregates in money' (Clarke, 1973: 159), they cannot be converted into constant-value sums. To attempt to do this is not to measure taxes in 'real' terms but to make money unreal (Rose and Peters, 1978a: 144ff.). Taxes are not related to a particular volume of goods and services; they are transactions denominated in actual money.

A third way to measure the growth of public revenues is to calculate revenue as a proportion of the national product. As long as the nation's economy grows at the same rate as public revenues, then there is nil change in the percentage of a nation's wealth claimed by government. The logic of this measure is that citizens will not notice or object to paying more taxes as long as their take-home pay is rising. Measuring revenue as a proportion of the national product is also useful in cross-national comparisons, for it provides a base for comparison independent of fluctuations in currency values. Tax revenues in OECD nations have increased their share of the gross domestic product from an average of 24.7 percent in 1965 to 36.6 percent in 1980.

The three measures give very different pictures of the growth in taxation. When changes in the current money value of total tax revenue are the measure, then on average in Western nations taxes have increased more than five times from 1965 to 1979, whereas when deflated in terms of a constant volume of goods, taxes may be said to have doubled. When total revenue as a proportion of the gross domestic product is examined, the increase is about one-half. Whatever the measure, one conclusion is consistent: total tax revenue has been rising throughout the Western world.

Statements about taxes in aggregate are often not true about particular taxes. Aggregate growth is consistent with some taxes rising and others contracting. The point is illustrated by a detailed examination of British taxation since 1948 (Rose and Karran, 1983). First of all, it shows that there are noteworthy changes in the taxes levied. Of the 20 taxes at some time contributing at least 1 percent to total revenue, only 11 were continuously in effect for three decades; 9 were either introduced or repealed within the period. Among the 11 continuing taxes, 7 actually decreased their share of the national product in the period, as against 4 increasing their share. Altogether, the 11 taxes displayed four different dynamic trends: a cyclical up-and-down pattern with little long-run change; a predictable pattern of growth; a predictable pattern of contraction; and an unstable course showing substantial changes without any consistent pattern.

While the pattern of growth in taxation is clear in aggregate, disaggregating total revenue into its constituent tax components shows that some taxes contract while others grow in their share of the national product. Of the principal taxes reviewed here, five account on average for 90 percent of revenue among OECD nations: income tax, social security tax, VAT and sales taxes, excise taxes and corporation tax. When we examine the direction of change in the share of the national product of each of these taxes from 1965 to 1979 in 20 OECD countries the overall conclusion is clear: in each country, at least one of the five taxes has decreased. Even though taxes in aggregate have everywhere gone up, in no Western nation has every major tax moved in the same direction.

To understand the dynamics of taxation, we must understand *which* taxes grow. The three largest taxes — income tax, social security tax, and VAT and sales taxes — have almost invariably grown. Income tax has increased its share of the national product in all 20 nations reviewed here; on average, its share of the national product grew by half to 12.2 percent. Social security taxes have increased their share of the national product in every country except one, Denmark, averaging an increase in their share of the national product by two-thirds to 8.8 percent. VAT and sales taxes have increased in every country where they are collected except Australia and Canada, with an average increase of two-fifths, to claim 5.2 percent of the national product.

Simultaneously with the growth in total taxation, excise taxes on such products as tobacco, beer and wine have been decreasing their claim in the national product in 13 OECD nations. In 1965 these excise taxes usually accounted for a larger amount of revenue than did general sales taxes. Governments have boosted net revenue by increasing the relative yield from across-the-board sales taxes and decreasing the yield from specific excise taxes. There is also a consistent decline in customs as a source of revenue in 16 nations. Governments have reduced trade barriers while simultaneously widening the tax base for sales tax. Corporation tax has tended to contract too.

The aggregate upward trend in tax revenue can be explained simply: government needs money. If public spending increases, revenue must be found. The push given taxation by public spending is illustrated by asking: What makes social security taxes much higher as a proportion of national revenue in some OECD nations than others? Social security benefits show a significant positive correlation (0.48) with social security taxes. High social security taxes are one price paid for high levels of pensions. To explain the growth of taxes as a reflection of growth in spending on public programmes is logical, but it begs the question: Why does public spending grow? This question is best considered in Chapter 7, which examines the causes of growth in the government programmes requiring most of the increase in public revenue. In this chapter attention will concentrate upon three causes of growth in taxation likely to affect every Western nation: the inertia of established commitments; changes in the national economy; and political choice.

1. The inertia of established commitments

This is a particularly appropriate explanation for taxation, because the two principal determinants of tax revenue at any one point in time — tax laws and the structure of a nation's economy — reflect decisions and events in the more or less distant past.

Revenue-raising does not start from scratch each year; it follows from the persistence of tax laws. A government does not need to pass new legislation to raise taxes; a host of taxes authorized by statute ensure government a continuing flow of revenue. Nor could any government revise the whole of its tax code within a year. To do so would jeopardize the monthly flow of revenues needed to meet the continuing costs of public expenditure.

In any given year the great bulk of a government's tax revenue is the product of applying established tax laws to the tax base, the national economy. The actual amount of revenue collected depends upon the size and composition of a nation's economy as well as upon tax laws. The point is specially relevant in international comparisons. Two countries may levy income tax and sales tax at the same rate, but the tax will yield more money in the country where incomes are higher and a bigger national product generates more sales. Whereas economies differ substantially among OECD nations, within a country there is very little difference in the structure of the economy from one year to the next. There is thus a steady, predictable flow of revenue from the interaction of established laws and a given economic structure.

The short-term stability sustained by the inertia of established commitments can be cumulatively modified by changes in tax laws and in the national economy. By definition, the national economy is continuously in motion, and the national product usually expands from year to year, in part because of inflation and in part because of an increase in the volume of national output. The effect of applying established tax laws to an expanding economy is to increase the revenue yield without any overt decision by government. Inasmuch as economic growth and inflation increase the size of the economy at a cumulatively compounding rate, the medium-term impact of non-decision making upon revenue can be substantial. For example, an economy that expanded 6 percent a year because of economic growth and inflation would double in size within 11 years, and within eight years if it expanded by 8 percent. In such circumstances, the inertia of established tax laws can quickly double the amount of revenue produced.

The annual Budget cycle forces a government to review its sources of revenue every year, and each year it usually makes a number of alterations in its repertoire of tax laws. To raise more revenue, a government does not need to introduce a new tax, with all the political and administrative uncertainties that this causes. Instead, it can simply adjust existing tax rates, which involves virtually no administrative difficulty, and limits political controversy. For example, increasing a sales tax from 5 to 6 percent will increase by one-fifth its revenue yield.

In an inflationary era, changes in the nominal value of income force government to index tax rates to avoid collecting 'too much' money in tax. Inflation increases nominal wages, thus pushing more and more people into higher tax brackets for the calculation of income tax. If government did nothing, people could find their income tax demand rising 20 or 30 percent a year. In reaction, most Western nations have introduced an element of indexing in tax rates, altering the level at which higher marginal rates of taxation apply and the nominal value of deductions as inflation increases current money earnings.

In so far as inertia properties of tax laws and of the economy tend to determine current tax revenues, the proportion of the national product claimed by each tax component should remain constant, as pervasive changes in the economy affect all taxes equally. To what extent did the share of the Gross Domestic Product taken by each tax component in fact remain the same from 1965, the earliest year for which there are detailed data, to the present? Stability is measured by comparing the proportion of GDP claimed in 1965 and 1979, and reckoning the smaller of the two numbers as the constant element.[5] For example, if income tax accounted for 9 percent of GDP in 1965 and 12 percent in 1979, then it accounted for a stable 9 percent of GDP. In a complementary manner, if excise and use taxes accounted for 8 percent of GDP in 1965 and 5 percent in 1979, the constant element is 5 percent. The sum of the constant terms indicates the proportion of today's total revenue provided by inertia commitments.

In every OECD nation, established commitments effective in 1965 accounted for more than half of all revenue raised in 1979. On average, established commitments accounted for 71 percent of 1979 revenue, and as much as 81 percent in Britain. Inertia sustains a dynamic, not a static, equilibrium. By definition, laws that claim a constant proportion of the national product yield more and more revenue as the economy expands. Table 4.3 shows the extent to which taxation has increased faster than the national product as a whole. In the median OECD nation, tax revenues have increased their share of the national product by 6.8 percent.

TABLE 4.3
The inertia of established commitments in revenue-raising

Nation	Total tax revenue as % GDP		1979 revenue accounted for by established commitments[a]
	1965	1979	
			%
Britain	31.0	34.0	81
Austria	34.5	41.4	79
Canada	26.0	31.0	79
France	35.0	41.2	79
Germany	31.6	37.3	79
Australia	24.4	29.7	79
Finland	30.1	35.0	77
Italy	27.2	30.1	76
USA	26.5	31.3	75
Japan	18.1	24.8	70
Netherlands	35.5	47.4	69
New Zealand	24.3	29.8	69
Norway	33.3	46.1	69
Belgium	31.2	44.7	68
Luxembourg	30.8	46.2	66
Switzerland	20.7	31.1	64
Sweden	35.6	50.3	63
Denmark	30.1	44.1	61
Spain	15.1	24.3	58
Ireland	26.0	33.8	54

a. The sum of calculations for 12 tax components in each country, counting separately social security revenue from employers, employees and the self-employed.
Source: Calculated from OECD, *Revenue Statistics of OECD Member Countries 1965-1980*, Paris, 1981.

2. Changes in economic conditions

These can influence tax revenues in several ways. Inflation is the first cause. Secondly, economic growth can increase tax revenue, for some taxes can grow faster than the rate of growth in the national product overall. Income tax revenue is buoyant because income tax is levied at a progressive rate. As incomes rise — whether that rise is the result of inflation, actual growth in the economy or both factors — then revenue from income tax will rise disproportionately. Thirdly, tax revenue can also change because of cumulative changes in the structure of the economy. For example, an increase in private motoring will increase revenue from user taxes on motor vehicles and excise taxes on petrol.

When changes in taxes from 1965 to 1979 are examined in current money terms, inflation accounts for nearly all the increase and economic growth for very little. This is demonstrated with statistical precision by stepwise regression equations in which inflation rates and growth in GDP are tested for their ability to explain growth in five major tax components. Inflation is consistently more important than economic growth as the explanation of increases in current-money tax revenues (Table 4.4). Inflation on average can explain 93 percent of the increase in current-money revenues, and economic growth explains only 2.7 percent. Inflation has had a far greater effect upon the tax base, the national product, than has the fiscal dividend of economic growth.

The political implications of Table 4.4 are pervasive. Inflation is pushing up taxes in every OECD country, and it affects every major source of tax revenue. Politicians can direct blame for the escalation of taxes at inflation. Given inflation, the money collected as taxes is bound to increase. Yet the fact that several hundred per cent increases in taxes can be 'explained away' by inflation does not dispose of all political problems. Citizens who complain about increased taxes are likely to complain about inflation too.

Analysing taxes as a proportion of the national product controls for much of the effect of inflation. In so far as taxes and the national product both increase equally with inflation, the share of the national product claimed by a given tax should remain constant. This procedure also controls for the effect of established commitments upon revenue-raising by concentrating upon changes in the share of the national product taken by a given tax component.

TABLE 4.4
Inflation the principal cause of increasing revenue

Principal taxes	Increase 1965-1979 explained by:		
	Inflation	Economic growth	Total explained
	(Average r^2 for OECD nations)		
	%	%	%
Income tax	98	0.4	98
Corporation tax	93	1.5	95
Social security	89	1.0	90
VAT and sales	93	5.2	99
Excise and use	92	5.6	98
Average	93	2.7	96

Source: Calculated from data in OECD *Revenue Statistics of OECD Member Countries 1965-80*, Paris, 1981.

Even when much of the effect of inflation is thus controlled, inflation remains important. Inflation and economic growth each account for a substantial amount of change in the revenue yield in each of the five major sources of tax revenue. Inflation is slightly more important in explaining increases in income, corporation and social security taxes, whereas economic growth is relatively more important in explaining changes in expenditure taxes. Together, these changes in economic conditions on average explain 72 percent of changes in the principal tax components' claims upon GDP. Economic growth and inflation each account for half of the explained change (Table 4.5).

TABLE 4.5
Inflation and economic growth as principal causes of change in tax components' share of GDP, 1965-1979

Principal taxes	Change 1965-1979 explained by:		
	Inflation	Economic growth	Total
	(Average r^2 for OECD nations)		
	%	%	%
Income tax	43	40	83
Corporation tax	32	26	58
Social security	55	32	88
VAT and sales	31	37	68
Excise and use	20	49	69
Average	36	36	72

Source: Calculated from data in OECD *Revenue Statistics of OECD Member Countries 1965-80*, Paris, 1981.

The impact of inflation and economic growth upon taxes does not show significant differences between OECD nations. In high-inflation, high-growth Sweden, economic growth on average accounts for 35 percent of changes in the share of GDP taken by major revenue components and inflation for 41 percent; in high-inflation, low-growth Britain economic growth accounts for 36 percent and inflation for 22 percent; in low-inflation and high-growth Germany inflation accounts for 41 percent of change and economic growth for 28 percent. Inflation and economic growth are each independent and substantial causes of change in the size of major taxes, irrespective of economic conditions within a particular country.

When the conjoint effects of established commitments and changes in economic conditions are taken together, nearly the whole of the growth in major taxes (and therefore, in total tax revenue) can be explained. In any one year, the inertia of persisting laws and the economic base is of greatest importance. But in an inflationary era the amount of revenue raised in current-money terms substantially increases, as the money value of the economic base is inflated. When inflation is discounted by examining taxes as a proportion of the national product from 1965 to 1979, established commitments account on average for about 71 percent of the share of GDP claimed by an average tax component in 1979; inflation for about 10 percent; and growth in the economy for another 10 percent.

3. Political choice

Given the influence upon taxation of established statutory commitments and changes in economic condition, what role if any is left for political choice? The significance of political choice for taxation is best appreciated when time horizons are greatly lengthened. The crucial question to ask is: *When* are significant choices made? The answer given by established commitments is: A long time ago. In almost every OECD nation, the proponents of the initial income tax legislation have made the most important choice affecting government revenue. In Britain income tax was introduced in 1799. Deciding whether to vary slightly the rate at which an established tax is levied is the only choice that a policy-maker need make in any given year.

Efforts to explain the growth of taxation as a function of party political choice are deficient for a number of reasons. The first and most important is that a governing party cannot determine the established tax structure, but can only make changes at the margin. Second, analyses (e.g. Cameron, 1978) may confuse the source of revenue (a tax) with its use (public spending programmes). A statistical association between socialist parties in office and high levels of taxation can be explained as a reflection of socialist preferences for high-spending welfare state programmes rather than as an indication of a liking for high taxes per se (cf. Castles, 1982b). Third, statistical studies usually analyse total taxes and do not explain why, within a given nation, some taxes will change in the predicted direction, and others in the opposite direction from that assumed to follow from a left-wing or right-wing government being in office.

Every party newly entering office is likely to promise some changes in tax laws or tax rates, and a particular change may excite political controversy in a given session of Parliament. But that does not mean that the change introduced has a substantial effect upon total tax revenue. British experience is particularly instructive. The two most important postwar tax innovations did not greatly alter government revenue flows: replacing a tax on corporate profits with a different corporation tax in the mid-1960s, and substituting a value added tax for a variety of purchase taxes in 1973 (Rose and Karran, 1983; Robinson and Sandford, 1983). If changes in technical features in tax laws are set aside because of involving a swap of taxes rather than an additional revenue source, then more than nine-tenths of total British tax revenue today can be attributed to taxes that have persisted since 1948, regardless of the rotation of parties in and out of office.

The longer the time perspective, the greater the impact of political events upon tax systems, and especially tax rates. Financing a war raises the greatest challenge to established patterns of revenue-raising. Pressures for more revenue also come from the cumulative increase in spending commitments. When events force substantial changes in tax rates or the introduction of new taxes, it is less an expression of what politicians choose to do than a reaction to events and pressures beyond their control.

In the period under review, political parties and politicians have had little scope to alter tax laws. Aggregate revenue requirements mean that abolishing one tax must lead to the introduction of another tax or an increase in the rate of established taxes in order to compensate for revenue forgone. Politicians tend to avoid the alternative way to cut taxes, abolishing programme commitments that create the pressure for revenue. Whatever their partisan orientation, politicians usually accept the inertia of established taxing commitments as the least painful way of financing government programmes. The taxes about which voters may complain were enacted not by the government of the day, but by their predecessors years ago.

Intentions and consequences of increasing taxes

A diverse repertoire of reasons are offered by politicians, economists, administrators and social policy experts for increasing or cutting taxes. Macroeconomists can view taxation as an instrument of short-term demand management, raising taxes to counter inflation and lowering taxes to stimulate the economy in accord with Keynesian doctrines. Applied economists can view alterations in specific taxes as means to influence particular sections of the economy, for example, encouraging investment or discouraging petrol consumption. Theoretical economists may construct an ideal tax system intended to achieve an optimal distribution of welfare in the abstract. Social policy experts view taxes in terms of their impact upon the distribution or redistribution of income from the well-to-do to the poor. The most ambitious social policy experts attempt to examine the conjoint effect of taxes and spending programmes upon income distribution, since a tax may be notionally regressive in incidence yet progressive in its programme outputs, as is social security (OECD, 1980). Politicians may view taxes in terms of their impact upon broad sections of the electorate or in reaction to ideological values, whereas pressure group leaders will be concerned with the specific impact of a particular tax upon their group. Tax collectors usually evaluate taxes according to administrative goals, concentrating particularly upon the efficiency and certainty of administration.

While it can be intellectually interesting to explore a variety of putative goals of taxation, the practical relevance of these discussions is often limited. To analyse the conjoint impact of all taxes as if they constituted a coherent system planned so that all the parts fitted together logically is to misunderstand the historical process. Actual tax systems have evolved by adding and amending taxes one at a time. As two tax experts (Kay and King, 1980: 18) note, 'While there is room for argument about the effects of the tax system, it is really very difficult to argue that many of them have ever been explicitly intended by anyone.'

Predicting the consequences of taxes, especially new taxes, can be difficult. New taxes are little used by governments for revenue-raising because their practical effect is so uncertain, and may even be counter-productive. While economic theory can predict what ought to happen if certain assumptions hold true, differences between actual consequences and theoretical assumptions are usually such that the ways in which actual taxes differ from these theoretical taxes are often of much greater economic significance than the ways in which theoretical taxes differ from each other.

The consequences of taxation that are important for understanding big government first of all concern revenue, for without a continuing or growing flow of tax revenue, big government cannot be sustained. Increases in tax revenue in the postwar era have made big government financially possible. But it does not necessarily follow that high levels of current taxation make further increases easy. The higher the level of taxes, the harder it may be to increase taxes further. Taxation with representation is consistent with doctrines of political consent — but it also encourages people to search on their own for ways to limit tax liabilities. People may evade taxes illegally or avoid them legally by making use of statutory tax deductions or by demonetizing work. Government may accede to popular anti-tax pressure groups by increasing 'tax expenditures', that is, loopholes legally reducing tax liabilities. But since this lowers tax revenue, as long as big spending programmes are the rule, government must seek revenue elsewhere. In consequence, it will turn to borrowing to meet the deficit between what it wants to spend and what it wants to tax.

The most immediate impact of tax trends is often overlooked or explained away: the very great increase in current-money sums paid in taxes. The increase reflects the conjoint effects of inflation, economic growth and higher tax rates. On average, total tax revenue has been increasing by 15 to 20 percent annually in OECD nations from 1965 to 1980. In this 15-year period, per capita taxes have cumulatively increased nine times in current-money terms. Analytically, the significance of higher money payments could be ignored by discounting for the effect of inflation. In fact, empirical studies by economic psychologists have demonstrated that a substantial proportion of the taxpaying population does not know how much tax it pays, and is a fortiori even more incapable of determining the effects of inflation upon taxation (Lewis, 1982: 217ff.). The one thing certain is that nearly everyone will correctly perceive that the current-money value of taxation is increasing.

The impact of taxation is felt far more widely throughout Western societies today than a generation ago. VAT and sales taxes affect almost all purchases, bringing into the tax collector's net people who do not pay income tax. The chief principle of progressive taxation — taxation according to ability to pay — has caused more and more wage-earners to pay income tax, as real incomes have risen. For example, in Britain in 1939 only 4 million persons, one-fifth of the work force, paid income tax; today 20 million, four-fifths of the labour force, pay income tax. When Ireland introduced Pay-As-You-Earn taxation in 1960, the total tax levied on the average single male industrial worker was equal to 10 percent of income. Today, in a more prosperous Ireland (and an Ireland with a much higher-spending government), the tax is more than 27 percent of income.

The impact of taxes on income is felt particularly strongly at the margin, for the principal of progressive income tax is that the more money a person earns, the higher is the rate of tax for each additional pound or dollar earned. When only a small fraction of persons paid any income tax, marginal rates concerned only the wealthy. Today, industrial workers in countries such as Sweden can find that the marginal rate of income plus social security taxes claims more than 50 percent of every extra 100 kronor earned. Where the standard rate of income tax is 30 percent and social security taxes are 10 percent, the great bulk of taxpayers will be subject to a marginal tax rate of at least 40 percent on increased earnings. Because marginal income tax rates are peculiarly sensitive to the number of deductions a worker can claim (and whether there are one or two wage-earners in a family), there are very big disparities betweeen the marginal tax rate of a single person and a married man with two children, or between the marginal tax of the first pound earned by a wife who goes out to work to augment her husband's earnings, as against the first pound earned by a widow or a single person.

From an individual citizen's point of view, the cumulative effect of the totality of taxes is a magnitude greater than that of any one tax. Many studies of public revenue concentrate upon only a single tax or a single tax jurisdiction. To write about cuts in central government taxes when their consequence is an increase in local authority taxation is to confuse shifting taxes with cutting taxes. From a taxpayer's point of view, the fact that many hands are dipping into his pockets in many different ways makes the total impact of taxation far greater than the impact of any one particular tax (cf. Table 4.1).

In a period of increasing affluence, citizens could pay increased taxes from the fiscal dividend of economic growth. Today the annual claims of government for increased revenue can exceed the total annual growth of the economy. Major Western governments are threatening to reduce individual take-home pay — that is, what individuals have left to spend of their earnings after taxes — when claims for increased taxes cannot be met solely by the fiscal dividend of economic growth. In the extreme case of Sweden, even though the economy had grown by about one-fifth from 1970 to 1979, take-home pay is now lower than in 1970. While an absolute reduction in take-home pay is not common in OECD nations, the growth of government's tax claims is reducing the scope for take-home pay to rise, bringing close the time when take-home pay can be under continuous pressure to decline (Rose and Peters, 1978a: Chapter 7).

How do we expect people to react when government's claims for increased taxes threaten to reduce their earnings? To speak of a tax revolt is to substitute hyperbole for analysis. There is no reason to believe that most citizens could or would want to take up arms against perceived increases in taxes (Rose, 1980b). But it is equally unwise to assume that citizens would completely ignore a government-imposed reduction in their earnings. The steps taken might not replace consent with active dissent, but they could encourage civic indifference.

The immediate consequence of increased taxes reducing take-home pay is that individuals who are not the direct beneficiaries of welfare state spending will find their standard of living threatened. How can people maintain their standard of living against pressures of rising taxes? The easiest way to do so is completely legal: avoid taxes. There is no obligation on a person to arrange his or her affairs so as to pay the maximum amount to the Inland Revenue. Tax laws contain many provisions (their critics call them 'loopholes') for reducing net tax liability. Surveys of taxation in Sweden have found that the number of people avoiding taxes legally exceeds the number of tax 'evaders' (those working in the illegal Unofficial Economy) by a margin of two to one (Warneryd and Walerud, 1982: 27).

Tax evasion is much more easily talked about than done. Tax laws are written with an eye to minimizing the opportunities for evasion by levying taxes upon economic activities that are difficult to hide from the tax collector, e.g. the payroll of large companies, or the sale of oil by a refinery. By definition, illegal activities such as tax evasion are not reported in government statistics. Careful estimates of the 'black economy' indicate that it comprises a very small portion of the total economy, about 5 percent in many Western countries, and that it shows no evidence of growing, even in high-tax countries (Smith, 1981; Blades, 1982: 33).

The biggest threat to public revenues comes from the prospect of individuals maintaining their living standards by *demonetizing* work, that is, making at home more of the goods and services that they need for themselves. Today, upwards of one-third of the work undertaken in a society is outside the tax collector's net, because it is part of the domestic economy (Rose, 1983a). Goods and services produced and consumed within the family are exchanged outside the market. Because money does not change hands, there is no basis for claiming a tax. In contemporary households, an employed person will spend 20 hours or more each week working in the domestic economy, and a women with children will spend far more. Since every family member has on average about 60 to 70 hours of leisure time per week, there is ample scope to increase activities in the domestic economy to maintain consumption, and thus avoid the effects of increased taxes and falling take-home pay.

Increasing civic indifference to tax claims can reduce government's effectiveness in collecting taxes. The collection of many taxes depends upon a measure of collaboration between taxpayers and public officials. Government cannot audit every tax return; it must trust most citizens and organizations to pay taxes honestly. In times past an absolute monarch could 'tax indiscriminately everything from belfries to playing cards', for the monarch's only goal was to raise more money (Caiden, 1980: 144). But a popularly elected government cannot levy taxes capriciously.

Raising taxes that appear likely to cause the least resistance among taxpayers is politically attractive. In principle, so-called 'invisible' taxes should be less irksome than 'visible' taxes (cf. Wilensky, 1981: Hibbs and Madsen, 1981). But no tax is nowadays invisible. A sales tax is technically described as an invisible tax, but every shopkeeper has an incentive to make it very visible by adding it on to the price in order to show that up to 15 percent of what the customer pays goes to government. In so far as an excise tax is passed on in higher prices, as in the sale of drink and tobacco, increasing such taxes is resented as an increase in the cost of living. Companies asked to pay social security and payroll taxes that are a 25 or even 50 percent additional charge on wages may hire fewer workers, thus causing political complaints about unemployment.

Within any given country, the level of tax resistance is likely to be greater when taxes are high rather than low. The existing composition of the national tax system can influence which tax is most likely to increase. In a country where income tax is relatively low by international standards, such as France, Italy or Ireland, it would be expected that this tax would be raised when government needed more revenue, since other taxes, such as social security, are unusually high. From 1965 to 1980, revenue from income tax rose twice as much as tax revenue generally in Italy and Ireland, and also disproportionately in France. In a complementary way, in Britain and America, where social security taxes have been relatively low by international standards, these taxes increased by a greater percentage than total taxes.

While raising relatively under-utilized taxes may be reasonable analytically, it still produces political problems, for the total claims of taxation upon citizens are increased. Governments have responded to this pressure by back-door means, reducing net tax claims by so-called tax expenditures. Tax expenditures are legal provisions in the tax code that allow individuals and corporations to reduce their effective tax liability. For example, people who pay for their housing by borrowing money on a mortgage can usually deduct interest payments from their gross income, thus enjoying a substantial rebate on the cost of housing. By contrast, people who rent housing pay the rent with post-tax net earnings. Companies that invest in ways that government wishes to encourage, for example in oil exploration or in new factories in economically depressed regions, may be allowed to write off investment costs rapidly, thus reducing their net tax.

Tax expenditures can be significant sums of money. In Britain, for example, allowances given to married and single taxpayers are worth the equivalent of £17 billion, allowances for interest on mortgages more than £2 billion, and allowances on corporation tax about £5 billion (Treasury, 1983, Vol. 2: 121). Tax expenditures in the United States involve a similarly large discounting of federal taxes (US Budget, 1982). Comparative analysis of the scale and dynamics of tax expenditures is not possible, because there is no agreement among economists or governments about what is and is not to be considered a tax expenditure: the OECD has yet to agree a common international definition of the concept. As Richard Goode (1977: 27) notes, 'The present tax expenditure budget rests on shaky conceptual foundations'.

Whatever definition is used, the important point about tax expenditures is that their primary impact is upon the distribution of the tax burden. No government would repeal tax expenditures without simultaneously adjusting tax rates. For example, abolishing standard deductions from gross family income could be offset by reducing the rate of income tax in order to keep revenue the same in aggregate. To eliminate tax expenditures without adjusting tax rates would impose a great shift upward in the tax burden of most families.

When government finds that pressures of spending programmes exceed the revenue that it can raise from taxation, then it must either put the brakes on public expenditure or find a way of covering the resulting deficit by borrowing. Western governments have usually preferred to increase borrowing. The extent to which government prefers to raise revenue by borrowing rather than by taxes can be most immediately expressed as the percentage that borrowing adds to current tax revenues. The greater the importance of borrowing, the more the government of the day is temporarily able to claim the political benefits of increasing expenditure without increasing taxes. The extent to which borrowing augments tax revenue can be very large. For example, in Italy, for every 1,000,000 lira that the government raised from taxes in 1979 it borrowed an additional 364,000 lira; borrowing equalled 13 percent of the gross domestic product.

There has definitely been a secular upward trend in government borrowing (Table 4.6). In 1960 three of six major Western nations were net lenders, not borrowers: on average, major Western nations ran a surplus of 0.2 percent of revenue. By 1965 the balance had altered, but the change was relatively slight; on average, major Western nations augmented taxes by borrowing an additional 3.4 percent. In 1970 a more favourable economic climate meant that borrowing on average augmented revenues by only 1.4 percent, and three countries ran a surplus. The intensification of world recession in the 1970s has brought about greater borrowing. In 1975, a very bad year for the world economy, borrowing added an average of 15.0 percent to revenue. By 1980 most governments had reduced their reliance upon borrowing, but it still provided a 10.0 percent supplement to tax revenue, far more than in the pre-1975 days. Without recourse to borrowing, governments would be faced with the unpleasant alternatives of substantially putting up taxes or reducing programme expenditure.

In the contemporary welfare state, the taxes levied by govern-ment directly affect every household, whether its income is large or small. In the extreme case, people receiving income maintenance grants to alleviate poverty will lose them as their income rises above the officially defined poverty line. For people caught in the 'poverty

TABLE 4.6
Borrowing as a percentage of current taxes, 1960-1980

	US	UK	France	Germany	Italy	Sweden
1960	1.5	7.6	−0.9	−8.0	4.5	−3.4
1965	3.7	9.0	0.0	2.8	13.9	−9.1
1970	6.3	−3.4	−0.3	0.3	12.5	−6.8
1971	8.8	−0.5	0.0	1.6	17.7	−8.3
1972	3.9	8.1	0.3	2.6	24.9	−6.6
1973	1.0	13.2	−0.3	−1.7	24.3	−6.3
1974	3.1	12.7	0.8	4.6	23.9	−1.6
1975	16.4	15.2	7.9	15.4	38.5	−3.3
1976	9.2	15.8	3.5	9.7	28.3	−6.1
1977	5.3	11.9	4.2	6.9	23.9	−0.8
1978	2.5	14.4	6.9	7.4	28.1	2.9
1979	0.9	11.5	3.9	8.2	27.4	14.4
1980	1.5	10.4	1.8	9.6	21.6	15.1

− indicates surplus.
Source: Calculated from OECD, *Economic Outlook*, December 1982.
Borrowing = total outlays (Table R8) − current receipts (Table R9).

trap', the *marginal* rate of taxation can be more than 100 percent, because of the conjoint effect of paying taxes and losing social security benefits as their income rises (Kay and King, 1980: 115). A leading British Fabian, Brian Abel-Smith (1973: 172), has argued, 'What is absurd about our present arrangements is that we are taking in income tax, national insurance and rates from the same families to whom we are offering help in means-tested benefits.' Both British and American governments have seriously considered removing the anomalies arising by adopting a Negative Income Tax. But this rationalization of revenue-raising and spending has not been achieved, because of the inertia of established tax commitments and of entitlements to welfare benefits.

Notes

1. Note that the ratio of tax revenue to GDP will differ from that of public expenditure to GDP because borrowing is also used to finance expenditure; see Table 4.6.

2. When a least squares regression trend line is fitted to the path of total tax revenue as a percentage of GDP from 1965 to 1979, there is usually a very steady trend: the median r^2 value for 20 OECD nations is 0.85. When the same procedure is applied to each of the 12 major components of tax revenue into which the total can be disaggregated, none of the means for individual revenue components approaches this figure, and the median r^2 among the 12 components is only 0.49.

3. In addition to taxation, government may also raise revenue from trading enterprises that are not run at a loss and by selling capital assets. The sums involved are usually relatively small. Since there is no satisfactory source of cross-nationally comparable data, these revenue sources are not examined further here.

4. Portugal, Greece and Turkey have been excluded, for their political systems were non-democratic for most of the period under review here.

5. Each type of social security tax — employer, employee and self-employed — is here calculated separately to produce 12 tax components. The effects of taxation upon intergovernmental relations are not considered here because they require a book in themselves.

5 THE WORK OF PUBLIC EMPLOYEES

In a very real sense, public employees put flesh on the bare bones of government. Public employees are a qualitatively different resource from laws and money. Laws by themselves are inert; people are needed to decide what statutes authorize, and to enforce laws. Money too is passive; it cannot be spent without action by public officials. Public employees actively run the multiplicity of organizations that collectively constitute government.

Analysing public employment raises fundamental questions about the institutions and activities of government. One conventional picture of a civil servant is a member of an elite or mandarin class, the power behind the throne, assisting or manipulating ministers elected to give direction to government (Dogan, 1975; Aberbach et al., 1981). Another is of faceless bureaucrats sitting in a ministry, producing memoranda that will never be read. In fact, in every Western nation civil servants are a relatively small portion of total public employees, and high ranking civil servants comprise much less than 1 percent of the total. Most public employees work in local government, the health services or nationalized industries; some, such as doctors or university professors, may not think of themselves as government employees. Equally important, the great majority of public employees do not work in a nation's capital, and most who do work there are not advising ministers. Most public employees are dispersed nationwide, delivering government programmes locally.

In an era of full employment, distinctive characteristics of public employment, especially security of tenure and index-linked pensions, are often ignored. The best jobs will usually be defined as the jobs paying most money; invariably, the top jobs in the private sector are better paid than in the public sector, because salaries are not subject to political scrutiny. In the private sector there are more employers competing against each other for workers than in the public sector; government is often a monopoly employer of particular occupations. In a period of high unemployment, however, such distinctive characteristics of public employment as job security and inflation-proofed pensions look much more attractive, compared with the insecurities of jobs in the private sector.

Public employment is both a consequence and a cause of the growth of government. When labour-intensive service such as education and the health service grow, public employment will grow too. In so far as public employees have an active interest in the programmes for which they are responsible, they can promote their programmes like any pressure group. Public employees can claim that they are recommending more health care, more roads or more military defence in the national interest. Their own self-interest in expanding their activities need not be mentioned. In so far as public employees are successful in promoting programme expansion, more tax revenue will be needed, and new legislation may be enacted.

The purpose of this chapter is to marshall evidence about the size and growth of public employment. Too often general assertions are made about public employees without considering where they work (e.g., in the ivory towers of ministries; at the coal face; delivering services in hospitals and schools), when (under government of a left-wing party, or under all colours of government) or why (e.g., to provide more benefits of public policy, or more jobs for themselves). The first section defines the scope of public employment, and presents quantitative evidence about public employment in major Western nations. The causes of change are the subject of the second section; a multiplicity of causes must be tested, since different sectors of public employment change in different directions. The concluding section considers the dynamic consequences of public employment in terms of the effectiveness of government, and continuing popular consent to their position.

The scale of public employment

To identify the employees of government, we must first of all identify the employers, that is, the organizations that collectively constitute government. Most cross-national compilations of public employment statistics are infirm because they start from each nation's own definition of public employees. The linguistic differences between *beamte*, *la fonction publique* and the civil service are nothing as compared to the differences in the legal and historical circumstances that have led some officials to be called civil servants, and others not. 'The legal definition of civil servant (whatever that may be) is a combination of various formalities, not a deduction from wider concepts' (Mackenzie, 1967: 185). In Britain, the civil service accounts for less than one-tenth of public employment, and in Germany the *Beamtenstande* accounts for about one-quarter. To make cross-national comparisons of public employees, we must have a generic definition.

The definition of public employment used here is political and organizational. Public employees are individuals who work for organizations that are headed by elected officials (e.g., ministers or local government councillors) or by appointees of an elected government (e.g., nationalized industries) and/or that are principally owned by government or funded by government grants (e.g., most universities). Defining employees by organizations facilitates cross-national comparison, for public organizations are usually good record-keepers.

In every Western nation, government is today a big employer. Whether its employees are numbered in the hundreds of thousands or millions depends upon a country's population. In the United States, where public employment is relatively low in percentage terms, government none the less employs 18.7 million people. In Sweden, where a national population of 8.2 million limits the size of employment, the government none the less employs more than 1.5 million people (Table 5.1). Collectively, government agencies are the largest single employer in every Western nation. This is true whether one tabulates the number of public employees (whether full-time or part-time), or the hours worked (OECD, 1982b: 20-21). The former definition is used here, because a person with a part-time job, for example a woman supplementing a husband's income by working in a school or hospital, is just as much a government worker as a full-time employee.

While public employees can be reduced to a single analytic category, the variety of public employees should always be borne in mind. Even in a normally unitary government, such as Britain or Sweden, two-thirds to five-sixths of public employees will not be working for central government ministries. Instead, they are scattered among hundreds of local governments and among public corporations whether market-oriented nationalized industries, non-trading public corporations, or health service institutions. Among the five countries surveyed here, central government is the largest employer only in Italy. Local government is the biggest employer in Britain, the United States and Sweden, and trading enterprises rank first in Germany. Each of these categories could be further divided into a host of different local authorities and trading enterprises. Within each local government, subdivisions exist between types of public employees, such as teachers, health officials and policemen.

TABLE 5.1
Public employment by type of government organization, 1980[a]

Type of organization	Britain		Germany		Italy		Sweden		USA	
	'000	%	'000	%	'000	%	'000	%	'000	%
1. Central	1,056	14	855	13	1,882	37	293	19	3,797	20
2. Intermediate	0	—	1,713	26	60	1	352	23	3,685	20
3. Local	2,970	39	1,010	15	586	12	488	31	9,763	52
4. Trading enterprises	1,918	25	2,361	36	1,542	30	351	23	1,361	7
5. Non-trading enterprises	1,726	22	695	10	1,000	20	67	4	101	0.4
Total	7,670		6,634		5,070		1,553		18,707	

a. Data are for 1981 (Britain) and 1980 (Germany, Italy, Sweden and USA). *Source*: Rose (forthcoming).

The organization of public employment reflects the fact that public employment is spread nationwide, because most public employees are concerned with the delivery of services. The most visible and authoritative officials are in a national capital, but by definition they will be relatively few. The great bulk of public employees are distributed in accord with population; they are found where there are people to consume public goods and services (Parry, 1981). Even in countries where central government employment is high, it is not because of a great concentration of personnel in Rome or London. Central government becomes a large employer by taking responsibilities for services that must be delivered nationwide; it does not do so by building up a large bureaucracy in the national capital.

The extent of public employment can be enlarged by using a transactional definition, that is, by regarding as public employees anyone who works for an organization that depends upon transactions with government for most of its operating revenue.

Firms producing military goods are the most obvious example of private sector corporations depending upon government for their revenue, for armaments cannot be sold in the private sector. These firms, small in number but large in size, are most significant in the United States, where there is a large defence establishment and where military goods are produced in the private sector rather than in the public sector, as is usual in Europe (Weidenbaum, 1980). In addition, many firms incidentally receive a portion of their revenue from their sales to government; for example, typewriter manufacturers sell their products to government as well as for private sector use.

The transactional approach is not used here for three reasons. First of all, it ignores differences in law and in practice between public and private sector organizations. Public sector organizations can be funded completely from tax revenues, whereas private sector firms are subject to market forces. Second, because there are two partners in a transaction, adopting this approach would involve counting every employee twice. Third, if dependence is the chief criterion for employment, then it could be argued that many public employees are dependent upon the private sector, for taxes generated from private sector activities account for the bulk of tax revenues paying the salaries of public employees.

In cross-national comparison, the size of public employment must be measured relative to the total number of persons employed in a country. Doing this (Table 5.2), confirms the importance of public employment; government activities account for 38 percent of all jobs in Sweden, and for one-quarter to one-third of employment in other major European countries. The only major Western nation in which public employment stands below 20 percent of the labour force is the United States. Among the nations reviewed here, the differences are very substantial. Public employment in Sweden is twice as high as in the United States, and half again as large as in Italy.

The scale of public employment at any one time is significant, but so are trends. A country may stand relatively high in public employment, but if it is growing very slowly, then this eminence will be gradually eroded. A country with a relatively low level of public employment may increase rapidly as it seeks to catch up with other countries in the provision of labour-intensive public goods and services. In so far as past differences in public employment reflect cultural differences and current programmes

represent influences common to Western nations, the pattern of
public employment should be increasingly similar cross-
nationally.

TABLE 5.2
Public employment as a percentage of national employment,
1951-1980

	Public employment		
	1951	1980	Change
	%	%	%
Sweden	15.2	38.2	+23.0
Britain	26.6	31.7	+5.1
Germany	14.4	25.8	+11.4
Italy	11.4	24.3	+12.9
USA	17.0	18.8	+1.8

Data for Germany and Sweden, 1950; and for USA 1952; for Britain 1981.
Source: Rose (forthcoming).

Trends in public employment differ greatly from among
Western nations. Three different patterns can be discerned among
the five nations analysed in Table 5.2.

1. *A big employer levelling off.* In Britain, the leading nation in
1951, public employment as a proportion of the workforce
increased in the next three decades by only 5 percent.

2. *A big increase from a low base.* Public employment more than
doubled its share of total employment in Italy and Sweden. Italy
increased by 13 percent from a 11 percent base in 1951, and
Sweden by 23 percent from 15 percent in 1950. In Germany too
public employment has grown very substantially from a low base
to account for 26 percent of the labour force in 1980.

3. *No change or relative decline.* The United States is
exceptional, in that it had a relatively high level of public
employment in 1952, 17.0 percent, but since then has shown no
tendency to increase. Public employment fell to 16.7 percent of the
labour force in 1957, then rose to 19.8 percent during the Vietnam
War in 1972, and fell back to 18.8 percent in 1980 in consequence of
military demobilization. The American experience shows that a
government that was once a big employer does not necessarily
keep growing bigger.

Western nations demonstrate no uniform tendency in the dynamics of public employment, and there is no support for a theory of less well-off nations catching up by expanding employment more rapidly. The biggest rates of expansion have been achieved by a relatively poor country in 1951 — Italy — and by a relatively rich country — Sweden. Equally important, the absence of growth in a high public employment country, Britain, and in a low employment country, the United States, demonstrates that steady growth is not inevitable.

The causes of public employment

In analysing causes of change in public employment, it is important to distinguish between absolute and proportionate change. In the United States, where the percentage increase has been least, the absolute growth in numbers is greatest, because of the explosion in the size of the American workforce. In 1952, 10.8 million Americans worked in the public sector; in 1979, 18.7 million people were public employees. The total number of public employees could remain constant, yet their share of the labour force would alter, if the number in private sector employment increased or decreased.

Changes in the total number in work are immediately affected by fluctuations in unemployment levels. Since most unemployed workers are drawing a cash benefit from government, they cannot be reckoned to be in the private sector. Yet the unemployed cannot be counted as public employees; by definition, they are out of work. Inasmuch as private sector workers are more vulnerable to market fluctuations than public sector employees, any increase in unemployment should reduce the number of private sector workers disproportionately, and thereby increase the proportion of public employees.

At the start of the period under review, 1951, unemployment was very low in most Western nations; by 1981 it was substantially higher, and rising. This has had the greatest effect in Britain. If the 2.6 million unemployed in 1981 are added to the labour force, public employment's share of the labour force drops from 31.7 percent to 28.5 percent — assuming that the unemployed would all be working in the private sector if at work. Of the 5.1 percent increase in public employment in Britain since 1951, more than half is explained as a byproduct of rising unemployment.

Changes in the composition of the labour force can also affect the
level of public employment. The size of the agricultural sector has
a   significant   impact   upon   total   public   employment.
Notwithstanding the importance of government price support and
market subsidies, the agricultural sector is considered to be
entirely in the private sector, for farmers are self-employed or
work for entrepreneurs with whom they share the risks of farming.
Moreover, people in rural areas tend to make fewer demands for
public services than do urban or suburban residents. The higher
the proportion of the labour force in agriculture, the lower the
expected level of public employment. The greater the decline in
agricultural employment, the greater is the likely rise in public
employment.

In the postwar era, agricultural employment has contracted in
every Western nation, as farms have become larger and more
mechanized. Of the five nations reviewed here, agriculture has
contracted most in Italy, where 5.7 million people left the land
between 1951 and 1980, and agriculture has declined from 43
percent of the Italian work force to 14 percent. Public employment
as a percentage of non-agricultural employment in Italy has risen
from 20 percent in 1951 to 28 percent in 1980. The decline in
agriculture has also boosted public employment in Germany and
Sweden, both countries with a substantial farming population at
the beginning of the 1950s. In the United States, nearly the whole
of the 1.5 percent increse in public employment can be accounted
for by the decline in agriculture.

Another reason why public employment is growing in
importance is that private sector employment is growing more
slowly, or even contracting (OECD, 1982a: Table 2). Whereas
private sector employment in postwar Germany has grown by 6
percent, public sector jobs have increased by 111 percent. In Italy,
a private sector decrease of 11 percent was countered by a public
sector increase of 123 percent. The paths of public and private
sector employment diverge most in Sweden and Britain. In
Britain, for every 10 jobs lost in the private sector, 17 new jobs
have opened up in the public sector, and in Sweden, for every 10
jobs lost in the private sector, 100 jobs have been created in the
public sector.

To deal with public employment in aggregate figures can be
misleading, for total public employment is not decided in
aggregate. No government agency is responsible for saying what
the level of public employment is or ought to be, as there is a

finance ministry seeking to determine total public expenditure. Public employment figures are the byproduct of many decisions taken in many places by many government agencies. To understand the totality of public employment, we must understand its parts.

In the public as in the private sector, people are employed for specific purposes or functions. Some jobs are specific to a particular programme, such as health care or road maintenance; other tasks are common to all government agencies, such as the work of secretaries. Public employees are added to or subtracted from the public payroll as means to the end of modifying particular programmes.

Disaggregating total public employment into employment by major government functions tests the relative importance of government-wide as against programme-specific causes of the growth of public employment. In so far as the factors influencing public employment are common to all government programmes, changes should occur at much the same rate in programmes as diverse as military defence, education and nationalized railways. In so far as programme-specific characteristics of employment are important, there should be big differences within a country in the rate (or even in the direction) of change. If this is so, the way to understand changes in public employment is to understand the programmes that create the jobs.

Given that public employment has been increasing in absolute and percentage terms in every Western nation, we would expect increases in all functional headings. In fact, this does not happen. An analysis of five major labour-intensive programmes — education, health, the post office, public transportation and defence — shows that programmes can change in opposite directions within the same country (Table 5.3). Employment in defence has actually contracted in absolute numbers in the four nations for which there is relevant data; Germany's defence circumstances were unique in 1950. Employment has also contracted in absolute terms in public transport in Britain, Germany and Sweden; it did not do so in the United States only because mass transport was not in government hands in 1951. In Britain total employment in nationalized industries has contracted by 25 percent since 1951, notwithstanding further nationalization, because of the massive contraction of employment in public transport and in coal mining.

In the past quarter-century, 'armies' of social welfare workers have replaced armies of soldiers as the characteristic employees of government. In Britain, for example, employment in education has increased by 998,000 from 1951, and in the health service by 824,000. Employment in education has increased by more than 100 percent in every Western country analysed, and the same is true of employment in the health services. These two programmes were substantial public employers in the early 1950s; today, they have become predominant.

TABLE 5.3
Changes in employment in major functional programmes,
1951-1980

	Britain	Germany	Italy	Sweden	USA
		(% increase in numbers since 1951)			
Social programmes					
Education	161	225	298	123	270
Health	167	217	289	628	209
All social	163	182	283	455	244
Nationalized industries					
Post Office	31	79	105	130	27
Transportation	−48	−27	50	−27	660
All nationalized industries	−13	65	120	76	134
Defence	−54	n.a.	−19	−10	−39
Total change, all programmes	22	111	123	217	72

Source: Rose (forthcoming).

The sum total of public employment reflects a large number of contrasting programme changes. In all the countries examined, social programmes increased in employment faster than the national average, and nationalized industries have grown less than the national average in every European country. Defence does not share in the overall pattern of growth; instead it contracts. The scale of the swings and roundabouts can be illustrated by Britain. For every 100 posts in public employment in 1951, 31 have been abolished since, but 50 new posts have been created. In the United States, for every 100 employees in 1952, 18 posts have been abolished, but 71 new jobs created. In Germany, changes in the oldest established trading enterprises, the Deutsches Bundespost and the Deutsches Bundesbahn, nearly cancelled each other out: the former added 200,000 employees, and the latter shed almost

200,000. In Italy and Sweden changes have usually been upwards, but the rates of change vary greatly, from a 628 percent increase in health employment in Sweden, to a 27 percent decrease in public transport.

The growth of public employment is selective, not uniform. The question thus arises: What causes some programmes to expand employment more rapidly, and others to expand less or even contract in employment? To answer this question, one must not only identify the causes of programme growth, the subject of Chapter 7, but also distinguish between labour-intensive and non-labour-intensive programmes.

One reason for differential growth is differential productivity of highly mechanized or computerized goods, as against labour-intensive services. Productivity tends to grow fastest when goods are mass-produced by technologies that can increase output by increasing the input of capital goods, such as automated assembly lines, computer-controlled production systems and robots. In such circumstances output can increase and employment decrease by the substitution of capital for labour. By contrast, most services are the product of the labour of individuals, whose own handiwork and skills require only a modicum of equipment, for example, the work of doctors, lawyers, teachers and restaurant staffs. In labour-intensive sectors of the economy, an increase in the output of services invariably requires an increase in employment, for the service *is* the work of employees. New technologies may enable service workers to be more effective and more efficient, but cannot substitute for them in large numbers.

Public employment tends to grow faster than private employment because more public programmes are labour-intensive services (e.g., health, education and police protection) than are private sector activities. While some economies of labour can be made in service activities and some workers are required even in automated production processes, the overall pattern is clear. In both the public and private sectors, employment in service industries is growing faster than in the production of manufactured goods (OECD, 1982b: Table 2). It is the specific characteristics of public programmes, not the ideological distinction between the public and private sector, that principally determine the productivity of a given activity (see Baumol, 1967).

The growth in labour-intensive social welfare programmes has been the principal cause of the expansion of public employment in every Western nation. The whole of the increase in public employment in Britain can be accounted for by the growth of labour-intensive social welfare programmes, which added 2,137,000 to the public payroll from 1951 to 1981, far more than the total net increase in public employment of 1,314,000. In the United States too, the social welfare sector increased by 6,027,000, accounting for three-quarters of the net increase in public employment. In Sweden, welfare services accounted for 64 percent of the total increase in public employment; in Germany, for 53 percent of the increase in non-military employment; and in Italy, for 51 percent of the total increase in public employment.

Because most nationalized industries are capital-intensive, employment has not had to increase output. Producing more electricity requires investment in more electrical generating equipment; producing more telephone calls requires the automation of work formerly done by operators; and producing more motor cars or steel requires investment in high-technology production processes that minimize the use of labour. Structural differences between public trading enterprises and social welfare programmes result in employment in social programmes growing seven times more than nationalized industries in Britain; six times more in Sweden, almost three times more in Germany, and about twice as much in Italy and the United States (Table 5.3).

Growth in public employment is also influenced by whether public employees sell their services or provide them on non-market terms. Some government agencies give away their products without charge instead of selling goods and services, as private sector firms do. This analytic distinction does not assume the intrinsic superiority of any of the three types of government outputs. That is a question of political values, and more than one alternative is technically practicable. Public employees can be divided into three groups, according to their relationship to the market in distributing their goods and services.

1. *Collective goods and services that cannot be marketed.* Collective (or public) goods, such as military defence and anti-pollution measures, must be made available to everyone within a society, because there is no way to exclude from their benefits people who do not wish to pay for them. Government pays for these goods.

2. *Marketable goods that are marketed.* Industries such as the railways, post office, electricity, public transport, gas and steel industries produce goods and services that have identifiable consumers, and therefore can be marketed. Where government has

nationalized these industries, it chooses to sell their products at more or less the cost of production. There is no expectation that they will be given away simply because they are produced by government.

3. *Marketable goods that are given away.* As a matter of political choice, goods and services such as education and health are given away without any charge, or with only a token charge. They are sometimes called merit goods, because they are normally thought of as 'good' goods, which everyone ought to have as a right of citizenship. They are not free goods, for even though no charge is made to the consumer, the cost of providing these services, including the wages of the providers, must be met by government.

TABLE 5.4
Changes in public employment according to market characteristics of products, 1951-1980

	Britain	Germany	Italy	Sweden	USA
	(% change in share of total public employment)				
Give-away goods					
1951	25	36	22	36	33
1980	49	44	38	62	61
Change	+24	+8	+16	+26	+28
Collective goods					
1951	31	20	47	27	59
1980	22	26	31	16	29
Change	−9	+6	−16	−11	−30
Marketed goods					
1951	44	44	31	37	8
1980	28	31	31	22	11
Change	−16	−14	0	−15	+3

Source: Rose (forthcoming). A small portion of total public employees is omitted, because they are unclassified.

The answer to the question — Which type of public programme is likely to grow fastest? — is clear on a priori grounds. We would expect public employment to grow fastest in the production of give-away goods and services. When no charge is made, there is no price barrier to citizens demanding more and more services and there is no measure of effective demand to regulate the number of producers employed. Public employees producing goods given away to individuals without charge comprised upwards of one-third of all public employees in 1951; three decades later, employees producing give-away goods had increased to an average of 51 percent of total public employment (Table 5.4). The proportion has doubled in Britain, and nearly doubled in the United States. More than half of public employees are today producing goods and services that could be marketed, but are given to citizens without charge as a conscious choice of public policy.

Since collective goods have no identifiable beneficiaries, being produced for the good of all, demand-stimulated employment should increase more slowly than in the provision of give-away goods. But employment in the production of collective goods should increase faster than in marketed goods, since no charge is made for the former, and a charge is made for the latter. In fact, employment in producing collective goods has undergone greater relative decline than employment in producing marketed goods (Table 5.4). Whereas collective goods accounted for 37 percent of public employment on average in 1951, by 1980 the proportion had dropped to 25 percent because there is a finite demand for collective goods. Once a government provides a certain level of military defence, courts of law, diplomatic representation and administrative services there is little pressure to expand these services further in the absence of identifiable beneficiaries. People would rather pay government to produce goods and services that they can benefit from as individual consumers than have government produce more collective goods that no one in particular regards as their own.

Public employment in marketed goods has not risen as fast as in the production of give-away goods because of the capital-intensive nature of many nationalized industries, e.g. electricity, gas and telephones. Increased market demand has been met by increased capital investment. When demand for marketed goods falls, employment falls too. In every European country surveyed, employment on the railways and in public transport has fallen, because of the shift to private transport. The government can subsidize the losses of nationalized industries with tax revenues, but sooner or later it will cut down employment in recognition of falling demand.

In the 1980s the conjunction of low rates of economic growth and high levels of unemployment faces governors with a particularly awkward policy choice: Is the principal objective of the nationalization of industries the promotion of economic growth, as measured by greater output for a given volume of inputs, or maintaining employment, even in firms losing money and declining in productivity? In so far as government regards guaranteeing high levels of employment as a major responsibility, whenever a large private sector firm threatens to go bankrupt with the resulting loss of many jobs, the argument will be heard that it should be taken into public ownership or publicly funded by non-economic soft loans. The ability of government to nationalize companies to protect employment is limited, and contraction of employment in some nationalized industries shows that it is not a certain guarantor of maintaining jobs.

The pressures to increasing public employment grow with the increase in unemployment. It is particularly noteworthy that in Sweden, where socialists long resisted nationalization of industries in their profit-making days, the bourgeois government from 1976 to 1982 nationalized firms to preserve employment. A review of the results, by two Swedish economists (Eliasson and Ysander, 1981: 62) concludes: 'The story of Swedish industrial policy in the 1970s does not sound very edifying to an economist.' The reason for this is that government programmes have not been concerned with increasing economic efficiency, but 'with proper and less proper ways of handling losers'.

Political choice, the conscious decision of politicians about a given labour-intensive programme, is a third reason for changes in public employment. This is most evident in military defence. The level of military defence required at any given time reflects a political judgement about the risks of war. Governments can increase military defence, as in the build up of NATO forces in the Cold War era of the 1950s, or decrease military forces, as in the period of detente in the 1960s and 1970s. The choice has significant implications for public employment. Political choices also determine whether a given industry or firm is subject to nationalization. Nationalizing a single industry, such as the railroads or steel, can significantly boost public employment. Choices about the provision or scope of welfare programmes also affect public employment. If American politicians chose to introduce a national health service on the European model, then public employment would be increased by the transfer of hundreds of thousands of doctors, nurses and medical aids from the private to the public sector.

Political choices are not necessarily determined by partisan ideology. The size and growth of public employment is not a simple reflection of left-right differences in the control of government. Public employment has grown most in Sweden (which was under a socialist government for nearly the whole of the period) and in Italy (which was under a Christian Democratic government for the whole of the period). In Germany there was a switch from right to left in control of government in 1969, but public employment actually grew more in two decades under a right-of-centre Christian Democrat government (up by one-third) than under a Social Democratic government (up by one-quarter). In Britain the alternation of Conservative and Labour governments has not been marked by a great change in public employment patterns. The slight fall in public employment in Britain from 1951 to 1961 is explained entirely by the reduction of 390,000 defence forces by Conservative governments, not a policy choice characteristic of right-wing ideology. Social welfare services have gained employees under governments of each party. In the United States, Democrats and Republicans have alternated in the White House with little effect on the level of public employment.

Contrary to what has been found in taxation, the inertia of established commitments is not of pervasive importance in the growth of public employment. If that were the case, then the oldest concerns of government, responsibility for defence and public order, would show the greatest growth. There would be a continuing build-up in military forces, not the great cutback witnessed in the 1960s and 1970s. There would also be a large increase in police services instead of average growth. The greatest increases in public employment have been in health and education. Health services are relatively new commitments of government. In education, statutory commitments have contributed to the growth of public employment by establishing an open-ended entitlement to education for all children, whatever their number.

Public employment does not grow simply in response to growth in the economy. Nor does growth in public employment, especially in the production of give-away goods and services, necessarily reduce the rate of economic growth (cf. Bacon and Eltis, 1976). The evidence here does not support such an hypothesis. Both public employment and the economy as a whole have tended to grow faster in Sweden, Germany and Italy than in Britain (cf. Table 5.2; Martin, 1982: 41). The virtually nil rate of growth in public employment in the United States has not been associated with a faster-than-average rate of economic growth. In so far as public employment is more secure than private sector employment, in an economic recession public employment may vary inversely with economic growth. Government may continue to employ the same number of people or add to its numbers by overt or covert job creation schemes, while the private sector slows down.

Growth in public expenditure does not translate automatically into growth in public employment. A modicum of expenditure increase is a necessary condition or consequence of increasing the number of public employees (OECD, 1982a: Table 6), but a significant portion of public expenditure growth consists of cash transfer payments to pensioners, the unemployed and others not in work. While such programmes make intensive demands for public revenues, they are not labour-intensive; for example, payments to pensioners can be made by computer. An expansion of nationalized industries does not imply an increase in public expenditure, for nationalized industries are meant to generate their own operating revenue, and a loss will not be as costly as employing teachers or doctors to give away services without charge.

Nor does the desire of bureaucrats for self-aggrandizement lead to a growth in public employment. Ironically, it is in the United States, where public employment has grown least, that writers frequently hypothesize that public employment will grow steadily because public employees wish it to grow (Downs, 1967; Niskanen, 1971). An increase in the number of public employees is assumed to be in the self-interest of bureaucrats, because more staff to supervise means higher salaries, greater prestige and power for the heads of these organizations, and promotions further down the hierarchy too. But such a model of bureaucratic growth is over-simple in two senses. First of all, it assumes that there are no constraints on the power of bureaucrats to augment their own number. These constraints are multiple, including opposition by other bureaucrats who fear that they will be taken over by empire-builders. Second, it ignores the fact that growth brings many problems and risks. Maintaining an organization at a constant size is less work than expanding it, and bureaucrats are trained to economize effort and to work to rule rather than to be entrepreneurs (cf. Rose, 1978: 87ff.).

If bureaucrats were able to increase their numbers out of self-interest, then they should grow steadily through the years, at the same rate in all programmes, and at the same rate in all Western nations. In fact, this is not the case, as Tables 5.2 and 5.3 show. There is no common across-the-board influence promoting the growth of public employment in all levels of government or in all programmes within a nation. Hence, the attempt to explain change by invoking a universal and general propensity to bureaucratic growth is faulty, especially in America, where growth in public employment is caused principally by population growth.

The benefits of public employment

Many of the characteristics of public employment are not specific to government; instead, they are conditions of work in large organizations, whether in the public or the private sector. The similarities may appear greater than the differences to a worker in a firm that has been nationalized, or to a secretary transferring from a private sector insurance company to a government agency. Yet there remain significant differences in the consequences of public sector employment for the relative effectiveness of government, and for popular consent.

As far as effectiveness is concerned, one can start with the proposition: more educated employees should be more effective producers of goods and services than less educated employees. The logic of this statement is that in a post-industrial society the capacity to produce goods and services is heavily dependent upon what Daniel Bell (1973) has called the 'new knowledge class', that is, people who have relatively abstract intellectual skills. Analytic skill is replacing brute human or mechanical force in producing big results from things invisible to the naked eye (e.g., microchips or atoms). Government should be particularly well suited to apply new knowledge, since the results of the new technology are capable of being reproduced on a routine basis by sophisticated machines or by less skilled workers, basic characteristics of bureaucracy. Even if one does not accept the whole of Bell's analysis, few would endorse the opposite proposition, namely, that less educated people are more effective producers of goods and services.

Public employees tend to be more highly educated than employees in the private sector. Definitions of a high standard of education vary from country to country, but the tendency of government to employ a disproportionate number of highly educated people is constant. When education to the level of university entrance qualification or professional training (e.g., English A levels, German *Abitur*, etc.), is defined as a higher educational qualification, then the proportion of educationally qualified employees in the public sector is four times greater than in the private sector in Italy and Germany, and about twice as great in Britain, France and the United States (Rose, forthcoming; OECD, 1982a: 39f.).

The typical educated civil servant is not a legally trained bureaucrat but a teacher or a doctor trained in relatively effective social technologies. Teachers know how to teach literacy and numeracy to children, and doctors and nurses can cure most ills that they diagnose. Given the public sector's tendency to recruit people trained in tested skills, they should be effective in their work. It is because these skills are labour-intensive that an increase in educated public employees does not increase productivity.

Nationalized industries are a major exception to government's use of educated personnel. The great bulk of employees in public transport, the post office, electricity, gas, coal mining and steelmaking are manual workers lacking higher education. However, the lack of educated personnel (which is slowly changing with increasing automation and the substitution of jobs such as airline pilot for that of a railway engine driver) does not mean that effectiveness is low. Nationalized industries, like private sector industries, tend to use sophisticated machines and tested engineering technologies applied the world over to produce energy, transport, communications and other basic utilities.

Public employees are also effective in the narrower sense of looking after their own economic self-interest. Historically, public employment was a public service, a status in a *Standestaat*. The person served was the King. Public servants were not only privileged in being free from the drudgery of agricultural labour and wearing the livery of their monarch, they were also privileged to serve the state, which represented the summation of the public good. This status and ethic was not confined to an elite at a royal court; it was diffused widely throughout society, including manual workers such as uniformed railwaymen. It was part of an organic society's conception of social relations between estates that antedated the conflict view of industrial relations.

Today public employment is in impersonal offices in large bureaucratic organizations. Individuals are meant to be recruited by rules, and to work according to rules. Moreover, many jobs in the public sector have counterpart posts in the private sector; there are thus many alternatives to working for the state. In so far as public employment has become a modern occupation rather than a traditional status, the rewards will be instrumental. Public officials will value work more in terms of money than social status. The cash nexus rather than a service ethic becomes crucial.

Membership in a trade union is the best indicator that workers value a job in money terms. Unions are the primary means for large groups to bargain impersonally and collectively for material gains. In so far as the older service ethic remains important, unionization of public employees should be less than in the private sector. In so far as public officials are more materialistic and government less able to resist unionization on political grounds, unionization should be higher in the public sector.

The cash nexus is normally more important among public employees than in the private sector, for union membership is usually higher among government's employees than in the profit-making sector of the economy (Rose, forthcoming). In Britain, Germany and Italy, public employees are as much as twice as likely to be a member of a trade union as are private sector workers. In each of these countries, a majority of public employees (and 75 percent in Britain) belong to trade unions, whereas in the private sector only a minority (no more than 34 percent in Britain) belong to trade unions. In the United States unionization is much lower all around, but public employees are more likely to be organized than are workers in the private sector. Only in Sweden is union membership equal (and equally high) in both the public and the private sector.

Public employees today tend to receive higher salaries and wage-related benefits than do employees in the private sector (OECD, 1982a: 33ff.). In part, higher wages reflect higher qualifications, and jobs requiring skill and responsibility; in part, they reflect more generous wage settlements by government as an employer. In pay bargains in the public sector, unions have two advantages lacking in the private sector: the threat of political embarrassment to politicians if a favourable settlement is not made, and the employer's lack of a need to make a profit, for wage increases can be paid by raising taxes. In addition to higher money wages, public sector employees usually enjoy better fringe benefits than private sector employees.

The growth of union membership among public employees not only increases the intensity of wage-bargaining, but also reduces the effectiveness of government control of its employees. Government today must bargain about conditions of work with trade union representatives; enacting a law is not sufficient to change the behaviour of public employees. This is most obviously the case in nationalized industries, where government takes over pre-existing industrial relations practices when it nationalizes firms. But it is also true in classic public employment functions, such as teaching and health care. Employee associations represent not only an organized work force, but also a professionally expert force claiming to understand better than elected officials the programmes for which they are jointly responsible.

In a democracy, popular consent to the actions of public employees should follow automatically from the fact that public employees are meant to be public servants, responding to the wishes of elected representatives and the electorate as a whole. But accountability is not so easily realized in practice. Public employees are organized to serve their own interests as well as being employed to serve the public interest. The institutions of government and the conditions of producing many public programmes make it difficult to discern what the public interest may be. Public sector unions can use their numbers and organization to influence (or critics would say 'capture') elected officials on behalf of their members. Public employees advocate a definition of the public interest congruent with their own values and welfare.

The lines of communication between an individual voter and an individual public employee will be too remote for the former to regard the latter as his servant. Nor can a public employee respond to individual wishes, for bureaucrats are rulebound, and adherence to rules is an important procedural means of giving equality of treatment to different citizens. Because a citizen can withdraw his custom in the market place, it can be argued that citizens have a better chance of holding public employees in nationalized industries accountable than elected officials. Dissatisfaction with public transport can lead a person to make more journeys by automobile, and dissatisfaction with the postal service can lead to greater use of the telephone. Where a buyer has an effective choice between a public and a private sector supplier a citizen may vote with his or her purse as effectively as by a ballot.

· The problem of determining what citizens want (and, therefore, what they have given their consent for) is clearest in assessing the level of non-marketed goods and services that government supplies. The conventional justification for providing education, health care and other welfare services without charge is that they are the right of every citizen; economists refer to them as merit goods. As Musgrave notes (1969: 12), merit goods involve the 'substitution of imposed for individual choice, a clear departure from the basic principle of consumer choice'. Because merit goods are popular goods, the provision of education, health and social services without charge is considered a benefit. Political values take precedence before the values of the market economy. In the absence of conventional market measures of demand, government must decide how much of these welfare services should be produced.

There is no way to get a precise answer to the question: how much is enough? The problem is worst in social work services, for there is no general agreement among social workers about what is or ought to be the level of services provided by social workers. Nor is it easy to measure the need for health services. If health is the objective, there are many ways in which an individual can maintain good health without recourse to any public employee, for example by frequent exercise or a balanced diet. In education, population statistics disaggregated by age provide guidance about the number of pupils that should receive compulsory schooling. But educators resist the use of performance measures (examination successes or scores on standard tests of reading and arithmetic) as a measure of how much children learn from compulsory education: They say that this would impoverish education by confining it to testable activities. No measurable alternative is offered instead. In practice, the provision of non-marketed public services tends to be supply-determined, reflecting what professional experts think is the appropriate amount for government to provide.

Even if government ministers knew precisely how much education, health or social work services they wished to provide citizens, they could not convert their preferences into programme outputs, for there is no measure of the programme output of these services. The volume of output is measured by the cost of inputs, of which the largest portion is the wages of persons employed to provide a service. If the total wage bill of teachers increases by 10 percent, the national accounts report this as a percentage increase in the amount of education produced. But paying 10 percent higher wages to a given number of teachers does not guarantee a proportionate increase in the quality of their work. It clearly benefits teachers to whom a significant portion of the increase in education expenditure in the 1960s and early 1970s went (OECD, 1976). The benefit to students is very difficult to measure directly.

While the number of public employees in the social welfare services is broadly likely to bear a positive relation to the output of benefits, in the absence of reliable and valid measures of these outputs it is impossible to calculate the effect of marginal changes in public employment upon labour-intensive government programmes. In the 1980s, confusion is most evident in education. In a period of falling birth rates, the argument used to expand the number of teachers when birth rates rose now implies reducing the number of teachers. But there is no political agreement that what goes up must come down. Instead, professional educators and teachers' unions are organized to advocate that the decline in birth rates is only temporary, that quality should be raised by improving the pupil/teacher ratio, and that services should be expanded to infants and adults. Organized producers of public programmes wish to maintain public employment for their members, whatever occurs in society.

Popular consent to public employees can turn into popular resentment among the two-thirds to three-quarters who are not working in the public sector, because private sector employees are relatively deprived in comparison with public sector employees. The deprivation starts early. The majority of the workforce in every Western nation lacks further education and is thus less well qualified to obtain public employment than the well educated minority. Relative deprivation also arises from the fact that public sector employees tend to have higher wages, and enjoy such important fringe benefits as greater job security in an era of rising unemployment, longer holidays, and more favourable pensions. A dual economy appears to be emerging, in which the division is not between capital and labour, but between the minority of the labour force working on very favourable terms in the public sector, with a first claim on tax revenues for their wages, and the majority, working in less well paid and riskier jobs in the private sector.

Theories of relative deprivation suggest that disadvantaged persons will feel frustrated and will direct aggressive behaviour against the perceived causes of their deprivation. Public employees today risk becoming the object of resentment from ordinary citizens because of the benefits they receive, financed to a significant extent by taxes paid by private sector workers. The expression of this resentment can be found in campaigns that swept Ronald Reagan to the presidency in the United States, and Margaret Thatcher to the prime ministership in Great Britain. It can also be found in Italy, where Italian Communists rail against 'parasites', defined as public employees who treat their jobs as a personal benefit rather than as an obligation to serve the public. Public employees today are not only regarded as public servants working in the public interest; they are also seen as a class that benefits by working for government.

6 THE ORGANIZATIONS OF GOVERNMENT

Organizations are central in government, providing structure and continuity for the activities of government. The difference between government as a set of elected officials constituting the government-of-the-day and government as a set of persisting organizations is the difference between the ephemeral and the durable. Elected officeholders come and go, whereas government organizations can persist as long as a constitution endures, or even from one regime to another as the experience of France, Germany and Italy illustrates.

Organizations give effective substance to the legitimacy that popular election confers upon politicians. Politicians claim the right to give direction to government; the winners of an election win government office. The offices gained place politicians at the head of the major departments of government; a ministry with tens of thousands of employees greatly augments the effective power of the minister in charge. The powers that elected officials seek to assert are vested by law in the organizations they head and the offices they hold.

Organizations are the chief active force of government; they mobilize laws, money and public employees in order to produce programme outputs. Organizing these resources in a particular agency transforms resources in the abstract into programme outputs. The inertia commitments of public programmes are sustained by government organizations that effectively institutionalize the activities of government. To reduce government to a handful of leaders, Cabinet ministers and their advisers is to confuse formal authority to make decisions with the role of organizations in determining what government does to implement decisions and, even more important, to ensure that the inertia of past decisions persists.

Government is a plurality of organizations; they are so numerous that neither social scientists nor politicians can easily count how many organizations constitute a government. For example, a survey of Washington by President Carter's Reorganization Project (1977) required 45 pages to catalogue one-line descriptions of organizations in the executive branch of the

151

United States federal government. This having been done, the compilers cautioned:

> It is important to emphasize that this categorization of organizational elements does not constitute an exhaustive accounting of the whole federal government. Rather, its purpose is to establish a definition of the executive branch for the reorganization process. We anticipate changes as the reorganization study groups learn more about the executive branch.

Collectively, government organizations are heterogeneous. There are a few features in common between a country's army, schools, health service, electricity generating industry and its courts of law. The differences further multiply if one also considers such public organizations as broadcasting corporations, a national theatre, a state church and quasi-official advisory bodies. The heterogeneity of government means that it is misleading to generalize the characteristics of all government bodies from the attributes of any one. Differences between public organizations within a country, such as armies and museums, can be greater than the differences between the same type of organization in different countries, e.g., armies.

Because the institutions of government are varied and numerous, much of the process of governing is about relations between government organizations. Any public agency must be understood in an ecological setting. A government organization depends upon other government organizations for its statutory authority, finance and personnel. Many do not actually deliver the service for which they are formally responsible. Central government ministries often delegate responsibilities to local authorities, independent boards and public corporations. In federal systems, central ministries may even lack original jurisdiction for such important programmes as education and police. Government organizations are interdependent, each relying upon the other to undertake activities necessary to implement a public programme (Hanf and Scharpf, 1978).

Inter-organizational relations inevitably involve inter-organizational politics. Organizations within government often disagree, and compete against each other for scarce public resources. Heterogeneity also means that organizations will have things to exchange with each other. While a central government ministry and a local government may disagree about who should pay for a service such as education, each must rely upon the other for funding or delivery of education programmes. The process of inter-organizational politics is not only about conflict; it is also about conflict resolution through political bargaining.

The first and most difficult task of this chapter is to establish a definition of government organizations that can be used to indicate how many organizations government consists of. Measurement is particularly important in discussions of big government, for the phrase does not specify whether it is the total number of organizations or the size of a few organizations, such as an army, that makes government big. Given that some types of organizations have been contracting in number while others have been growing, the second section considers the causes of these changes, and how, if at all, changes in the number of organizations are related to the resources claimed by organizations. The third section starts by asking what consequences, if any, result from changes in the number and type of government organizations. Does an increase or decrease make government more or less effective? It is also important to ask what influence organizational changes have upon popular consent, by their impact upon the accountability and responsiveness of public organizations to citizens.

Identifying government organizations

Organizations are ubiquitous features of modern society. We cannot think of the production of familiar goods and services, whether military defence, motor cars, television programmes or frozen foods, without thinking of organization. Unlike a village organized around face-to-face informal contacts, a modern society depends upon organizations. To reduce social and political life to relations between individuals, whether voters and politicians or producers and consumers, is to gain simplicity at the cost of understanding.

Organizations are purposeful; they seek not only to maintain their existence but also to advance instrumental goals. The word 'organization' is derived from Latin and Greek words describing a tool or instrument. Organizations are instruments of policy, not just ends in themselves. The assessment of organizations cannot be undertaken independent of their programmatic purposes.

Organizations are formal institutions with a legal status that makes them different from and greater than individuals working within the organizations. A formal organization commands far greater resources than any one individual; a prime minister or president has a very small personal staff by comparison with the impersonal resources of the government bureaucracy. A formal organization is a stable body with established rules and activities that constrain the individuals holding office within it. An organization persists, in contrast to the informal and transitory networks that sociologists refer to as social institutions. Organizations have a cohesiveness and capacity for action different from categoric groups. A well organized pressure group, though small, can exert more influence upon government than can the unorganized categoric group of people who share the same opinion but have no organization to advance it. The post office, collecting and delivering mail daily through a network extending nationwide and internationally, is another example of an organization that differs in kind from unorganized informal communication.

The political system can be conceived of as a set of organizations, but there are very sharp distinctions between government organizations (for example, the Ministry of Defence or the office of the Prime Minister) and extra-governmental organizations (for example, a pressure group promoting nuclear disarmament, or a party organization). The same individual may have an office in both governmental and extra-governmental organizations (e.g. as prime minister and as party leader), but authority over public officials and public money comes immediately from office in government. Extra-governmental organizations can influence government, but cannot legitimately supplant it. Government differs from market organizations, whether profit-making firms or trade unions, because of what Lindblom (1965: 12) has described as the 'troublesome concept' of sovereignty. In bargaining between a government organization and a private sector organization, the government can invoke its sovereign authority to change the rules by which disagreements are settled and, in the extreme case, to abolish an organization.

Government organizations were defined in Chapter 1 as organizations established by the constitution or public law, headed by elected officials or having their heads appointed by elected officials, and/or principally financed by tax revenues or owned by the state. This definition emphasizes the constitutional and legal status of public agencies, political accountability for direction, and reliance upon public finance. The use of a multiplicity of attributes is common to virtually every empirical attempt to enumerate government organizations, reflecting the diversity of government's forms.

A strictly legal definition would be inadequate, for countries differ in the legal status they confer upon publicly funded agencies, and cross-national differences between legal systems further inhibit comparison. For the same reason, it would be misleading to identify government organizations by formal status of employees, for civil service status is a privilege accorded a limited fraction of public employees. Most workers in nationalized industries are organized like manual workers in the private sector, albeit their employing organization is publicly owned and its losses funded by public revenues. In Britain, bodies headed by appointed rather than elected officials have come to be known as 'quangos', that is, QUAsi-Non-Governmental Organizations. The definitions attached to this label are numerous and the overtones pejorative. The coiner of the word, Anthony Barker (1982b: 3), has concluded, 'As a means of describing anything, however, the word is useless; it has been applied to anything from a local council for the welfare of elderly people, running with the help of a town hall grant, to the National Coal Board' (cf. Hood and Mackenzie, 1975: 422-423; Hood, 1982: 57).

Any government organization can be disaggregated into a large number of small units concerned with specific tasks, whether functional (a staff cafeteria or a computing centre) or territorial service delivery units. A study of the structure of the 20 major federal government agencies in the United States found that they consisted of 14,818 separately identifiable units, an average of 740 units for each organization (Goodsell, 1983: 112), plus an additional 30,613 post office units. More than half of all these units of federal departments employed fewer than five people. The same phenomenon is found in local government; most local government units in the United States employ fewer than 24 people (Goodsell, 1983: 115). While government organizations can be large in aggregate resources and responsibilities, the typical unit within the organization is small.

Public organizations are often multi-functional. A local government is a single organization for most legal and revenue purposes, but is also authorized to carry out a variety of programmes within a circumscribed geographical area, such as police, fire, roads, public health, housing, social work and education. The approach adopted here is to treat the politically

responsible body, the local authority, as the unit of analysis. At
central government level, the government ministry is treated as
the unit of analysis, because it has a single minister politically
accountable to Parliament for the department's varied programmes. When the same function is performed by separately
organized and accountable organizations — for example, the
provision of education in the United States by thousands of
separately elected school boards — it is necessary to think in terms
of thousands of education organizations, rather than a single
abstract education function or service. Even though there are
substantial similarities between different organizations, separate
structures of accountability create the possibility of differences
between them.

The identifying criteria of government organizations — directed
by elected or publicly appointed officials, and owned by the state
or funded by tax revenues — yield 16 logically possible types of
organizations. Five categories account for an overwhelming
number of government organizations: (1) headed by elected
officials and publicly owned and funded (e.g., central and local
government organizations); (2) headed by appointed officials,
owned but not funded by government (e.g. nationalized industries
receiving most of their revenue from trading activities); (3) headed
by appointed officials, owned and funded by government (e.g., a
national broadcasting service); (4) organizations whose heads are
neither elected nor government-appointed but are government-
owned or principally funded by government (e.g., universities); (5)
fringe organizations, small but distinctive in their organizational
forms.[1]

1. Organizations headed by elected officials,
state-owned and principally funded by tax revenues

Central government ministries are the most prominent
organizations that meet this definition, for Cabinet ministers are
usually MPs or hold office at the discretion of Parliament, and
ministries normally depend upon tax revenues to meet their
operating costs. Local government also meets these criteria.

The eminence of central government ministries is derived from
their fewness. This is most evident in the post of prime minister,
which gives one politician a unique claim to be a nation's political
leader. At any particular time there can be only a relatively small
number of departments of great political importance, with a

minister of substantial political status. Juridicially all government departments are equal, but in political terms a few ministries are of disproportionate importance, for example, finance and foreign affairs.

There are also functional reasons for keeping a Cabinet small. A Cabinet can deliberate collectively only if its members are sufficiently few to meet for intensive discussions around a table. An assembly of 100 is not a deliberative body but a debating chamber or a public meeting. In Western nations the average Cabinet contains ministers for 19 departments (Table 6.1). If anything, this exaggerates the size of the average meeting of Cabinet ministers, for a Cabinet usually has a dozen or more committees despatching the bulk of Cabinet business, each having half a dozen members or less (Mackie and Hogwood, 1983).

TABLE 6.1
The growth in central government departments, 1849-1982

	1849[a]	1982
	(number of ministries)	
France	10	42
Canada	8	36
Italy	11	28
United Kingdom	12	22
Denmark	8	20
New Zealand	19	19
Sweden	7	18
Germany	12	17
Norway	7	17
Belgium	6	15
Finland	11	15
Ireland	11	15
Australia	7	14
Austria	9	14
Netherlands	9	14
USA	6	13
Switzerland	7	7
Average	9.4	19.2

a. Or a date shortly after national independence, if later.
Source: Compiled from Rose, (1976a), and up-dated by the author. Non-departmental ministers are included; a ministry also having an assistant or deputy minister in Cabinet is counted only once.

Western governments usually have much the same number of Cabinet ministries, from 14 to 22. Only two governments have a smaller Cabinet. In Switzerland this is because of the relatively few responsibilities of the Federal Council by comparison with the cantons, and in the United States it is because of the very substantial responsibilities vested in the President and in such non-Cabinet bodies as the Environmental Protection Agency. A Cabinet with more than two dozen ministries is exceptional. Moreover, the number of ministries has grown far less since the mid-nineteenth century than have government's resources overall.

Local governments are usually created by acts of a national parliament or by a national constitution, but their raison d'être is different from a central government ministry. A local government can claim to be better informed, because closer to those who receive its services, and its elected political heads are responsible to a smaller electoral constituency. In federal systems of government, intermediate-tier *laender*, states or regions can introduce further political complications. Like central government ministries, local authorities are headed by elected officials, and fund the programmes they operate with tax revenues (cf. Newton, 1980).

There is great variation among Western nations in the number of local authorities. The number of basic (that is, lowest-level) units of local government ranges from 36,391 in France to 277 in Denmark (Table 6.2). In smaller European democracies, the number of local government units is counted in the hundreds rather than the thousands, but the total remains far greater than the number of central government ministries. In the four most populous European countries, the average number of local government units is 13,360. In the six smaller democracies examined the average is 481 units.

When allowance is made for population differences between countries, there is a considerable degree of similarity in the size of local government units in the Western world. The average unit of government has a population of 20,500, that is, about 5,000 households (Table 6.2). The median country, Finland, has one local government unit for every 10,400 people, and in Germany, Italy, the United States and France local government is even more local, for the population of the average unit is less than 7,500. Every country has some very large cities that inflate the average. In France the average population of a commune, 1,500, is higher than the population of five-sixths of communes; in 16,550 of France's 36,391 communes there are less than 300 people.

TABLE 6.2
The contraction in local government units, 1951-1982

Country (basic unit)	1951	1982	Change, 1950-1982	Population per unit 1982
	(N units)		%	
France (commune)	37,983	36,391	−4	1,500
United States (townships, municipalities)	33,980	35,744	+5	6,300
Italy (commune)	n.a.	8,053	n.a.	7,100
Germany (*gemeinden*)[a]	24,500	8,510	−65	7,200
Norway (municipalities)	746	454	−39	9,000
Finland	547	461	−16	10,400
Belgium (commune)	2,670	596	−78	16,700
Netherlands (municipalities)	1,014	820	−19	17,000
Denmark (commune)	1,388	277	−80	18,400
Sweden (commune)	2,500[b]	279	−89	29,800
United Kingdom (districts)	1,932	548	−72	102,500

a. Includes *kreisfrei gemeinden* (92), *einheitsgemeinden* (2,170) and the 6,248 villages that are the units constituting *verbandsgemeinden*. If the *verbandsgemeinden* are reckoned as the basic units, the German total is 3,353 units, with an average population of 18,400. See Gunlicks (1981: 175).

b. Local government reorganization in Sweden in the 1950s reduced the number of basic units to 1,032, which were subsequently reduced by reorganizations in the 1960s and 1970s.

Sources: *The Stateman's Year Book 1951, 1982-83*, London, Macmillan; Gunlicks (1981).

The number of local government units has declined in Western nations in the postwar era by an average of 45 percent. Units of government that serve a small number of people today had even fewer constituents in 1951. Reorganization has reduced the number of local government units by as much as 89 percent in Sweden, and by more than two-thirds in Denmark, Belgium and Britain. In the United States, where population has increased by 50 percent and suburbanization and interregional migration has led to a major redistribution of population, the number of local government units has not grown in proportion to the population.

The number of local governments cannot be compared with the number of central government ministries because of fundamental differences. First of all, ministries normally have nationwide jurisdiction, whereas local authorities have their activities circumscribed within a limited territory. Local authorities ought to be far greater in number, because each is confined in its territorial scope. Second, each local authority is multi-functional; it usually has responsibilities for a multiplicity of programmes, looking after education, social services, public health, housing, refuse collection and police, which are divided among four or five ministries in central government. Within its limited territory, any one local authority will do a greater variety of things that any one central government ministry, though the resources it commands are much less (Rose, 1982a: Chapters 5-6).

2. Organizations headed by appointed officials and state-owned but not primarily financed by public funds

Nationalized industries are owned by government and have directors appointed by government, but the market is their principal source of revenue. Even if a nationalized industry loses money, the losses are almost always a small fraction of operating revenue. Public enterprises differ from private enterprises, having a direct claim upon the public purse for operating subsidies and investment capital. Moreover, the directors of a public enterprise are accountable to politicians rather than to private owners.

Nationalized industries can take any one of several very different forms. A government can establish a single corporation for a single industry, e.g. a national coal board. This is invariably the case with the post office or the railways, because of the nationwide interdependencies in such services. Public ownership is also consistent with a multi-organizational industry; for example, a nationalized water industry may involve dozens or hundreds of different water authorities, each covering a single locality or watershed. Whereas an inter-city bus service is likely to be run by a single government corporation, each municipal bus service is likely to be owned by a different local authority. A nationalized corporation may be multi-industry if, for historical reasons, the nationalized company retains interests in a variety of firms and fields.

The number of nationalized industries and public enterprises varies substantially among member-states of the European Community. Post offices and telecommunications, electricity, gas, coal, the railways and airlines are almost invariably government-owned. The position of steel, motor cars and shipbuilding is usually complex. The comparability of data is limited, given the very great cross-national differences in legal and organizational forms between ministries, public corporations and companies that are technically private but have substantial state shareholdings (cf. Vernon and Aharoni, 1981). On the basis of available data, Germany leads the list with more than 1700 public enterprises, principally because of a tradition of municipal ownership of public utilities. While the number of German public enterprises is large compared with other European countries, it is a small proportion of the total number of German enterprises. While there are 635 German limited liability companies in public hands, this is a trivial proportion of the 86,820 limited liability companies in Germany (CEEP, 1981). By contrast, in Britain public enterprises are far fewer in number, but because they operate on the same scale as central government each commands large resources.

Collectively, the resources commanded by public enterprises are large. In every major European country public enterprises account for about one-quarter to one-third of total public employment (Table 5.1 above), and thus for 5 to 10 percent of total national employment. Moreover, in primary industries and manufacturing, state-owned enterprises are dominant, or even claim a national monopoly. Public enterprises have substantial financial resources, whether viewed in terms of investment or gross trading revenue (cf. OECD, 1981).

Government ownership of banks and other financial institutions can further extend its influence upon trading enterprises. Government can influence these organizations by making direct loans, or by guaranteeing loans made by private sector banks in order to encourage investment in housing, rural electrification, small businesses, the exploitation of energy resources and other government-endorsed policy aims. In the United States federal financial institutions use loan and loan guarantee powers as a principal financial resource (Musolf and Seidman, 1980; US Budget, 1982: 65ff.).

3. Organizations headed by appointed officials, and owned and financed by government funds

This type of public enterprise differs from trading enterprises, for it is dependent upon tax revenue rather than on revenue from the market. For example, a state-owned television company is a non-trading enterprise if it receives most of its revenue from government grants or a compulsory user license, but it is a trading enterprise if it receives most of its revenue from advertising. Dependence upon the public purse for funds is likely to make this type of public organization closer to central government than is a trading enterprise, which generates a large cash flow.

A central government may choose to deliver a given service by establishing an extra-ministerial agency headed by an appointed official, thus divesting itself of unwelcome routine activities, for example operating hospitals or administering a health service; or to give authority to experts, as in the operation of a national space agency or a museum; or to distance itself politically, as in public broadcasting. By giving responsibility to appointed officials rather than another set of elected officials, a central government greatly reduces its risk of involvement in controversy while retaining substantial influence through the power of appointment, control of finance and responsibility for its statutory powers.

4. Organizations principally financed or owned by government, but headed by officials appointed independently of government

A small fraction of public organizations, such as universities, religious schools, hospitals or charitable and philanthropic bodies, may be owned and directed by non-governmental bodies. For example, a university may be run by a self-perpetuating board of trusteees or an academic senate, and a school by a religious body. None the less, if operating funds come from government, it will be a government organization, since primary dependence upon public funds brings with it government regulation. Just as nationalized industries put a limit to the power of political appointees by their market operations, so these organization limit the power of the purse by having directors appointed independent of government.

The most extreme example of distancing from government, while still remaining financially dependent, occurs in national health services. The great majority of medical doctors are self-employed professionals, or are organized into small group practices owned by their members. Only a minority of doctors are salaried employees in the military, schools and other public agencies. But doctors are part of a national health service because they are paid principally by government, and not by the patients they treat.

5. Fringe organizations

In addition to the four different types of organizations collectively responsible for executing the programmes that account for the great majority of government resources, every country has hundreds of advisory or consultative committees. In many cases these bodies are not organizations, for they meet only once a month or so, rely upon civil servants drawn from other organizations, and lack responsibility for delivering public programmes or disbursing public funds. The membership of advisory and consultative committees often is not determined by government, because the committees are meant to represent the views of interest groups. Interest groups can nominate members, or their officers may sit ex officio on the committee. Some committees, such as a British Royal Commission, are ad hoc, advising on a specific problem, whereas others offer continuing advice to a government ministry, e.g. a standing committee of agricultural interests.

Counting the number of advisory and consultative committees is misleading, albeit a favourite device of their critics, because it suggests a vast number of bodies 'overrunning' government, when in fact they are so insubstantial in resources that it is doubtful whether they can be properly classified as organizations. In Britain the lowest official estimate is of the order of 250 to 300 fringe bodies, but as many as 1000 have been identified (cf. Hood, 1982: 52; Hogwood, 1982: 73). In the Netherlands, a similar scale of activity is found, with 525 permanent advisory boards in national government. These boards are relatively recent in origin; less than one-eighth date from before the Second World War and more than one-half have been created since 1966 (Wassenberg and Kooiman, 1980: 129). The total number of advisory and consultative bodies in government is likely to be far greater than the number of local authorities and trading enterprises, but their resources are far less.

There is great semantic and conceptual confusion about organizations that are relevant to the public interest or interact with government but are not a part of government. In continental Europe there is a public law framework which explicitly identifies organizations as state organizations. But there has also been a growth of organizations headed by publicly appointed officials, and owned and/or financed by government. In Italian these are called the *parastatale*, organizations on the fringes of government but without the legal attributes of state organizations. From a natural law perspective, the proper functions of government are meant to be undertaken by state organizations, with para-state organizations undertaking functions not identified traditionally as 'proper' or 'natural' to government. In Italy and Spain, the weakness and inefficiency of the state has promoted the growth of para-state organizations as an effective alternative means to carry out conventional government tasks.

In most Western nations legal recognition is given to organizations considered as operating in the public interest but not part of government. Non-profit organizations often receive statutory recognition for their activities, for example trade unions, churches and philanthropic bodies. Their activities may substitute for public programmes, e.g. education provided by churches, or may complement programmes, for example, the role of political parties complements the role of public organizations administering elections. The number of non-profit organizations is substantial and their financial resources significant (Weisbrod, 1977). Although affecting the public interest, these bodies are not government organizations so long as they have independent legal ownership, do not have their directors appointed by government, and are not dependent upon government grants as their principal source of income.

Private sector organizations differ greatly from each other; the Ford Motor Company, which operates worldwide with greater resources than some member-states of the United Nations, is in most respects very different from a corner shop. But private sector organizations have common characteristics differentiating them from government organizations. Their directors are not elected by citizens, or appointed by government; nor are they state-owned or funded by tax revenues. Government organizations lacking one or two of these three defining attributes of government by default share characteristics with private sector organizations. For example, public enterprises sell their goods in the market to gain most of their revenue as do private sector organizations. But this does not make public organizations any less public; they are simply a different type of government organization.

In a mixed economy, private sector organizations will sell a significant portion of their output to government. In a complementary way, public enterprises will deliver a substantial portion of their output to private sector organizations. A few large organizations depend very heavily upon government contracts, for example construction and civil engineering firms specializing in public works, and the so-called military-industrial complex in the United States. The purchase of goods and services from private sector firms can involve the inclusion in contracts of clauses that regulate employment practices of the private sector bodies, drawing them closer to government (cf. Sharkansky, 1980; Weidenbaum, 1981).

Interaction and interdependence between public and private sector organizations has undoubtedly grown with the growth of government. In a society in which 10 percent of organizations were part of government and 90 percent were in the private sector, then if interaction between organizations were strictly proportional to numbers, 81 percent of a society's organized affairs would involve only private sector organizations, 18 percent would cut across the public-private boundary, and 1 percent would be solely within government. But if the proportion of organized activities under government auspices rose to 30 percent (less than government's proportionate share of the GNP), then 42 percent of all interactions would cut across the public-private sector divide, 49 percent would remain exclusively within the private sector, and 9 percent would be exclusively within the public sector.[2] The numbers are hypothetical, but the substantive point is clear: an increase in the activity of government organizations disproportionately increases contacts between the public and private sector.

In order to understand the policy process and, even more, the impact of government upon society, it is important to understand the relationships between organizations. But this can be done only if there continues to be a recognition that the formal structure of each organization establishes boundaries that separate it from every other organization. The point is important, for there is a tendency to submerge organizations in a single abstraction, such as the political system, issue networks or corporatism (cf. Heclo, 1979; Jordan, 1981). To speak of a system emphasizes the interaction and interdependence between organizations. But a system exists only by virtue of the different organizations that form its constituent parts.

Notwithstanding major differences in institutional structures of government, the foregoing review has found a common pattern among major Western governments. Everywhere, ministries at the top of government are very few in number, usually fewer than two dozen. The number of public enterprises are also relatively few,

numbering in the dozens or hundreds, depending upon the extent
of government intervention in industry and the number of
subsidiaries of major state enterprises. Local governments are
more numerous, numbering in the hundreds or thousands,
depending upon the recognition given to small towns and villages
by a country's structure of government. If only because each
government organization can have more than one advisory body,
they are likely to be very numerous, even though each has few and
insubstantial resources.

Counting government organizations is not the same as weighing
them. If government organizations are weighed by their resources,
there is likely to be an inverse relationship between the number of
organizations in a category and the resources that each commands
individually. This is most evident in central government, for the
fewness of ministries assures each a sizeable amount of legal
powers, public revenue and civil servants.

Causes of organizational change

If government is treated as a single organization, a state in terms
of international law, then it cannot grow or contract; a state can
only persist or cease to exist. The history of Western states since
1945 has been extremely unusual; there has been no change in their
number since the settlement of the Second World War, and
boundary changes have been trivial. In the world as a whole, by
contrast, there has been a great growth of independent states
resulting from the ending of colonial empires.

Within an independent state, organizations are of two types:
those established by the country's constitution and those
established by laws which are altered far more easily than
constitutional provisions. Government organizations established
by the constitution are relatively few and fixed in number. If the
principal political organizations of government are defined as the
parliament, the courts of law, the central machinery for directing
the executive branch of government, and in federal systems the
territorial partners to the federal compact, then there has been
virtually no change in their number in any postwar Western
government. Constituent alterations are minor, such as the
addition of two states — Hawaii and Alaska — to the United
States, the division of the canton of Jura into two cantons in
Switzerland or the abolition of the upper house in the Swedish
parliament.

Most organizations of government are not embedded in a country's constitution. Even as legalistic a country as the United States gives constituent status to 0.01 percent of its total number of government organizations. Central government ministries, local authorities and public enterprises can be created or abolished by amending an Act of Parliament or by executive action. The evidence reviewed here shows a limited tendency for central government ministries to increase in number and for local government units to decrease in number. Evidence about trading enterprises is inconclusive. Nationalization can reduce a large number of separate private sector bodies into a single organization owned by central government, or sustain a large number of municipally owned organizations.

The simplest explanation of changes in the number of organizations — that organizations increase in response to an increase in programmes — is of greatest significance in understanding long-term changes. The number of ministries has increased in every Western nation in response to a growth in the programme commitments of government. In the mid-nineteenth century, government was responsible for a relatively limited range of programmes; on average, a Cabinet was responsible for only eight separately identified major programmes, such classic concerns as finance, police and justice, defence and foreign affairs. By 1936 the average Western government had increased its ministerial functions by half, adopting programme commitments promoting the economy in agriculture, industry and trade and minimal welfare provisions for education and (usually) health. The growth of welfare state commitments since the Second World War has further expanded the number of central government ministries (Table 6.1). A few governments have abolished ministries where they no longer have responsibilities; for example, the end of the British Empire meant the abolition of the India Office and the Colonial Office.

A Cabinet can grow slowly in size while each individual ministry grows in complexity by adding bureaus to deal with an increase in its programme responsibilities and a local government can increase the number of departments within a town hall. The redefinition of programme responsibilities sometimes contracts the number of organizations. This is most obvious in the case of military services. A half-century ago nearly every Western government had separate ministries for the Army and the Navy; the Air Force established a claim to parity of organizational treatment in the Second World War. Since 1945 every major Western government has redefined its military programmes in terms of a single overall mission, national defence. This has resulted in the creation of a single integrated Ministry of Defence, and the reduction of the former Army and Navy ministries to subunits of the new ministry. While the number of defence ministries was reduced, the old ministries were not abolished: they have been merged. A systematic analysis of organizational change in the United States has shown that organizational succession (that is, merger or division) is more likely than the creation of new organizations or the termination of old ones (Hogwood and Peters, 1982: Table 4.1).

The most straightforward way to reduce the number of government organizations is to abolish the programmes for which they are responsible. Today this is central to the idea of the privatization of public programmes. Privatization often means that government is no longer the organization responsible for delivering a service, contracting out responsibility to a private sector firm. Instead of maintaining a large number of its own office buildings and its own property management agency, a government can rent building space, or a local authority can abolish its municipal refuse collection department and contract with a profit-making firm to collect local rubbish (cf. Savas, 1982). In such circumstances, government continues financing the service, even though it has reduced its organizational capability. The only way in which privatization can lead to government's reducing both organizational and financial responsibilities is if it sells a state-owned enterprise to private sector investors, who then become responsible for financing it. This is infrequently done, for most government organizations produce goods and services that are not sold, and many public trading enterprises are run at a loss subsidized by tax revenues.

Changes in the structure of central government ministries can also reflect changing fashions in reorganization programmes, usually favouring a reduction in the number of separately identified organizations, but an increase in the number of subunits within the new organizations. Britain illustrates the tendency to reshuffle programmes and organizational labels while tending to make nil change in the total number of government ministries. Since 1900 there have been 111 different ministries in British government. The creation of the great majority of so-called 'new' ministries has involved re-labelling or reorganization rather than innovation in form or changes in programme content (Butler and

Sloman, 1980: 65, 78; Clarke, 1973). A new ministry is unlikely to consist of bureaus and programmes that previously had no place in government. It will first of all consist of bureaus and programmes assigned to it from already established ministries. A 'new' ministry, such as the Ministry of Technology created by Harold Wilson in 1964, may commence on its first day with 25,000 employees, because it takes over old programmes, personnel, money and legal responsibilities from its predecessors.

By contrast with very substantial growth in tax revenue and public employment, government organizations have not increased in total number to anything like the same extent. The principal organizations delivering programmes — local governments — have actually contracted in number. This seeming paradox can be explained by turning attention from the number of government organizations to their weight, that is, their claim upon government resources. In the postwar world, the organizations of Western government have increased much more in weight than in number. What most distinguishes a ministry of defence from a large number of municipal bus companies is not that the latter are more numerous, but that the former makes far more claims upon government for money and personnel and has greater statutory powers.

Public organizations can increase their employees or expenditure very substantially without increasing the number of their programme commitments if their principal activities are routine and easily reproduced in a large number of parallel and more or less identical operating units carrying out the same programme in different places (cf. Kochen and Deutsch, 1980: 35ff.). The directing minister remains in charge at the top, while the organization grows at the base through the multiplication of service delivery units. The military is one familiar example of expansion. An army grows by increasing the number of its military divisions, a navy by increasing its number of ships, and an airforce by increasing the number of planes and missiles. At the end of a war, a military force contracts by reducing the number of its divisions, laying up ships and not replacing aircraft as they become obsolete. At all times, the military remains an organization under a single command.

The multiplication of programme delivery units — whether army divisions, primary schools or hospitals — need not increase the number of organizations or programmes within government, but it does increase the weight of resources claimed. When an organization is doing more of the same thing, e.g. teaching more pupils or caring for more hospital patients, it does not need to establish new bureaus or agencies: it simply needs more resources to expand the number of standardized service delivery units. By contrast, when a government increases its number of programme commitments, the initial addition of resources may not be large, but there is usually pressure to create a new bureau or agency to be responsible for the new programme.

In local government, the reduction of the number of local authorities found throughout Europe (Table 6.2) reflects distinctive political and economic values. Local government is of particular importance as a means of realizing political participation through elected officials. The total number of elected councillors in local government is hundreds of times greater than the number of politicians elected to a national parliament. Moreover, the much smaller size of the local government electorate increases contact between voters and their elected representatives. Local governments (and, in federal systems, provincial-level governments) are the most numerous elected organizations in a country.

Proponents of political participation advocate an increase in decentralized organizations headed by elected officials. Such organizations are assumed to be 'closer' to the people, and therefore better. Elected organizations are often praised as being better than bureaucratic or market organizations (Lindblom, 1977; but contrast Dahl, 1970, Huntington, 1974). Nationalist, autonomist and regionalist groups add ethnic claims as an additional political justification for decentralization. The vogue for political participation in the late 1960s was coincidental with the expansion of the resources of government organizations, and in many countries with local government reorganization.

Criteria of economic efficiency normally assume that bigger organizations are more efficient producers of services. From this perspective, a reduction in the number of local government units would be regarded as desirable, notwithstanding the potential loss of opportunities to participate in locally elected councils. Moreover, in countries with many very small local jurisdictions, a reduction in numbers is often considered necessary to increase the powers and responsibilities of local agencies. An authority with a population of 10,000 or 100,000 people can have more service delivery powers than a commune with 5,000 or 1,000 people.

Whereas liberal political values have favoured increased individual participation, collectivist and socialist values have tended to favour fewer separate local government units in order to maintain minimum standards in all units, reduce the extent of variation in service provision between communities, and redistribute resources through central government financial powers. In its extreme form, the doctrine of territorial justice would favour central government provision of all major programmes to ensure that all citizens throughout a country receive much the same benefits, regardless of their local resources (cf. Davies, 1968). Equality in programme outputs prescribes centralization, whereas increased opportunity for participation prescribes decentralization.

Local government reorganization in Europe is clearly not explained as a response to demands for participation. Notwithstanding spurts of support for minority regionalist or independence parties in Europe in the 1970s, there has not been a large-scale transfer of powers from central government (cf. Cornford, 1975; Rose and Urwin, 1975; Rose, 1982a). The number of elected officials heading government organizations has been drastically reduced almost everywhere in Europe in the belief that this will cause greater economic efficiency, and will lead to a more equal territorial distribution of programme benefits (cf. Gustaffson, 1980). The majority of European states interpret better government to mean fewer rather than more organizations headed by elected officials.

Do organizations matter?

Does the necessary concern of public administrators with the forms of government organization have any practical consequences for the programmes of government? Even if organizations can be shown to make a difference, what are the consequences of changes in the scale of government organizations, regardless of whether size is measured by the weight of resources that a single organization commands, or by the number of organizations concerned with the manifold programmes of big government?

Politicians believe that organizations matter. Schattschneider's (1960: 71) dictum, 'Organization is the mobilization of bias', is the premise that makes politicians jockey for position within government in order to secure an office with maximum organizational impact. The importance that politicians attach to organizations is also shown by the frequency of attempts to reorganize one or more major institutions of government. Reorganization is an almost chronic concern of postwar American presidents (see e.g. Szanton, 1981), and it is also recurrent in European political agendas (see e.g. Leemans, 1976; Caiden and Siedentopf, 1982). Concern with governmental reorganization is not just a matter of good government doctrines. Lester Salamon (1981: 81) argues: 'The purposes of reorganization go well beyond the narrow confines of economy and efficiency to embrace the purposes of politics itself.' Changing the structure of organizations delivering programmes is meant to influence the programmes too.

Any consideration of effectiveness must start with the recognition that all organizations, including public organizations, are inevitably imperfect. A perfect organization is no more possible in a complex modern society than is the perfect market of economic theory. No government organization can meet all the criteria for perfect administration, for government lacks unitary organization with a single unambiguous line of authority, uniform rules, clearly defined and ranked objectives, freedom from time pressures, perfect information, and consensus about goals among organizations. Each government organization is deficient to some degree in each of these attributes (Hood, 1976).

The programme goals of government organizations vary in the extent to which they are achievable. Some tasks are inherently more 'do-able' than others, because of the existence of known and effective means-ends technologies. A department of highway engineering can more easily be effective in building roads than a department of social engineering can be in reducing poverty. When attempting to evaluate the effectiveness of organizational structure, it is necessary to make considerable allowance for differences in their programme goals. Any organization can achieve relatively simple goals, whereas no organizational form can guarantee success if its assigned goal is 'mission impossible'.

Public administration experts do not agree about the empirical consequences of different organizational forms. In the absence of such agreement, it is not possible to hypothesize with confidence what result to expect from organizational changes. If public administration or management is a science, it is a science like meteorology, which is better at offering explanations after the fact than at prediction. Practical politicians also lack understanding sufficient to guarantee the success of their reorganization efforts.

In view of the confusion about the likely effects of changes in organizations, the simplest hypothesis to propose is the null hypothesis: changes in form make no difference to organizational effectiveness. The null hypothesis does not assume any particular level of effectiveness of a government organization before it adds weight. In Mediterranean countries, for example, the state has been relatively small in terms of the resources it commands, yet complaints about the failure of the state are frequent. In Scandinavian welfare states, government's claims on resources are large and public organizations have been assumed to be effective though big in weight. In each of these countries, political culture is thought more important than size in determining the effectiveness of government.

Bigger is necessarily better only in such atypical programmes as the military. Everything else being equal, an army of 50 divisions is likely to be more effective than an army of 10 divisions. Moreover, a noticeable loss in efficiency is not tantamount to the complete loss of effectiveness. By definition, a decline in efficiency is relative; more resources are needed to maintain a given level of effectiveness. It does not mean that an organization is completely ineffective.

The chief condition that allows organizations to increase their scale of resources without losing organizational effectiveness is that the activities of the organization are suitable for pluralization. The multiplication of service delivery units within an organization need not lead to a loss of effectiveness, as long as the means-ends technology of an organization is amenable to replication. The growing weight of education and health ministries is not evidence of declining effectiveness, because these services can be provided by a plurality of delivery units within a local education authority or health authority.

Weightier organizations lose effectiveness only in so far as an increase in the volume of resources cannot be managed by pluralization. For example, growth in the size of a police force (particularly a national police force) will greatly increase the difficulties of inspecting the force for illegal actions by policemen. Inspection must be a centralized function, for policemen or police stations cannot inspect themselves, yet knowledge of malfeasance is greatest where illegal acts occur. In a small organization inspectors can become aware of illegal activities through informal as well as formal channels. In a very large organization, inspectors are likely to be so remote that they rely very heavily upon formal channels of information, with a consequent loss of effectiveness.

An increase in the number of organizations that collectively constitute government is very different from an increase in the weight of resources commanded by any one public organization. There is an increase in the number of co-ordinating activities required to bring together separate organizations with related tasks. Political conflicts and bargaining between organizations increases too.

Every organization within government has a distinctive cluster of interests and goals. A ministry can become a spokesman or 'captive' of its clients, for example, Agriculture for farmers, Industry for business and Labour for trade unions. The more numerous the organizations within government, the greater the number of interests articulated within government, and the greater the number of potential conflicts between government organizations. The result is sometimes referred to as a problem of co-ordinating organizations, but it is better referred to as a problem of conflict management (Schick, 1981a). Only in exceptional circumstances will a co-ordinating organization have the political power to enforce its will against all parties to a conflict. Instead of searching in vain for a lost or imagined simple structure of accountability, an Anglo-American group of researchers advise: 'Let us instead talk of the optimal degree of disorder' (Hague et al., 1975: 374).

The mechanisms for managing conflict within and between government organizations are multiple (Rose, 1982a: Chapter 7). Within an organization, hierarchical theories posit that decisions should be made at the top, and services delivered at the bottom. But the more complex an organization is, the greater the variety of problems flowing to the top, and the greater the potential conflicts between different sides of an organizational pyramid. In such circumstances, any attempt to resolve conflict will be unlikely to be acceptable to all sides. At the other extreme, a theory of stratarchy prescribes that, in order to avoid conflict, organizations should avoid intervening in each other's affairs. But such a prescription can apply only when organizations need not interact with each other. In contemporary mixed economy welfare states, interdependencies between organizations concerned with a given programme increase contacts. For example, local government is less and less insulated from the fiscal stress facing central government, and central government is less and less insulated from the problems that local authorities face in delivering programmes. In practice, inter-organizational politics within government is most likely to follow a model of oligopoly, that is, conflict between a relatively few interdependent and unequal organizations. An increase in the number of government organizations will also increase the number of problems to be resolved within an oligopolistic framework.

The multiplication of government organizations can reduce effectiveness, as more organizations become involved in implementing a given programme. While problems of implementation are limited with established programmes, because inter-organizational relations are well established, new programmes have yet to demonstrate any effectiveness. Pressman and Wildavsky's (1973) pioneering study of implementation argued that there was an almost exponential increase in the probability of failure of a new programme with an increase in the number of organizations involved in delivering it. The argument depended upon the crucial assumption that the need for clearances between organizations increased disproportionately with an increase in the number of organizations involved, and that each clearance is independent of every other, thereby increasing the probability of failure if any one organization refused co-operation.

In fact, an increase in the number of organizations need not prevent the effective implementation of new programmes. Bowen (1982) has shown that the assumptions of Pressman and Wildavsky are of limited applicability. Many clearances depend upon each other, and organizations often combine to deal with a multiplicity of problems simultaneously. Furthermore, success at the initial stages of implementation greatly increases effectiveness at subsequent stages.

The growth of supranational and transnational organizations such as the European Community and the International Monetary Fund have further increased the complexity of inter-organizational politics (Wallace et al., 1977; Keohane and Nye, 1977). Major government organizations, of which the foreign ministry is the most obvious example, deal with their opposite numbers in other states as well as with other ministries in their own country. A study of Norwegian public officials found that the majority dealt with some international issues each year; the higher their position, the more likely they are to become involved in international as well as domestic negotiations (Egeberg, 1980). In a national Treasury, one side of the ministry will be continuously dealing with problems of the international economy, represented by foreign government and banks, and another, with domestic issues. The incorporation of conflicting pressures within a single ministry increases communication between the responsible units, but it does not thereby make it easier to remove conflicts inherent in contrasting domestic and international pressures.

Popular consent for public organizations is not simply a function of size: the demand for representative and responsive government antedated the creation of the mixed economy welfare state. The creation of big government forces a reconsideration of conventional assumptions, for theories and practices of representation suited to a small, face-to-face community are not necessarily suited to the government of a country with 40 million or 140 million electors. As government grows, the importance of national government tends to grow, thus shifting the locus of decision-making to the national parliament from local government, where in principle representatives and voters could meet daily, and know each other personally.

The simplest indicator of a direct relationship between electors and elected officials is the number of electors per representative. The lower the ratio, the greater the possibility of direct communication between the two, and the greater the potential influence of an individual vote. Since the size of national parliaments has not been enlarged in proportion to the growth in the electorate, increasing the size of national electorates has reduced greatly the prospects for personal communication and influence between individual voters and their representatives in parliament (Table 6.3). The ratio of electors to representatives is now so large that the link between the ordinary elector and a representative in parliament must be impersonal and indirect. Whereas nineteenth century elections typically involved a few thousand voters per constituency, contemporary elections involve tens of thousands of voters — or hundreds of thousands, when multi-member proportional representation constituencies are taken into account. The ratio of electors to representatives has increased most in Belgium (43 times) and the United States (37 times). Where the change has been least in relative terms, this is because the number of electors per representative at the first national competitive election was already high.

The influence of a voter upon government today must operate through organizations. The growth of the electorate and disciplined parties has reduced the role of individual influence, as assumed in nineteenth century liberal theories of representative government. Masses of voters must hold a party (or a coalition of parties) collectively accountable for the actions of government. Referendums cannot give voters the opportunity to determine public policies. The measures voted upon in a referendum are usually drafted by a national parliament, and the decision to hold a referendum is usually taken in parliament. Except for the egregious example of Switzerland, referendums are usually held once a decade in European nations (cf. Butler and Ranney, 1978: 227f.). The limits upon individuals giving their direct consent to public policies are thus very great.

TABLE 6.3
The increasing number of electors per representative in Parliament

Country	1st competitive election			Latest election		Increase in ratio voters/ MPs
	Year	No. MPs	Ratio voters	No. MPs	Ratio voters	
						%
United States (Congress)	1828	213	9,464	435	360,857	3,713
Germany	1871	382	20,041	497	86,983	334
France	1849	750	13,116	474	74,970	479
Italy	1895	508	4,175	630	66,953	1,504
Netherlands	1888	100	29,261	150	66,934	129
United Kingdom	1885	670	8,519	635	64,716	660
Belgium	1848	108	732	212	32,444	4,332
Denmark	1901	114	3,546	175	21,579	608
Norway	1882	114	873	155	19,374	2,219
Finland	1907	200	6,364	200	19,293	203
Sweden	1887	214	1,284	349	17,308	1,348
Ireland	1922	128	11,172	166	13,707	23

Source: Mackie and Rose (1982).

Because government is a set of formal organizations, individuals must organize to negotiate agreements that involve collective questions of public policy. This is most evident in the development of quasi-corporatist tripartite institutions involving government, business and trade unions to discuss the problems of a mixed economy (cf. Schmitter and Lehmbruch, 1980). The institutions of so-called corporatism are not actually corporate, in that they are not a single formal organization with the resources to achieve their goals. Typically, they are advisory committees for discussion and negotiation about economic problems, a place where government officials try to 'jawbone' business and unions into adopting courses of action that government believes will be desirable for the economy as a whole. A corporatist body can hope to be fully effective only if it has statutory authority to resolve differences between business and labour, and the staff and funds to enforce any decision it takes against business and trade union organizations. Most corporatist institutions lack compelling powers.

The dilemma facing individuals is that they must allow government organizations to act in their name in order to achieve collective ends, yet they do not wish to lose all power to act on their own behalf.

> By giving the corporate body power to act, each member largely loses his power over the direction its actions will take; but by withholding this power through a more restrictive decision rule, the potential benefits brought by the corporate actor vanish. [Coleman, 1974: 40]

In Western democracies, governments usually prefer to trade off effectiveness for consent. The quasi-corporate institutions that they establish have little or no coercive power; they act by agreement or not at all. By contrast, in Eastern Europe Soviet-style regimes are ready to sacrifice popular consent, compelling their subjects to accept the unilateral government regulation of wages, prices, investment decisions and trade unions.

The problems of securing consent exist within the state too. Elected officeholders are caught up in a network of organizational pressures that inhibit elected politicians from determining what government does. A Cabinet minister, in principle one of the two dozen most important people in the whole of government, is subject to the organized inertia force of the ministry's commitments in law, expenditure and personnel. None of these is immediately changed by the appointment of a new minister, or by a change in the party control of government. Officials can run government programmes without direction by elected politicians because they are numerous, informed, and interested in the success of their programmes; but professionalized decision-making cannot be described as government by elected representatives. Moreover, officials usually have a bias towards growth.

Sample surveys of high-level civil servants in countries as different as Denmark (Damgaard, 1982) and the United States (Aberbach and Rockman, 1976) find that agency officials usually believe that the programmes and expenditure of their agency should be increased.

An elected officeholder, placed in charge of a government ministry by virtue of winning popular support, becomes immersed in face-to-face relations within an elite community. His immediate problems are managing the ministry for which he is responsible and engaging in inter-organizational or inter-governmental politics in order to advance his organization. In the words of Dahl and Tufte (1974: 75f.), politicians move from a situation in which citizens can be present in the calculations of leaders, albeit 'treated as an audience', to a world in which 'top leaders communicate with one another through intermediaries if at all'. Simultaneously, popular pressures from outside government may threaten structural overload, that is, the imposition of more demands than an organization can meet. In response, officials may resort to 'defensive closure', reducing their openness to popular pressures (Wassenberg and Kooiman, 1980: 143).

So great are the obstacles to directing government organizations in accord with conventional democratic theories of popular electoral control that individual citizens are often said to 'become alienated and impute the blame for much that goes wrong to the bureaucracy' (Johnson, 1982: 216). But does the failure of theories of small government actually result in popular frustration with the institutions of big government?

The answer is: No. There is a relatively high level of popular confidence in the principal institutions of big government today. Popular confidence in major government institutions consistently tends to run higher than popular confidence in major non-governmental institutions (Table 6.4). In six major Western nations — America, Britain, Ireland, Germany, France and Italy — a majority of people show confidence in the police, the armed forces, the legal system and the education system, and nearly half show confidence in Parliament and the civil service. On average, 58 percent of respondents report confidence in public institutions. By comparison, confidence in major non-governmental institutions — the church, major companies, the press and trade unions — is on average expressed by only 39 percent. The organizations in which confidence is shown are central to the state. Three — the police, the armed forces and the legal system — are involved in

collective defence; education, a major welfare state service, also
ranks relatively high.

TABLE 6.4
Popular confidence in major institutions of society

	USA	GB	Ireland	France	Germany	Italy	Average
	%	%	%	%	%	%	%
Government							
Police	76	86	86	64	71	68	75
Armed forces	81	81	75	53	54	58	67
Legal system	51	66	57	66	67	43	58
Education system	65	60	67	55	43	56	58
Parliament	53	40	51	48	53	31	46
Civil service	55	48	54	50	35	28	45
Average	64	64	65	56	54	47	58
Non-governmental institutions							
Church	74	38	78	43	38	60	55
Major companies	50	48	49	42	34	38	43
Press	49	29	44	31	33	46	39
Trade unions	33	26	36	36	36	28	32
Average	33	35	52	38	35	43	39

Source: Calculated from Heald (1982: Table 4) reporting research by the European
Value Systems Study Group.

Individuals clearly discriminate between institutions that are
thought to merit confidence and those that do not. There is no
generalized tendency to trust or distrust large social
organizations. People are more likely to trust government than
private sector institutions. The difference is greatest in the United
States and Britain, where levels of confidence in public
institutions tend to be almost twice as high as levels of confidence
in private sector institutions (Table 6.4). The evidence of the
European Values survey is supported by very detailed studies of

user satisfaction with a variety of public sector services conducted at the state and local as well as federal levels in the United States (Goodsell, 1983: Chapter 2). Voters do not evaluate government organizations according to their congruence with classic democratic norms of representativeness: they appear to judge them by their performance in delivering services. Anti-bureaucratic fulminations may be easy to find in the press, but they are not endorsed by public opinion generally.

Notes

1. Other logically possible categories are likely to involve very small numbers. Organizations without any of the attributes of a government constitute the private sector.

2. The calculations assume an equi-probability of interactions between the public and private sectors. In fact, most interactions of an organization are with bureaus within it or proximal organizations (cf. Rose, 1976b). The basic logic of interdependence is unaffected by this fact.

7 COMBINING RESOURCES INTO PROGRAMMES

Analysing public programmes puts the purposes of government first. Government is about doing things to some purpose; it is not just a combat between politicians, between abstract philosophies or between competing statistical formulae. Without considering purposes, a quantitative description of the activities of government risks becoming a stream of numbers that has no meaning in itself. The resources of government are mobilized not in order to produce changes in quantitative indices; they are mobilized for public purposes. Programmes are concrete legal and bureaucratic attempts to translate general policy intentions into specific government actions. They are means to the end of realizing larger if not necessarily well-defined political goals and values.

Programmes are the policy outputs of government. A programme mixes government resources, combining legal authorization, revenues and public personnel into a package of activities undertaken by a particular public organization. Programme outputs are a primary concern of ordinary citizens. From a programmatic perspective the money that government collects in taxes is not a burden imposed upon citizens but rather a boon, financing the benefits of public programmes. It is the programmes of government that constitute the benefits and create the costs of a mixed economy welfare state.

The particular mix of resources varies greatly from programme to programme. For example, pensions are money-intensive; they do not require a large administrative apparatus, and the most important pension legislation is not easily altered. Education is labour-intensive, for the services of teachers are required to educate young people. Marriage and divorce are classic examples of law-intensive programmes: laws regulate under what circumstances people may make or end a marriage. Environmental pollution programmes are a contemporary illustration of government using laws and regulations to achieve its purposes. Because the mixture for a given programme is highly variable, the full repertoire of government programmes cannot be measured by a single resource; to do so would create a one-dimensional picture of public policies. Seeing public programmes in terms of laws and employees as well as money gives a three-dimensional view of government.

Thinking of government in terms of a plurality of programmes emphasizes the multiplicity of activities of a mixed economy welfare state. Contemporary government is large in scale; at any given moment it is responsible for hundreds of programmes. Government is also varied; maintaining an army, providing health care, subsidizing agricultural production and regulating the adoption of children are not identical activities. To understand what government does we must understand both its variety and its scale.

The size of government is the collective sum of all the programmes for which government is responsible. In the first instance, causes of government growth must be sought in the causes of change in major programmes. It is growth in particular programmes that results in the aggregate phenomenon commonly known as big government. Government is big today because it mobilizes large resources for a few major programmes.

The object of this chapter is to examine the ways in which contemporary government combines resources into programmes that constitute the outputs of government for ordinary citizens. The first section identifies the major programme areas of government and shows how they differ from each other. The second section considers different types and rates of change among programmes, and alternative explanations of the growth of specific programmes. The third section considers the consequence of programme growth for government's effectiveness and for popular consent.

The manifold of government programmes

Politicians must be interested in issues. Even a politician consumed by personal ambition learns to rationalize ambition in terms of achieving broad public purposes. Much of the agenda of politics is set by events, such as the threat of war, an economic boom or recession, a nationwide strike, a natural disaster, or a scandal with little relation to the programmes of government.

Politicians show concern with an issue by talking about it. The act of giving an issue public attention in Parliament, on television or in party meetings can place or keep a subject on the political agenda. Showing concern about an issue can be non-directive in the extreme. A politician need do no more than ask the government of the day to do something about a topic. Such a demand simply asserts that the status quo is unsatisfactory. To endorse a particular programme of action to meet a problem invites conflict, in so far as the programme prescribed is far from the position of the government of the day or of groups with an interest in the status quo. Programmes emerge from conflicting answers given to the question: What shall we do about this issue?

The mass public gives limited attention to issues. At any given time, a few issues will dominate popular attention. In 1983 unemployment was deemed the most important issue in most European countries. A few years earlier, inflation was widely considered of greatest importance.

At any given moment, only a small number of topics can be high on the political agenda. Issues high on the political agenda must be visible and controversial. Visibility is determined first and foremost by the media's interpretation of what is news: an unexpected event can become a crisis issue (for example, a few poor people freezing to death during a cold spell) whereas a persisting condition (say, 5 million people remaining poor) can become a media issue only if a politician is able to publicize the subject. Controversy is the stuff of politics. Politicians may agree on the ends (e.g. to reduce poverty) but they can dispute endlessly the programmatic means to a desired end. It is continuing controversy about means or ends that sustains attention for a political issue.

Policy objectives are often vague, multiple, contradictory and unstable (Rose, 1976b: 5ff.). Policy objectives are vague, (for example, to secure the maximum reduction in full employment consistent with preventing inflation) because vagueness gives a politician room to manoeuvre between disputing groups, thus reducing the risk of being identified with failure. Policy objectives are multiple because the concerns of government are multitudinous. The activities of government cannot be reduced to a single goal, whether social, economic or political. In a government with all the policy concerns of a mixed economy welfare state, politicians must bear in mind the impact of one policy upon another, such as unemployment policies upon inflation rates. When there is a conflict between policies, a government trying to provide something for everybody can adopt contradictory objectives — for example, stressing to bankers that it wishes to reduce inflation, and to trade unions that it wishes to reduce unemployment — even though measures necessary to achieve these two ends will tend to contradict. Policy objectives are unstable because mobility is the salvation of a politician pressed hard to do many things. By re-interpreting objectives without necessarily changing laws or programme budgets, a politician can adapt intentions to the electoral calendar and to the audience.

Stating a policy objective is no guarantee that it will be realized in practice. The record of any government is full of good (and sometimes not so good) intentions that never come to pass. To have a chance of realizing a policy intention, politicians must have a programme that mobilizes resources for public purposes. A statement of a policy intention without a programme may be effective as political rhetoric, but it is irrelevant to the activities of government. To have a programme as well as a policy intention does not guarantee success, but it is a necessary step in the process of governing.

At any given point in time, a government is responsible for hundreds of programmes. In addition to the small number of new programmes that a government adopts, it remains responsible for thousands of programmes that it has inherited from its prede-cessors, each enshrined in public laws and revenue allocations, and in the responsibilities of public employees in particular organizations. The rhetorical description of a programme intention may change with the political weather, but ongoing programme activities are much harder to alter. The inertia pressures to persist are reinforced by the pressure of client groups to continue receiving a programme's benefits.

Programme outputs — the actions of government — are not to be confused with programme outcomes — the impact of a pro-gramme in society. A programme may not produce an intended outcome. For example, a programme to improve educational achievement among disadvantaged children may be frustrated by youths refusing to attend the schools provided, or refusing to learn the lessons offered. A programme to promote employment may be frustrated by changes outside a government's control, such as a change in international oil prices. A government-funded programme to find a cure for cancer may fail, notwithstanding research efforts by hundreds of skilled doctors. Government programmes are no more and no less than inputs to society; effectiveness is contingent, not certain.

The activities of government are not all of equal importance. The logic of a government ministry is to aggregate programme responsibilities in bureaus, so that related activities will fit

together and can be better appreciated by the minister responsible. Policy-makers do not concern themselves with the details of
every programme for which they are normally responsible; often
they are concerned with the relationship between programmes. In
this chapter, the term programme is used to describe a range of
activities in a given policy area. This focuses attention upon
activities that make major claims on public resources, and avoids
becoming bogged down in a plethora of details or case studies
within a programme area. A macroscopic review of government
must concentrate upon the forest in order to identify those
activities that make government big.

National budgets provide a clear example of the way in which
policy-makers disaggregate the activities of government. In a
budget, total expenditure is the sum of spending in many different
programme areas. In Britain the Treasury divides total expenditure into 17 functional categories, covering such topics as
defence, health, education, housing, agriculture and transport. In
turn, each of these major programme areas is disaggregated into a
dozen or so more narrowly defined categories. For example, the
budget of the Department of Education and Science is disaggregated into schools, higher and further education, adult education
and research councils; and each of these categories is further
subdivided. The schools budget is subdivided into schools for the
under-fives, primary schools, secondary schools, special schools,
other services, transport, school meals, school milk (Treasury,
1983, II:45). In the 1983 United States federal budget, the whole of
some $800 billion of expenditure is initially summarized under 17
functional headings, which are then disaggregated in a series of
stages that take 173 pages to list.

The major programme areas of government differ greatly in the
particular mixture of claims that they make upon public revenues,
employees and laws. The programme areas examined in Table 7.1
— education, health, income maintenance, debt interest, economic
infrastructure, public enterprises, defence and law and order —
were selected because each ranks relatively high in its claim on at
least one major public resource. Collectively, the programmes
account for about five-sixths of public expenditure and public
employment and for a high proportion of laws as well. Major programmes can be differentiated into four different types, each
making a substantial but different claim upon the resources of
government.

TABLE 7.1
The scale of major public programmes compared

Resource claims	Public expenditure[a] (mean % GNP)	Public employment[b] (mean % labour force)
High in money and employment	%	%
Education	6.0	5.5
Health	5.4	4.8
Economic infrastructure	4.3	—
Public enterprises	—	6.7
High in money only		
Income maintenance	15.2	(very low)
Debt interest	3.5	(trivial)
Medium high in money & employment		
Defence	3.2	2.4
High in laws only		
Law and order[c]	1.1	1.5
Total all programmes	42.7	28

a. Data for Denmark, France, Germany, Italy, Japan, Netherlands, United Kingdom and the USA, latest available year, as reported in 'Big Government: How Big Is It?' *OECD Observer*, no. 121, March 1983: 8.

b. Calculated by the author from data for latest available year from Britain, Germany, Italy, Sweden and the United States, reported in Rose (forthcoming).

c. Public expenditure figures are for European Community countries as of 1970, as reported in Kohl (1979, vol. II: Table III.5). Employment estimates are based on totals for police and fire services, plus an allowance for courts and prison staffs.

1. *Money-intensive and labour-intensive programmes.* Education and health programmes make big claims on a country's national product, and also upon its labour force, and this pattern is found consistently in all OECD nations. The explanation is simple: *education* is provided by teachers, who are paid above-average wages because they are relatively well educated, have relatively prestigious middle-class jobs, and receive salary increments determined by years of service. The *health* services are also labour-intensive, and the quantity of lower-paid hospital service workers is offset by the highly paid skills of health professionals.

Government programmes for *economic infrastructure* and *public enterprises* are money- and labour-intensive, but each in a distinctive way. Public enterprises are substantial employers in European countries. Collectively, nationalized industries usually employ more workers than either the education or the health service. But the wages of most workers in nationalized industries are not paid from tax revenue, as is the case in education and health. Instead, wages are principally financed by the revenue that the enterprises earn in the market-place. Government need only subsidize losses (which are but a fraction of costs), and finance public sector investment. By contrast, government programmes to maintain the economic infrastructure tend to be money-intensive, such as cash grants to firms in the private sector, agricultural subsidies and the finance of capital investment in roads, transport and telecommunications.

2. *Money-intensive programmes.* The *income maintenance grants* to pensioners, the unemployed and others entitled to cash benefits make a great claim upon the public purse. Writing cheques is administratively easy; it requires a minimum of organization and manpower to verify that an individual is old enough for a pension, and once a person begins to receive a pension, he or she will do so for years. Income maintenance programmes make so low a claim upon the labour force that the numbers employed are not recorded in comparative analyses of public employment, and are less than 1 percent of the total labour force. By contrast, income maintenance programmes on average claim 14 percent of the gross national product of OECD nations, more than education and health combined.

Borrowing money is easy, but meeting the cost of debts is expensive. *Debt interest* payments account for a significant amount of the national product (3.5 percent) in the average OECD nation, more than is now spent on defence. The cumulative effect of government borrowing tends to increase total debt interest. Even though inflation reduces the relative significance of long-term debt, it increases interest rates on short-term borrowing. Administratively, government employs a trivial number of people to pay debt interest, and claimants are easy to identify, being banks and wealthy people. The number of employees in a country's central bank is small compared with the money a bank handles in paying interest on government borrowing.

3. *Programmes that are medium-high in money and employment.* Like health and education, *military defence* requires both money and manpower. Armed forces are labour-intensive. A bigger army (that is, an army with more people) is deemed a stronger army. But military forces today are also capital-intensive. A better airforce is a force with faster and more expensive planes; a better navy, a force with sophisticated surface, air and submarine weaponry; and armies too are becoming more mechanized and automated. In an era

of diplomatic detente, the resource claims of defence programmes have become medium-size, being outpaced by the rise of even greater claims from health and education; but they remain substantial in terms of both money and manpower.

4. *Law-intensive programmes*. The maintenance of *law and order* is norm-intensive, not money- or labour-intensive (cf. Table 3.7 above). Laws are a unique resource of government, because of the extent to which they are self-implementing. Their effect is achieved by the voluntary compliance of the great majority of citizens without further effort by the government. Police, court and prison officials deal with persons who dispute or break the law, a group that must be a relatively small proportion of society if law enforcement officials are to be effective. Whereas the number of laws regulating society's affairs is large, the proportion of public employees concerned with law enforcement is relatively small.

The size of a programme's resource claims is not the only evidence of its importance. To defend a country, diplomacy may be as important as military force, even though military defence makes a larger claim on a nation's money and labour force than does diplomacy. The cost of running a country's diplomatic service is small, the total number of diplomats is very small, and diplomacy also makes few claims on laws. The shift of emphasis from the cold war to diplomacy in the 1960s meant a relative reduction in the claims of defence upon resources, and greater reliance upon the intangible resources of diplomacy.

There are noteworthy differences between Western nations in the relative priority they give to particular programmes. For example, the United States is low in the proportion of the national product spent by government, but ranks second in the proportion of money spent on military defence, and first in the proportion of the labour force employed in education. Differences between nations tend to be less than the common factors that cause all Western nations to devote a substantial amount of resources to the major programmes reviewed here, and to vary the mixture of resources between programmes in similar ways cross-nationally.

Programme growth and change

The most striking changes in programmes occur when a government decides to do things differently than before; for example, it can decide to legalize the use of marijuana or repeal a welfare benefit. The termination of an established programme is exceptional; the inertia properties of laws and organizations, with attendant claims for money and personnel, maintain the great bulk of programmes from year to year and decade to decade. The adoption of a completely new government programme is easier said than done. There are only a limited number of areas of social life that today are unaffected by any government programme. Within a given policy area, the accumulation of pre-existing legislation means that there is limited room for completely new programmes.

When a new law is enacted, it is unlikely to be original in the sense of identifying a completely new programme goal, or a completely unprecedented means of reaching an established goal. The limits upon innovation are evident in the attention a new Act gives to pre-existing statutes that the new measure affects. In order to enact a new law, a government usually accepts many established laws and procedures as given. Often, a change in policy intentions can be achieved by altering actions within a given law, for example, in managing the economy or changing the amount of money and manpower committed to an established programme.

A study of British government from 1970 to 1979 found that what the government of the day identifies as new programmes make only small claims on public resources. From 1970 to 1974 the Conservative government added 16 new spending headings to the more than 100 programme headings into which the Treasury divided the Budget. In aggregate, these new headings (some of which contained pre-existing programmes) accounted for an additional 4.4 percent of total public expenditure by 1974. The 1974-79 Labour government, working under greater expenditure constraints, added eight new programmes to the Budget at a total cost equal to 0.8 percent of public expenditure in its final year (Rose, 1980a: 124). Rhetorical statements are frequently made offering new intentions or justifications for ongoing programmes, but they have limited effect upon inertia commitments.

The repeal of an existing law might appear the surest way to change government's programme commitments. But repeal of legislation occurs relatively infrequently, for every Act of Parliament creates a group of interested clients once it goes into effect. Notwithstanding the alleged adversary nature of politics in Britain, the 1970-74 Conservative government repealed only three measures enacted by its predecessor Labour government from 1964 to 1970. In 1974 a Labour government returned to office having voted against 36 bills of its predecessor, but it repealed only 11 of these Acts, 6 percent of the total legislation that the Conservatives enacted. Some repeal Acts simultaneously re-enacted a large number of clauses in the Act repealed, thus maintaining a measure of continuity even in an apparently adversary act (Rose, 1980a: 87ff.).

Between the extreme limits of a completely novel programme and the complete termination of a programme, there are many forms of programme succession (Hogwood and Peters, 1982: 62). New programmes do not originate de novo; usually they involve grafting new bits on to old programme structures until the changes have become so substantial that a 'new' programme is said to result in succession to a no longer recognizable original.

The evolution of unemployment benefit programmes in European nations illustrates the extent to which programmes develop through a succession of additions (Table 7.2). The median European nation adopted its first unemployment benefit programme during the First World War. But the measure adopted did not provide full coverage; usually the initial programme concentrated upon one category of workers, and was voluntary rather than compulsory. The number of people covered, the contingencies covered and the value of benefits have been increased and altered in the half-century since by a series of laws (see Albers, 1981: 153 ff.). On average, a European nation has taken 53 years to enact the laws that today constitute its unemployment benefit programme. Unemployment benefit programmes as they stand today are not produced by a single act and cause: they result from a process in which a multiplicity of influences leads to the adaptation and augmentation of established laws. Any attempt to fix a single date for the enactment of a programme will have an element of arbitrariness about it.

Measuring changes in programme resources is far easier than identifying novel programmes, for such a change is a matter of degree, not kind, indicated by the claims that a programme makes upon public revenues and public employment. A government programme does not require new legislation to grow. Without any positive action by government, the amount of money spent on pensions can increase as people live longer, and as cost-of-living indexing automatically increases the value of pensions. The number employed in education can grow slowly without a conscious government decision, as an increase in the number of young people of school age leads to an increase in the number of pupils. Statutory entitlements to education, pensions and health care mean that their resource claims are more likely to reflect citizen demand than a conscious choice of the government of the day.

TABLE 7.2
The evolution of programmes for unemployment benefits

Country	No. years between oldest/ newest law	Insurance[a]	Dependent's benefits	Extension to farmers	Other laws (range)
		(year of legislation)			
Austria	31	1920	1920	1949	1918-1926
Italy	40	1919	1937	1949	1917-1957
Finland	43	1917	1917	1917	1934-1960
Netherlands	48	1916	1921	1949	1964-1964
Ireland	50	1923	1923	1953	1933-1973
Germany	51	1927	1927	1927	1918-1969
Norway	53	1906	1938	1949	1959
Sweden	58	1934	1934	1934	1916-1974
Switzerland	59	1924	1924	n.a.	1917-1976
Denmark	60	1907	1919	1907	1921-1967
France	62	1905	1967	n.a.	1914-1959
Belgium	64	1907	1944	1944	1933-1971
United Kingdom	64	1911	1921	1936	1920-1975

a. Older of dates for voluntary or compulsory insurance.
Source: Adapted from Albers (1981: Table 5.1).

Whether changes are measured in terms of programme expenditure or public employment, a very similar picture emerges: the claims that a given programme makes change substantially through time. Growth has been greatest in health programmes; in the past quarter-century public spending on health in OECD nations has increased its share of the national product by an average of 190 percent, and public employment in health has increased by 220 percent (Table 7.3). Income maintenance grants rank second in expenditure increase, and education ranks second in the growth of public employment (see Appendix Tables A7.1, A7.2).

Within a given programme area, the direction of change — whether up or down — is usually consistent across nations. Changes in public expenditure as a share of the national product have consistently been up in education, health, income maintenance payments, defence and debt interest, and up for economic programmes in all but one country, and consistently down in defence. Similarly, change in public employment has been up in all countries examined for education and health and down for military defence (Appendix Tables A7.1, A7.2). Across Western nations there are substantial similarities in patterns of change within a given programme, just as within a nation there are big differences between programmes in the direction and extent of change. The major programmes examined here display four different patterns (Table 7.3).

TABLE 7.3
Changes in the scale of major public programmes

	Public expenditure (change % share GNP 1954-80)	Public employment (change % labour force 1951-80)
	%	%
1. Big increase in money and employment		
Health	200	243
Education	82	162
2. Big increase in money		
Income maintenance	105	(n.a.)
Debt interest	94	(trivial)
3. Little change in money and employment		
Economic infrastructure	16	(n.a.)
Public enterprises	(n.a.)	18
4. Big fall in money and employment		
Defence	−49	−35

Sources: Calculated from national data reported in Appendix Tables A7.1, A7.2.

1. *Big increase in both money and employment*. Education and health, two of the major cornerstones of the welfare state, have both grown greatly in their claims upon public revenues and employment in the past quarter-century. On average, public spending on health has trebled as a proportion of the gross

national product and has increased very much more in its absolute resources; the proportion of the labour force in health services has also trebled. Education too has grown greatly, increasing its share of GNP by four-fifths, and of total public employment, already substantial in the early 1950s, by one and one-half times.

2. *Big increase in public expenditure.* Income maintenance programmes have more than doubled their claims upon the gross national product in the past quarter-century. In 1954 pensions, unemployment pay and other cash benefits were the most expensive programme area in the public budget, on average claiming 7.4 percent of the national product; today they claim 15.2 percent of the national product, more than one-third of total public expenditure. Interest on the public debt has nearly doubled its claim on the national product. In 1954 debt interest was equivalent to 1.8 percent of GNP, compared with 3.5 percent today. Because both programmes concentrate upon money transfers, their share of total employment is relatively low.

3. *Little change in resource claims.* Economic infrastructure and trading enterprises consistently claim a significant amount of public resources — about 4 percent of public expenditure and 6 percent of the labour force on average — but their aggregate share has scarcely altered much in a quarter of a century. Expenditure subsidizing the private sector has been re-allocated among beneficiaries, and major changes in employment patterns have occurred within totals that are not much altered in aggregate.

4. *Big decrease in money and employment.* Defence programmes have contracted everywhere in the Western world with the thawing of the Cold War. The proportion of the national product devoted to defence spending has halved on average, thus releasing public revenues for allocation to public programmes with a rising claim on resources. The proportion of the labour force in the military, whether as volunteers or conscripts, has fallen by one-third.

Three points are specially significant about the pattern of changes. The first is that programmes differ in the direction of change. In order to understand the dynamics of government programmes, we must understand why some programmes grow, some remain much the same, and others contract. Second, if a programme is both money- and labour-intensive, public employment and public expenditure tend to rise or fall together.

Third, a given programme is likely to have more in common with the same programme in other countries than with other programmes in the same country. To understand changes in government programmes, we should look first to common cross-national influences. Nation-specific explanations invoking political culture, parties or individual politicians can account for variations in detail, but national events are not adequate to explain trends common throughout the Western world.

Observing programme changes invites questions about the causes of changes. It follows from the foregoing analysis that any attempt to explain growth or change in public policies should first of all be programme-specific. To focus exclusively upon aggregate public employment or expenditure is to build upon a fallacy, the assumption that what is true of the whole is equally true of the parts. Given observed differences between programmes, we must start from the assumption that no one cause, whether economic, social or political, can equally explain the variety observed.

Welfare programmes — education, health and income maintenance grants — have grown most in the past generation throughout the Western world. For that reason, OECD has undertaken an elaborate statistical analysis of the causes of growth (OECD, 1978: 26ff.). Four major causes have been identified as affecting programmes to a greater or lesser degree (Table 7.4).

TABLE 7.4
Causes of change in welfare expenditure, OECD analysis, 1960s-1970s

| | Total increase as % GNP | Increase due to: | | | |
Programme		Demographic change	Broadened access	Improved quality, quantity	Higher cost
		%	%	%	%
Education	1.1	n.a.	55	n.a.	45
Income maintenance	2.0	40	60	n.a.	n.a.
Health	1.9	5	26	58	11
Total	5.0	16	44	24	16

Source: Adapted from OECD (1978: Table 7).

1. *Demographic pressures.* These are a form of consumer demand that no government can resist, for statutes confer a legal entitlement to education, health care and pensions upon all citizens of a given age or condition of need. An increase in the number of children in the age bracket for compulsory education immediately creates pressure to expand spending and employment in education; an increase in the number of elderly increases the number of pensions paid; and an increase in young and old creates a bigger demand for health care. The benefit received by an individual can remain constant, but a programme will expand if more people receive the benefit. If the government of the day wishes to prevent growth in response to demographic pressures, it must make it harder for an increasing number of individuals to claim benefits, for example, lengthening queues for hospital admissions by not building hospitals in the face of a rising demand.

2. *Broadening programme access.* Even if the population of a country remains constant, a programme will affect more people if the government broadens the conditions that entitle a person to have access to a programme. Unemployment benefits have broadened coverage gradually. Income maintenance programmes have expanded by making it easier for people to become eligible for transfer payments, by such means as lowering the age at which a widow can claim a pension, or the extent of disability that a doctor must certify to claim a disability payment. A comprehensive national health service has usually been achieved gradually, first by providing a public health service for the low paid, the elderly or manual workers, and then by broadening the coverage to include the whole of the population. In education, expansion has occurred because of a voluntary increase in the numbers seeking access to further and higher education.

3. *Improving the quality or quantity of individual programme benefits.* If the amount of pension paid each elderly person increases, this is an improvement independent of any change in the number of people claiming a pension. Improving quality makes additional claims upon money and personnel. On a priori grounds one might think that quality would be most likely to improve when the numbers entitled to a programme benefit contract, increasing benefits to individuals while reducing resource commitments in aggregate. In fact, this has not happened. In health care the quality of service has improved substantially while the coverage has been broadening.

4. *Increasing the cost of programmes.* An increase in money spent is not necessarily an improvement in quality. For example, if interest rates rise and a government must spend more to service its debt, it is not thereby getting better loans: it is only spending more to borrow a given sum. In welfare services there has been a tendency for costs to rise because the services are labour-intensive, and productivity does not rise as fast as productivity in the more capital-intensive private sector. As long as government increases wages in tandem with increases in the private sector and public employees are effective in lobbying for increased wages, then the total public sector wage bill will rise faster than the private sector. In such circumstances, a programme will expand its claims upon public revenues without its observable output increasing. The OECD estimates that upwards of half the increased expenditure on education from the early 1960s to the 1970s was accounted for by increased costs unrelated to programme improvements (OECD, 1978: 26).

No attention is explicitly given to political factors in the OECD analysis, yet a little reflection shows that most of the causes identified by the OECD reflect positive preferences of politicians. Only demographic changes can be said to increase the scale of a programme with a minimum of government intervention — that necessary to mobilize the extra resources for extra claimants. The most significant influence upon programme expansion, broadening entitlements, is explicitly political; normally, a change in the law by the government of the day is required to broaden entitlements. Decisions about improving the quality or quantity of welfare services require the appropriation of additional public funds, and politicians will want to take credit for this. Increased costs arise when politicians accept that public sector pay should rise with private sector pay. Political decisions are also specially important in determining whether military defence should expand *or* contract. Policy decisions by government are the immediate cause of many programme changes often explained in apolitical terms, for example the presumed propensity of public consumption to rise with an increase in the national product.

Conventional democratic theories emphasized popular choice as the principal determinant of government programmes. But social and economic conditions set boundaries upon the extent to which popular demands can be realized. In India, where free competitive elections have been held regularly since independence, there is no way in which popular votes can quickly transform one of the world's poorest countries into a society capable of financing the programmes of a contemporary welfare state.

Within the OECD world, all countries have a relatively high material standard of living, yet there remain differences between nations in the resources that Western governments devote to particular welfare state programmes (see Appendix Table A7.1 and A7.2 and Castles, 1982b: 68). The differences between countries in a particular programme are less than differences between programmes within a country, yet they can be significant. To what extent is this evidence that voter preferences, or at least the preferences of the party in office, make some difference to major welfare state programmes?

An elaborate statistical analysis of the causes of expenditure change in major public policies, directed by Francis G. Castles (1982a), has confirmed the general proposition advanced here, namely, that causes of change in resource commitments differ from programme to programme. The Castles group correlated OECD data about changes in expenditure on education, health and income maintenance and defence from the early 1960s to the 1970s, with a variety of political, economic and social indicators. The conditions most conducive to making one programme grow are not necessarily likely to influence change in another programme (Table 7.5). None of the hypothesized influences showed a statistically significant influence on changes in health expenditure, and two of the three influences significantly related to income maintenance programmes are not significant for education.

Of the eight different influences tested, only one — the competitive or coalescent nature of government — is significantly related to spending changes in two major programmes. In countries such as the Netherlands, where government is usually a grand coalition of leaders from different parties, there has been a tendency for spending on income maintenance programmes and education to rise more rapidly than in countries where government control involves competition between adversary parties, such as Britain (cf. Peters et al., 1977). One interpretation of this relationship is that increased spending on welfare programmes is the price that political leaders have to pay to maintain a coalition of disparate political groups cutting across conventional lines between bourgeois, Catholic and socialist parties. While this interpretation fits evidence of income maintenance programmes best, and also education programmes, it is of no statistical significance for health.

TABLE 7.5
A test of political determinants of changes in welfare expenditure, 1960s-1970s

Influence	Education	Change in spending on: Income maintenance (Correlation)	Health	Defence
Growth in GNP	−0.53*	−0.06	−0.11	−0.42
Initial level of spending	0.04	−0.04	0.10	n.a.
Imports + exports as % GNP	0.40	0.64**	0.13	n.a.
Union membership	0.14	0.07	−0.01	n.a.
Socialist seats in Parliament	−0.14	−0.03	−0.12	0.45
Right-wing seats in Parliament	−0.33	−0.73**	−0.39	−0.11
Federal/unitary[a]	−0.16	0.32	0.14	n.a.
Competitive/ coalescent elites[b]	0.41*	0.58**	0.14	n.a.

*Significant at 0.05 level.
**Significant at 0.01 level.
 a. Federal coded 0; unitary, 1.
 b. Competitive coded 0; coalescent 1.
Sources: Compiled from Castles (1982b: 63) and Keman (1982). Change in education, 1960-70; income maintenance, 1952-72; health, 1962-74.

The success of particular parties in winning seats in Parliament influences the growth of welfare state spending to a very limited extent. There is no support for the hypothesis that the presence of a substantial bloc of socialist MPs, whether in government or pressing the government as a strong opposition party, leads to an increase in welfare state spending. Contrary to conventional expectations, all the correlations involving socialist parties are negative, and the only positive correlation is between an increase in defence expenditure and socialist strength in Parliament (cf. Keman, 1982). When parties are divided into three blocs — socialist, centre (American Democrats, Canadian Liberals, Irish

Fianna Fail, etc.) and right (Italian Christian Democrats, French Gaullists, etc.) — then the weakness of right-wing parties is significantly related to higher spending on income maintenance programmes; it is also related to spending on other programmes. A conventional left-right confrontation in Parliament is likely to depress the growth of the welfare state, whereas government by a grand coalition of parties or a by a centre-left or centre-dominant coalition is likely to expand the welfare state more quickly.

The chief economic correlate with an increase in welfare spending is growth in the gross national product, but contrary to many conventional expectations, the relationship is negative. The greater the growth in the economy, the less rapid the growth in spending on education; it is less too for other programmes. This challenges the idea that countries will inevitably spend a disproportionate amount of their increase in national wealth on welfare state programmes. The importance of foreign trade, as measured by imports plus exports as a share of the national product, is significantly related to spending on income main-tenance programmes, and also correlates positively with spending on education. Cameron (1978) interprets this as evidence of the readiness of governments of small open economies to give concessions to socialist and trade union groups to gain agreement for measures deemed necessary to maintain economic competitive-ness. While Cameron's argument is ingenious, Castles (1982b: 77ff.) shows that in fact international trade patterns and party system characteristics have been so intercorrelated for generations that the relationship is coincidental rather than causal. Moreover, Cameron's generalization from total welfare expenditure is not supported by the analysis of specific programmes, for there is no significant relationship between openness to international trade and growth in spending on education or health.

In any test of hypothesized influences upon public programmes, it is always important to note what is not statistically significant. This is particularly true here, for only one of the influences examined explains as much as half the variance of any programme. The weak influence of union membership is consistent with the weakness of socialist parties in influencing public expenditure. The absence of a relationship between initial levels of spending in 1960 and spending levels in the mid-1970s rejects hypotheses of a convergence in welfare state programmes (that is, that laggards tend to catch up with leaders) or of divergence (that is, that leading welfare states tend to grow faster than lagging welfare states). The absence of a relationship between a federal or unitary constitutional structure and spending changes is evidence that federalism per se does not weaken the welfare state by dividing responsibility. American government is federal and underwrites less welfare expenditure, but the relationship is coincidental, not the reflection of a general causal pattern.

The major overall conclusion from this analysis is that there is no single cause of changes in the scale of government programmes, just as there is no tendency for all programmes to change in the same direction or at the same tempo. Programmes differ fundamentally in their dynamics — contrast defence and income maintenance — and they differ too in the causes of change. No one type of influence, whether the colour of the party in office, the pattern of a country's economic growth, its constitution or its demographic structure, is sufficient to explain all the important changes that occur among the major programmes of the welfare state (see also Schmidt, 1982; Mazmanian and Sabatier, 1980). To understand what it is that makes big government grow, we must understand what makes each major programme grow.

The growth of government is collectively the result of the activities of many sub-governments, that is, issue networks that constitute the inertia force behind particular public programmes (Rose, 1980a; Heclo, 1978). The immediate determinants of education programmes are the cluster of influences specific to education, including the political direction of the ministry, the outlooks of public officials overseeing education, the interests of teachers, education pressure groups, and social, economic and demographic trends specific to young people. The link between sub-government and generic political system influences is contingent, not certain. Moreover, constraints upon the total number of programmes expanded by government at any one time imply some negative relationships between programmes. If some grow faster than average, then others must grow slower or contract. Understanding the causes of differences between programmes is necessary in order to understand change in aggregate.

Declining effectiveness and continuing consent?
To understand the consequences of public programmes for government's effectiveness and popular consent, we must

distinguish changes in established programmes and in new programmes. Whereas the expansion of established programmes involves familiar activities with known consequences, by definition new programmes are untested.

In the absence of constraints upon the aspirations of politicians, new programmes can be adopted without any prior consideration of an effective means-ends technology. The American War on Poverty under President Johnson is rich in examples of the introduction of new programmes inspired, as one Brookings proponent admitted (Aaron, 1978: ix), by faith and beliefs, not research. At the extreme, a policy may be adopted that is no more than an unforceable statement of what social policy experts think would be desirable. In 1979, the Swedish government went so far as to adopt a law that declared that parents should not spank their children. The Justice Department recommended that instead parents should rely upon 'a continual interchange with loving care'. It admitted, however, 'There is no way we could go into every home and check up' whether the law was effective (Justitiedepartementet, 1980).

Novelty receives much political attention, because novelty is newsworthy and often controversial. But evaluating the consequences of novel programmes is difficult. This is true whether they are intensive, increasing activity within a given area, or extensive, introducing government to an area where it had not previously been active. By contrast, evidence is at hand about established programmes.

Established programmes are usually based upon established means-ends technologies. This is particularly true of the defining programmes of the state, concerned with diplomacy, defence, law and order, and tax collection. These programmes were concerns of the ancient Greeks, and the Roman Empire developed a system of government effective at a great distance from Rome. If the modern state cannot be effective in these programmes, it will cease to exist. Moreover, technological developments make it easier today to run effective armies, courts of law or tax collection systems than centuries ago (see Tilly, 1975).

The creation and expansion of major welfare state programmes has been based upon the utilization of easily diffused and predictable technologies. This has been most evident in the state's mobilization of economic resources, which in France and Prussia antedated industrialization. Engineers can and do build roads, and railways, and run the posts, telegraph, telephone and latterly, satellites. In the field of welfare, the first advances were public health measures to prevent the decimation of urban populations by disease: water purification, public sewers and mass inoculation against epidemics all employ proven technologies. Compulsory primary education, another nineteenth-century programme innovation, used tested pedagogical techniques for teaching the rudiments of reading, writing and arithmetic. A national health service followed after the development of medicine as a science that predictably (even if only probabilistically) improves a patient's health. Income maintenance schemes were launched with the simple assumption that, if money is given to the poor it will be spent. To criticize these programmes for not attaining some ideal standard of efficiency is to overlook the primary point: the major programmes of the contemporary welfare state use relatively effective social technologies.

Government's postwar commitment to manage the mixed economy has introduced qualitatively different considerations about the effectiveness of government. Economics, which provides the theoretical base for programmes to influence the economy, is not a mechanical science with the certainty of some fields of engineering (Rose, 1982b). Instead, it is a probabilistic science, whose prescriptions invariably contain a ceteris paribus clause, warning any who rely upon it that the predictions hold good only if all other conditions remain equal, which often fails to happen. To the uncertainties of the subject matter must be added controversies between economists about policy prescriptions that are desirable (a question of political values), practical (a political and administrative judgement), and logically consistent (the judgement of an economist). If economics is a science, it more nearly resembles psychiatry than it does physics.

For two decades after the Second World War, the coincidence of unexpectedly high rates of economic growth and low rates of unemployment and inflation led many politicians and many economists to assume that there was an effective means-ends technology at hand for the management of the mixed economy. Keynesian theories and policy prescriptions were believed to give policy-makers the ability to make the economy achieve a multiplicity of desired programme objectives, and to fine-tune the economy by eliminating difficulties before they became great or chronic. But since the early 1970s, policy-makers and economists, each in their own way, have come to the conclusion that there is no longer an agreed and effective means of managing the economy (cf. Lindbeck, 1976; Lindberg, 1982).

Controversies between economists are now endemic. Politicians confronted with stagflation (which was assumed to be technically impossible in the 1960s) have reduced their claims to influence the economy, because they do not wish to be held responsible for the undesired state of many Western economies today. Policy-makers involved in economic management now emphasize that they are not decision-makers but decision-takers, reacting to events determined by forces outside their control in the world economy. In the words of the civil service head of the British Treasury, Sir Douglas Wass,

> In the past ten years or so both the Keynesian and the monetarist explanations, which are anyway not mutually exclusive, have been found to be inadequate. I think all economists are to some extent at sea in describing how the economy works! [Quoted in Young, 1982]

The effectiveness of untested new programmes is especially uncertain when growth is *extensive*, that is, when a new programme is launched in an area previously not the subject of government action. When growth is *intensive*, that is, when a new programme is launched within an area already covered by many measures, then there is a fund of relevant administrative experience providing a basis for forecasting how effective a programme may be.

The extension of government programmes to new areas can follow from the belief that it is more desirable to treat causes rather than symptoms of social problems. From this perspective it is no longer enough to apprehend and gaol criminals; government should also adopt programmes that cure people of their proclivities to crime. To ameliorate the condition of poor or handicapped people is inadequate; the causes of poverty should be eradicated, and the effects of handicaps should be negated.

Treating the causes of social problems is well intentioned in theory, but rests upon three highly contingent assumptions: first, that we know the causes of all social problems; second, that the causes are in principle amenable to influence by government; and third, that government has the knowledge, resources and political will to treat these causes. On a priori grounds it is at least as logical to assume that social conditions that have persisted for centuries will not be abolished by a single programme or Act of Parliament.

Typically, new programmes show a big gap between the issue that stimulated them, the intentions of their proponents and the actual content and resources mobilized by the specific measure adopted. A government pressed to do something about unemployment may announce its intention to secure full employment — a few years hence. The actual programme that it brings forward may preserve tens or even hundreds of thousands of jobs. Yet doing this will not necessarily reduce unemployment; it may only prevent unemployment from rising, or from rising more rapidly. A government may announce policy intentions that promise what the electorate would like to hear, but it must adopt programmes consistent with what can be done with the resources and technology that it has at hand.

Arguably, the adoption of new programmes without any assurance of effectiveness can be a step towards creating an organization within government that can learn how to develop an effective programme. From a review of the development of income maintenance programmes in the first half of this century, Heclo (1974: Chapter 6) concluded that the growth of social programmes is a process of gradual social learning. The public officials involved in programmes may develop a capacity to learn from their mistakes, promoting a succession of intensive and extensive measures that cumulatively increase programme effectiveness and expand programmes. But this is not the only gloss that can be put upon the immediate failure of new programmes. Wildavsky (1979) views government efforts to correct the faults of new programmes as a process of increasing ignorance, because the multiple consequences of programmes are likely to expand more rapidly than government can learn to deal with them.

When new programmes are intensive, by definition they are likely to have an impact upon already established programmes. Prior to the introduction of a new programme, efforts may be made to anticipate some likely consequences of change. But the linkages between programmes — and even more the interaction with programme recipients — cannot be fully known. Only if one believes in a hidden-hand mechanism, which assures that all government actions are harmonious, without internal conflicts or contradictions, can it be assumed that the accumulation of more and more programmes within a given policy area will be free of contradictions. As the space within a given policy area becomes more intensively occupied with programmes, the likelihood of unintended or unanticipated consequences grows disproportionately, and with it the potential for contradictions between programmes. In Heclo's (1975) words, 'As policy effects accumulate and interact, the explosion of costs becomes less important than the implosion of spillovers.'

Contradictions between programmes are as likely as contradictions within a programme area. Economic and social policy objectives often contradict. For example, spending on pensions immediately promotes consumption, whereas policies for economic growth are based upon deferring consumption to increase investment. Policies to protect jobs in regions of economic decline may be desirable socially, but they impose market costs, thus reducing the prospect of economic growth. Bureaucratic regulations designed to promote the reduction of environmental pollution may conflict with politicians' promises to do everything possible to encourage economic growth.

Conflicts between social preferences are not new; the conflict between borrowers and lenders is ancient in origin. What the growth of government has done is to internalize many conflicts *within* government. What is new today is that government wishes to protect the value of its currency by pursuing anti-inflationary policies, while simultaneously pursuing other programmes that result in inflation. Conflicts become institutionalized when different public sector organizations have conflicting goals. For example, there is a real conflict of interest about whether green-field sites in the countryside should be preserved for their environmental amenities, or used for industrial development. In Britain a number of land use disputes have arisen, with nationalized industries pressing to develop green-field sites in the public interest and local authorities invoking the public interest in opposing these claims. A third organization, a government ministry, determines which of these two public bodies better perceives the public interest (cf. Gregory, 1971).

In theory, contradictions between interdependent programmes could be resolved by trade-offs, that is, by accepting a marginal decrease in the effectiveness of one programme as the cost to be paid for increased effectiveness in another programme. The Keynesian model of economic management is pre-eminently a model for trading off between competing economic goals. Economic growth, price stability and full employment are all accepted as desirable goals, but the Keynesian model does not prescribe that all should be pursued simultaneously with the same intensity. The past decade has undermined the comfortable assumption that there is sufficient knowledge about programmes to enable government to decide the degree of effectiveness it would sacrifice in one programme in order to achieve greater effectiveness in another. In the absence of firm evidence of the relationship between competing programme goals, policy-makers cannot effectively make trade-offs.

Given the tendency for new programmes to be less effective than established programmes, the empirical question is: Has the growth of government been concentrated among established programmes, which are prima facie effective, or among new programmes, which are likely to be less effective?

The evidence is clear: the growth of government has been greatest among established and effective programmes. Income maintenance programmes, already the largest programme in OECD nations in the 1950s, have grown the most since. Income maintenance programmes now account for more than one-third of total public expenditure in the average Western nation. The object of these payments is to give a cash income to the elderly, the unemployed and others deemed in need. Input is easily converted into output; massive sums of public revenue become massive cash benefits. The recipients of income maintenance grants are free to spend their benefits as they wish, a procedure meant to assure optimum efficiency in market economics. The administrative costs of income maintenance programmes are very low relative to the total amount of money paid out.

Effectiveness is also reasonably high in the other two very large programme areas, which have grown greatly since the 1950s in their claims upon both public revenue and public employment. In education, every Western nation has seen the number and proportion of qualified school leavers increase in the past quarter-century, and the total number receiving a basic education has expanded greatly with demographic changes. In health, programme outputs are more difficult to evaluate for effectiveness, for health care is usually concentrated upon those lacking health. Infant mortality and life expectancy have improved in the past quarter-century.

The relative decrease in defence expenditure, which accounts for less than one-twelfth of total public expenditure today as against one-fifth a quarter-century ago, can also be considered evidence of increased effectiveness, since it has not been accompanied by an increase in wars. Most governments claim that the decline has made no difference for the intangible but important goal of maintaining national security. In analytic terms, one could say that an intangible — security — is now being purchased with the materially much cheaper intangibles of diplomacy. The revenue formerly spent on the uncertainties of military defence now finances more certainly effective welfare programmes.

In terms of resource claims, income maintenance, health, education and defence account for more than two-thirds of public expenditure, and about one-half of public employment. When one adds in employment in public enterprises, which are invariably effective in producing goods and services, then the major programmes account for about three-quarters of total public employment. Moreover, these programmes together account for the bulk of the increase in resource commitments of government from the 1950s to the 1980s. In 1954 they accounted for 64 percent of total public expenditure; by 1980 they accounted for 77 percent of total public expenditure and showed a similar proportionate increase in public employment.

In the span of a quarter-century it is easy to find examples of new programmes that have been completely ineffectual. But examples do not equal trends. The important point is that the growth of government programmes has principally meant an *increase in the scale of established and relatively effective programmes*. New programmes, and especially unsuccessful new programmes, invite controversy and publicity. But social scientists should be wary of generalization from atypical cases. The greatest growth has occurred in the most inconspicuous way because it has involved established programmes of proven effectiveness.

Technological effectiveness is not the only cause of programme success or failure. Popular consent is important too. Recurring efforts to introduce prices and incomes policies to combat inflation have shown that consent is a precondition for success. The nominal objectives of wage and price policies may be broadly agreed, but the means necessary to control them involves government's affecting the right of trade unions to bargain for wages, and of businesses to pursue profits. Voluntary controls are likely to erode rapidly, but statutory controls are also subject to erosion, because government cannot insulate a national market from the impact of changes in international markets. Nor can a government force businessmen to pursue policies that threaten bankruptcy, or force trade unions to ignore the wishes of workers who can turn to wildcat strikes in pursuit of demands for higher wages. The more effective controls are in keeping wage increases below the rate of inflation or squeezing business profits, the more likely those affected will be to withdraw cooperation and consent (cf. Goodwin, 1975; Schwerin, 1980).

If government programmes become more and more extensive, there is a risk of reducing popular consent by overstepping the line between public and private. The contemporary welfare state is a mixed society as well as a mixed economy; there is a more or less recognized limit to what government should or should not do. Political values rather than technological constraints are the ultimate determinants of what constitutes 'too much' government. In a field such as population policy, these limits depend upon qualitative values about the line between what is private and what is public. In the field of public morality, where consent is particularly important, private choice has replaced state religion as the arbiter. In a permissive era nearly every Western government has therefore reduced the scope of programmes that regulate morality, such as the prohibition of homosexuality and censorship of pornography. By doing less, government may increase effectiveness and consent for what it does do.

While questions of popular consent can affect the consideration of new programmes, they are not usually significant in relation to established programmes. Established programmes have the great asset of familiarity. Their durability is a prima facie indication of popular endorsement. A decade of complaints about alleged shortcomings of big government has yet to see popular support emerge for abolishing the programmes that have made government big: namely, pensions, education and health. While popular welfare state programmes are not necessary for consent, since many governments enjoyed consent before the welfare state was developed, the inability of conservative parties to repeal or greatly reduce the scale of these programmes is evidence of popular endorsement of programmes causing big government.

Everybody benefits at important times in their lives from welfare state programmes. In a typical European country the health service provides care for an expectant mother at birth and there is a children's allowance thereafter; the schools provide an education for a decade or more; the social services provide health care, insure a worker against a loss of income through unemployment, sickness, or disability, and may subsidize housing; there are income supplements for the working poor; and the elderly receive a pension and health care after retirement.

TABLE 7.6
The scale of individual benefits from the contemporary welfare state

	Education	Health & sickness benefit	Pensions	Other income maintenance	Children's allowances	Other programmes	Total	
			(percentage of population benefiting)					
Sweden	21	98	13	15	17	28	16mn	193
Britain	21	46	16	8	9	32	75mn	132
Italy	23	32	18	26	20	9	73mn	128
France	25	35	19	6	21	13	63mn	119
Germany	21	51	18	8	11	3	70mn	112
USA	28	9	11	17	0	14	166mn	79
Average	23	45	16	13	13	16	n.a.	126

Source: Rose and Peters (1978a: Table A 3.2).

Contemporary European governments provide an average of more than one major benefit each year for every person in society, and in Sweden almost two major benefits (Table 7.6). In the United States the proportion of benefits is less, because of the absence of a health service and children's allowances on the European model. None the less, the American government is a leader in providing public education and food stamps. The average European family annually receives an average of two or three benefits from government — for example, education and children's allowances, a housing allowance and sickness benefit, or a pension and hospital treatment. The benefits are dispersed among families, between generations and throughout the life-cycle. The big programmes of big government today are a basic social support system for most families.

The programmes that have tended to grow most are programmes that benefit almost everyone. At any given moment virtually the entire population of a European country is covered by the health service; about one-fifth are in school; a quarter are drawing pensions or other income maintenance benefits; and one-fifth draw children's allowances. There are other national programmes, such as housing in Britain, that provide benefits for up to a third of the population. Because many programmes have been promoted as social insurance, even though recipients' contributions do not usually meet costs, the benefits are often perceived as deserved as well as desirable.

Ironically, the greater the scale of a programme's benefits, the greater the potential for citizen complaints. In so far as the proportion of citizens dissatisfied with a programme is constant, then, however low that percentage is, the more parents with children in school or the more people in hospital, the greater the number of people likely to complain about public programmes. Grievances as well as satisfaction can increase with the growth of government. The point is most relevant in the United States, for the population explosion in the postwar era has added an additional 70 million Americans, equivalent to the population of a large European country plus Scandinavia. Moreover, the relatively late American adoption of welfare programmes means that it has a higher proportion of newer and untested programmes by comparison with a European state. These factors, as well as ideological differences between America and Europe, may explain why complaints about big government are most often written in the United States, where government is relatively but not absolutely small.

The political rationale of the expansion in major welfare state programmes in postwar decades is simply stated. It is to provide something for everybody. In so far as government does this, then the expansion of public programmes is likely to be popular, at least, as long as each programme is evaluated in terms of its benefits rather than its costs.

TABLE A7.1
Changes in expenditure on major programmes, 1954-1980

Country	Education		Health		Income Maintenance (percentage of GNP)		Defence		Economic infrastructure		Debt interest	
	1954	1980	1954	1980	1954	1980	1954	1980	1954	1980	1954	1980
Denmark	3.6	7.6	2.4	5.6	7.0	19.7	—	2.3	—	—	1.3	—
France	3.6	5.7	2.3	6.0	11.2	17.9	6.0	3.4	3.1	4.0	1.3	1.5
Germany	3.6	5.1	2.5	6.5	11.5	19.0	3.8	2.9	1.9	5.3	0.8	1.9
Italy	2.8	5.5	1.4	5.9	10.1	15.4	—	1.9	—	4.8	2.2	6.2
Japan	1.9	5.0	1.0	4.7	2.9	7.3	2.1	0.9	11.1	5.8	0.6	3.2
Netherlands	4.2	8.3	1.1	7.1	6.4	21.1	6.0	3.2	3.4	4.5	2.8	4.7
United Kingdom	3.9	5.4	2.9	4.7	6.4	11.7	8.5	4.7	1.1	3.0	3.9	4.6
United States	3.0	5.6	0.8	2.5	4.1	9.8	11.3	4.6	1.8	3.0	1.5	2.7
Average	3.3	6.0	1.8	5.4	7.4	15.2	6.3	3.2	3.7	4.3	1.8	3.5

Source: Calculated from OECD, 'Big Government: How Big is it?', *OECD Observer*, March 1983, No. 121, 8-9; for some entries, 1978 or 1979 data are used.

TABLE A7.2
Changes in public employment in major programmes, 1951-1980

Country	Education 1951	Education 1980	Health 1951	Health 1980	Public enterprises 1951	Public enterprises 1980	Defence 1951	Defence 1980
			(percentage of total employed)					
Britain	2.6	6.7	2.1	5.4	11.9	8.7	5.2	2.3
Germany	1.4	3.5	1.8	4.4	6.4	7.6	n.a.	2.7
Italy	1.4	5.2	0.9	3.5	3.5	7.3	2.6	2.0
Sweden	2.3	4.1	1.6	9.2	5.5	7.8	3.1	2.2
USA	2.9	7.0	0.8	1.7	1.2	1.9	7.8	3.0
Average	2.1	5.5	1.4	4.8	5.7	6.7	3.7	2.4

Source: Calculated by the author from Rose (forthcoming).

8 THE LIMITS OF BIG GOVERNMENT

Big government is distinctive because it has bigger problems. The difficulties as well as the rewards are much greater than in small-scale government. The claims of big government upon the resources of society give its programmes far greater impact than ever before. However, the opportunity cost is also great, for government pre-empts more and more of society's resources and fewer resources are available for new programmes.

Big government is here to stay. No popularly elected government is going to repeal the social, economic and defence programmes that make government big. Ironically, critics of the growth of government can see many reasons why it may continue to expand. Actions of the Thatcher and Reagan governments that have unintentionally made government bigger emphasize inertia pressures for continuing growth. Concurrently, proponents of big government programmes fear that economic constraints may make it difficult for government to grow in future as in the past; both conservative and socialist governments face pressures to put the brakes on the growth of government.

Whatever political perspective is adopted, within the immediately foreseeable future the size of government can change only marginally. This is true whether the margin for change involves growth or cutting back. The inertia forces that have created big government are not easily stopped or reversed. Keeping government big is not a problem of contemporary politicians; it is a condition that goes with the job.

In Chapter 2 four potential problems were hypothesized as resulting from bigness. The evidence in subsequent chapters has shown that in fact three of these hypothetical problems have *not* arisen. The growth of government has not caused a great reduction in organizational effectiveness, or contradictions between programmes; nor has it meant the proliferation of ineffective programmes based upon soft technologies. The programmes that have grown most are welfare state programmes which tend to retain their effectiveness with growth. However, big government does create one big problem: the problem of paying for its costs.

A second issue raised in Chapter 2 was the potential consequence of big government for political consent. A connection between government's effectiveness and popular consent is sometimes assumed, but not proven. The world depression of the 1930s did *not* lead to the abandonment of democracy by the great majority of Western nations, and the world recession of the 1970s was smaller in scale, and has had proportionately less of an impact upon regimes, although it has shaken the self-confidence (or over-confidence) of political leaders. The evidence herein has shown that government does not grow by introducing a large number of 'improper' programmes; growth has usually involved the multiplication of small units on a familiar scale, e.g., the primary school, the doctor's office or hospital, and the office for claiming an old age pension. There remain, however, questions about the impact of government's growing claims for national resources upon the extent to which citizens today give consent or are prepared to challenge the authority of government.

To speak of solving the problems facing government today is to misunderstand the nature of politics. Conflicts are endemic to politics. To ignore the inevitability of conflict is to lapse into the rhetoric of a consensus-mongering politician or a politically naive scientist. Governments can do no more and no less than cope with the problems facing them. To cope with problems does not promise the end of politics, but it does mean that the response is at least equal to the immediate challenge.

The central question today is not whether government can cope with the problems facing it, but *how* government can cope with problems on the scale of the 1980s. The coping strategies of policy-makers depend upon two conditions: the degree to which they understand the problems, and the impact that government can have upon these problems (Rose, 1974: 21). In a totally controlled world (which would lack the freedom and surprises of contemporary Western politics), policy-makers would have a high understanding of problems and their actions would have a major and consistently positive impact. This is not the situation of Western policy-makers in the 1980s. But the opposite is also untrue: few actions of government lack all understanding, and even actions deficient in understanding have an impact upon society.

Policy-makers have two alternatives for coping with the problems of big government. In so far as they understand the nature of a problem but cannot immediately affect underlying conditions, e.g. an oil price rise determined by OPEC nations, they can adapt in response to events they cannot control. In so far as actions have an impact that is not fully understood, then policy-makers can act in the hope of learning to understand the problem better by the feedback of information thus generated. Adaptation and learning are not so much alternatives as sequential ways of coping. Policy-makers can act with low understanding, in hopes of learning why their measures have a high impact, and adapt their programmes in a process of trial and error.

Any judgement about how to cope with the problems of big government must reflect political values as well as technical understanding. While policies can be supported by technical arguments, they are not created in a politically neutral vacuum. The problems that government faces today are man-made; they arise from political pressures, and there are political conflicts about how governments should respond. The state of economics, the most seemingly scientific of the social sciences, reflects the dangers of ignoring political values or assuming, without evidence, that there is a value consensus. In the words of a senior British economist, Alan Peacock (1982: 2), 'In the debate about the size of the public sector every contestant claims victory. The ideological split between economists is pronounced.'

The value that informs this chapter is simply stated; it is that political consent is more important than political effectiveness. An effective government can exist without consent: history records a plenitude of coercive regimes that have endured for generations or centuries. Today, Eastern Europe offers ample evidence of government without consent. But a regime that lacked the consent of the majority of its citizens would be very different from the governments of the Western world as we know them. To place political consent first is not to deny the importance of contemporary economic problems. In an ideal world, a government ruling by consent would be fully effective too.

The object of this chapter is first of all to examine the distinctive problem of big government today, the difficulty of balancing its claims for big resources against the limits of national resources. Second, the chapter examines the choice of policies for maintaining effectiveness. In the third section, the priority that government gives to consent is examined, and the final section examines the priorities of individual citizens.

The big problem: balancing fiscal loads

The biggest problems facing big government today are meta-problems, arising from the interaction between competing programme claims for resources. By definition, an overloaded government cannot be understood in terms of a single attribute; fiscal overloading reflects an imbalance in the ratio between government's resources and its inertia programme commitments. When government operated on a much smaller scale, the resources of expanding industrial societies far exceeded the claims of the Nightwatchman state. If anything, there was an under-provision of public programmes. Today, the risk is the opposite. Big government's claims upon society's resources may be growing faster than these resources, thus threatening fiscal overload (Rose, 1975).

Taken individually, every programme commitment of government may have much in its favour: it can be effective and popular with those who produce it and with its recipients. Yet collectively government can still face great problems, for the whole of government is different from the sum of its part. In the mixed economy welfare state, a sophist might argue that a £5 or $10 a month increase in pensions is not difficult for government to pay, because it is such a small sum for each person to receive each month. But when this sum must be paid 12 times a year to tens of millions of people, the annual total is a large sum, more than £500 million in a country the size of Britain, and more than $3 billion in the United States.

The major meta-problem facing Western governments in the 1980s is clear: how to reconcile the inertia commitments of the welfare state with the finite resources of the society it governs. Of course, the resources of government have always been finite; by definition, economics is about the allocation of limited resources. But the limits are not fixed. In a period of economic boom, like the 1950s and 1960s, the resources of society appeared to be expanding without limit. In the 1980s the picture is very different: claims upon resources appear to be expanding without limit, whereas resources are failing to grow as before, or even threatening to contract.

If democratic government is about giving people what they want, then economics is the dismal science of telling people what they can have with the resources at hand. In managing the mixed economy welfare state, politicians must learn to balance the competing claims of the happy science of politics and the dismal science of economics. While the parameters of the political economy do not prescribe how a nation's resources must be spent, they restrict how much can be spent. Money is not the measure of all things, but a government that raises and spends hundreds of billions of its national currency each year cannot be indifferent to an imbalance between its commitments and its resources.

At any given moment the size of the national product sets a limit upon the total material resources of a society. The national product of a country, augmented by foreign borrowing, sets a limit upon the material resources of a society. In the simplest model of the mixed economy, the national product can be divided into two portions: one portion claimed by government through taxation in order to meet the costs of public policy, and the other remaining in the hands of individuals as take-home pay, that is, post-tax pretransfer income (Rose and Peters, 1978a).

A nation's political economy is dynamic, not static. At a given point in time the sum of resources devoted to the public sector and private sector is fixed. But the national product can grow, and a bigger national product makes it possible for both take-home pay and public programmes to increase in size. Reciprocally, a contracting national product (an occasional but hardly normal phenomenon in OECD nations) compels a reduction in spending on public programmes, on take-home pay or both. A third possibility is that the growth rate of either the public or the private sector is so great that it forces a reduction in the other sector, claiming all of the fiscal dividend of growth and then some.

The course of major Western economies from the 1950s to the 1980s has been a gradual progress from treble affluence — a growing national product, a growing public sector and a growing private sector — to overloaded government. The inertia commitments of government have moved forward slowly but steadily. In consequence, the increasing claims of financing the public sector threaten an absolute and not just a relative reduction in the private sector.

Overloading is the cumulative result of different parts of the political economy growing at different rates. In the three decades from 1951 to 1980, the costs of public programmes have grown on average by 6.9 percent a year in major Western nations, as against an average rate of growth in the national product of 4.0 percent. Growth rates have differed in America, Britain, France, Germany, Italy and Sweden, but the pattern is everywhere the same: the costs of public programmes have been growing substantially

faster than the economy as a whole (Table 8.1). Thus, take-home
pay has grown more slowly, averaging a 3.1 percent increase a
year. For more than a quarter of a century every major Western
nation has enjoyed treble affluence: a growing national product
has financed a real growth in public programmes and in take-home
pay too.

TABLE 8.1
Inertia growth in the political economy, 1951-1980

	National product	Costs of public policy	Take-home pay
	(average annual rates of growth in constant prices)		
	%	%	%
Germany	6.0	7.8	4.3
Italy	4.5	9.3	3.7
France	4.5	8.3	4.1
Sweden	3.7	6.8	2.3
America	3.1	5.1	2.5
Britain	2.6	4.3	1.7
Average	4.0	6.9	3.1

Source: Rose and Peters (1978b), as revised by B. Guy Peters.

Past prosperity creates present trouble. The costs of public
policy have been growing relatively steadily in constant money
terms. In the 1950s this did not place a heavy burden upon the
political economy of a government claiming on average 29 percent
of the national product. A 6.9 percent increase in the cost of public
programmes required only a two percent increase in a country's
national product. In the 1950s Western economies were buoyant,
growing on average at a rate of 3.9 percent. In such circumstances,
half the fiscal dividend of growth could go to the public sector, and
half to the private sector. Public and private affluence advanced
together, producing 'policy without pain' (Heclo 1981: 397).

But the cumulative effect of the public sector growing faster
than the private sector has been to alter fundamentally the
distribution of the fiscal dividend of growth. By 1980 the cost of
public programmes on average accounted for 46.5 percent of the
national product in major Western nations. The annual growth in
the costs of public policy changed little in the 1970s, averaging a
7.1 percent annual increase. But much greater economic growth is

now required to fund the growing costs of public programmes painlessly, because the public expenditure base is much larger. In 1980 a 7.1 percent increase in the costs of public policy required a growth in the economy of 3.3 percent in order to be funded completely by the fiscal dividend of growth. Such growth does not now occur. On average, major Western nations grew at a rate of 2.5 percent in the 1970s, less than the amount needed to fund the rising cost of public programmes.

The result of different parts of the political economy growing at different inertia rates is a scissors squeeze. In 1951 the cost of public programmes was relatively small, and one year's growth of public spending claimed a limited portion of the growth in the national product. By 1980, however, the cumulative difference in growth rates had reversed the relationship: public programmes are now growing more rapidly than the economy as a whole.

Fiscal overload is a major concern today because government is tending to finance the rising costs of public programmes by cutting take-home pay. In every major Western nation take-home pay has fallen at least once since 1973, and there has been a secular trend down in Britain and in Sweden. The extent of the pressure on take-home pay varies between nations, but one thing is clear: *everywhere the growth of government threatens a real and continuing reduction in take-home pay in the 1980s* (Rose and Peters, 1978a: Chapter 7).

Notwithstanding fiscal overloading, the national economy of every Western nation is wealthier today than it was a decade ago; public programmes and take-home pay are both materially far higher than two or three decades ago. Most of the growth of government has concerned what are usually thought of as 'good' goods, such as increased public spending for pensioners, education and health services.

The incapacity of the national economy to bear the claims of big government painlessly has arisen gradually; it is not the consequence of a single shock event, such as an oil price increase. Instead, the fiscal overloading of the political economy is the consequence of a quarter-century of unrivalled national economic prosperity and of the unrivalled expansion in the spending commitments of government. Just as it would take a decade or more to undo the positive consequences of economic growth, so too it may take a decade or more to deal with the fiscal consequences of overloaded government.

Effectiveness: a choice between priorities

While every Western nation today is concerned about fiscal overloading (Tarschys, 1982: Table 3), the size of the problem is surprisingly small. In percentage terms the difference between a balanced and an overloaded political economy is equivalent on average to 0.8 percent of the national product. If a nation's economy could grow by 0.8 percent more each year, an increase of one-third, take-home pay would be secure. Alternatively, if public spending could grow by one-quarter less than its present rate of growth, public programmes could continue to grow without causing fiscal overload. This would not remove all of the anxieties about the mixed economy welfare state, but it would at least resolve the present scissors squeeze, in which public benefits grow by cutting take-home pay.

The good news for politicians confronted with the prospect of fiscal overload is that they have a choice of how to respond. But to identify a choice between policies does not mean that all are agreeable, or that there is any consensus. The alternatives differ in the fundamental assumptions they make about what can or should be done about the national political economy.

Increase growth in GNP

The first and most appealing alternative is to increase growth in the national product to at least 3.3 percent a year in order to finance the average increase in the cost of public programmes. By the standards of the 1950s and 1960s, this rate of growth is reasonable, for most Western economies actually grew faster then. But the growth rates of Western economies from 1951 to 1970 were unprecedented by comparison with the previous century and a half. In the 1970s growth rates slowed down, yet even the 2.5 percent growth rate of the 1970s was high by historic standards, surpassing that achieved in the industrial revolution from 1820 to 1870, and from 1913 to 1950 (Maddison, 1981: Table III.2). There is no reason to assume that national economies will cease to grow, but there are theoretical reasons as well as historical precedent to believe that Western economies are unlikely to grow at an accelerating rate in the 1980s (see e.g. Olson, 1982).

Because the future cannot be known for certain, it is possible to produce plans on paper that forecast the economy accelerating if 'correct' policies are followed, whether correctness is defined in monetarist or Keynesian terms, or by some combination of prescriptions deemed uniquely suited to the circumstances of a particular nation. Forecasts are necessary in order to anticipate expenditure commitments and revenue flows. A forecast is neither true nor false at the date it is made; it simply rests upon logical inferences from more or less credible assumptions.

The political process can convert economics from a dismal science into a happy art. Politicians confronted with awkward evidence about a downturn in the economy can produce a happy forecast simply by altering their forecasting assumptions. If there were no political bias in economic forecasts, then growth would as often be overestimated as underestimated. In fact, this does not happen; there is a persisting tendency for government economic forecasts to overestimate the size of economic growth in order to underestimate fiscal overloading (Rose and Peters, 1978a: 149-152).

International forecasts of economic growth tend to be over-optimistic too. A particularly relevant example is *Towards Full Employment and Price Stability*, a major OECD report produced by an internationally prestigious team of economists in 1977. The report granted that there had been economic difficulties, but argued that they reflected an unusual bunching of unfortunate disturbances unlikely to be repeated on the same scale, compounded by some avoidable errors in economic policy. It concluded, 'Reasonably rapid growth remains an appropriate objective' (OECD, 1977: 14f.). It suggested an annual average growth rate of 4.7 percent among major Western nations from 1975 to 1980. Even though the report was not published until halfway through the period that its forecast covered, it none the less overshot the target. The actual annual average growth rate was one-third less, 2.9 percent (cf. OECD, 1977: Table A.26; OECD, 1982a: Table 3.1). Furthermore, OECD has usually been forecasting lower growth in the 1980s than in the difficult enough 1970s, well below that needed to finance rising costs of public programmes.

Ignore fiscal overload

Ignoring fiscal overload is a second alternative, since the problem facing a government in any one year is only marginal. Elected officeholders have an immediate incentive to ignore the problem, for the measures required to redress a fiscal imbalance are likely to be unpopular, and unpopular measures are not willingly undertaken by elected officials. Particularly in advance of a general election, politicians will be anxious to temporize, buying at least a little time by adopting placebo policies, measures intended to reduce symptoms of anxiety without having any effect on the body politic. Because they have no effect, thus avoiding the political costs of acting upon fiscal overload, placebo policies can be attractive to politicians.

Borrowing is the simplest way for politicians to temporize, as the Reagan administration has demonstrated. Borrowing money bridges the immediate gap between the money a government raises in taxes and its spending commitments. From 1970 to 1980 borrowing quadrupled as a proportion of gross national product in most major Western nations, reaching as much as 18 percent of the gross national product in Italy. Borrowing can buy time in which a government may reorganize its economy, but it does not remove the causes of fiscal overload. It is a temporary placebo, only removing the immediate symptoms of fiscal stress. Gradually, borrowing becomes another cause of fiscal overload, for the cumulative effect of increased borrowing is an increase in debt interest. In the 1970s payments of interest on the debt of major Western nations nearly doubled.

Cutting waste is the most popular placebo, for no politician will defend measures that squander government's resources. However, there is no agreement among politicians about which programmes are wasteful. By definition, every programme will have advocates within government among those responsible for providing it, and beneficiaries outside government as well. To describe an entire programme as wasteful is to attack it head-on, and to invite a spirited defence. To attack wasteful elements in a programme presents another type of difficulty: identifying and agreeing upon which particular elements are wasteful, and securing agreement that they are to be eliminated.

Politicians elected to eliminate waste in government have given unintended testimony to the irrelevance of placebo programmes. When James E. Carter became America's President in 1977, he pledged to reduce waste in the federal government by reorganization. To this end, he created a large reorganization unit within the Executive Office of the President. Before his term of office was over, however, the reorganization office had been abolished without fanfare; it could not deliver the savings that Carter had promised. In Britain, the entry of Margaret Thatcher to Downing Street in May 1979 was followed by the appointment of a retail marketing expert, Derek Rayner, as her special advisor on eliminating waste in government. When Lord Rayner (as he became) retired as an advisor three and one-half years later, the Conservative government announced that savings of £170 million a year had been achieved. By comparison with the small cash cost of Rayner's unit, the sum saved appears substantial; but by comparison with the total cost of running British government it is trivial — slightly more than 0.1 percent of total public expenditure.

Privatization is a placebo policy when it simply alters the delivery of public programmes without altering responsibility for funding. Public goods and services can be delivered by a wide variety of institutional arrangements, including government contracts with private profit-making organizations for delivering public programmes on a fee-for-service basis. Making organizations bid competitively for work is assumed to make programmes more efficient and effective, thus reducing the cost to government (Savas, 1982; Meyer, 1982). Even in so far as this is true — and the evidence in support of the claim is not conclusive — privatization can contribute very little to reducing the fiscal overload of government. The services most often cited as readily amenable to contracting out to private firms, for example refuse collection, account for a small proportion of public spending. Privatization at most promises a marginal reduction in cost among a marginal range of services.

Radical privatization, that is the repealing of existing programmes, could in principle end fiscal overloading by reversing and not just slowing down the growth of public spending. The radical argument for repealing major welfare state programmes is an argument of principle based upon free market or libertarian doctrines. But any proposal to repeal a programme with major spending implications will stimulate a defensive reaction from those who support it in principle, and have an interest in it as providers and beneficiaries. The bigger the potential savings from repeal, the greater the political controversy; the repeal of all subsidies to agriculture or business, or a substantial cut in public expenditure on education, health care or pensions, would not be easy to achieve.

No political party in the Western world has publicized campaign pledges to make big cuts in the benefits of the contemporary welfare state and won an election in consequence. So-called anti-public spending parties promise placebo policies. Once in office there is little that they actually do to repeal or reduce the programme commitments of government. In 1983 Mrs Thatcher's Conservative government even campaigned for re-election by boasting how much it was increasing welfare state expenditure.

The problem of fiscal overload can be made to disappear — in theory at least — by selectively imposing economic accounting conventions upon the facts of political life. National income accounts conventionally distinguish government consumption (the money it spends for goods and services) from government transfer payments (the money spent for such cash benefits as pensions and unemployment allowances). The reason for this is that a transfer payment is not an act of final consumption; the individuals receiving the transfer payment can spend the money as they wish. If one is interested in consumer behaviour this point is meaningful. If government consumption is treated as the only measure of government's size, then government's spending can thus be made to appear much smaller, for income maintenance transfer payments are the largest programmes of government.

In political terms, ignoring transfer payments is fundamentally misleading. First of all, it disregards the fact that transfer payments must be financed by public revenue; the taxes levied to pay for income maintenance programmes are part of the cost of governing. Second, most of the people whose taxes finance transfer payments are not the immediate beneficiaries. While every taxpayer sooner or later can expect to draw a pension, these programmes immediately involve an inter-generational transfer between the elderly and the young and middle-aged, or from the working population to the unemployed. The argument for compelling the payment of social insurance taxes — that many people suffer from 'defective telescopic faculty, that is, an inability to allow sufficiently for future satisfactions' (OECD, 1976: 85) — implies that people who pay social security taxes do not see themselves as the immediate beneficiaries.

Follow the trend
A third alternative is to embrace the trend. Just as free market ideologues may recommend privatization as a good in itself, so collectivists can view as good in itself the increasing government control of the allocation of the national product and an absolute reduction in take-home pay. From a collectivist point of view,

increased public expenditure is considered good because it is public, determined by a popularly elected government rather than by market forces. The political values justifying collective action by the state are many, including non-economic conservatism, nationalism and catholicism, as well as socialism and communism. A general ideological preference for collective action by government can be reinforced by pressure from public employees and beneficiaries to expand programmes in which they have a material interest.

Egalitarians also wish to give first priority to public expenditure, in order to redistribute incomes within society. They assume that the purpose of welfare state programmes is egalitarian, notwithstanding historical evidence that the programmes were launched to provide a minimum or floor for every citizen, rather than to lower the income of the well-to-do for egalitarian ends (Plattner, 1979). From an egalitarian perspective, welfare state programmes are good in themselves, and desirable as means of redistributing resources, whatever the fiscal consequences. Evidence that redistribution does not happen is then interpreted as a failure of egalitarian aims. In fact, the distribution of public benefits to the well-to-do as well as the poor accounts for the widespread popular success of the social programmes of big government.

Proponents of giving public programmes an absolute priority in claims upon national resources face two principal problems. The first is determining how an increasingly large public revenue is to be allocated, if growth is not simply to proceed according to inertia commitments reflecting priorities of a quarter-century or half-century ago. Both market and state bureaucratic methods have inadequacies, yet no third alternative is readily at hand (Lindbeck, 1971: 32). The second problem is the absence of widespread popular support for greatly expanding the present mix in the mixed economy welfare state, once a basic level of welfare services is secured. A leading scholar of the welfare state, Hugh Heclo (1981: 397), has concluded that financing the post-1951 expansion of the welfare state from the fiscal dividend of growth has 'gradually devalued the political commitment necessary to sustain social policy', without creating a new collectivist commitment.

Put the brakes on public expenditure

The fourth alternative is the only one available when the room for manoeuvre is exhausted by a failure of the economy to grow, of placebos to produce satisfaction, and of the electorate to endorse a continuing reduction in take-home pay. It is to put the brakes upon the growth of government's resource claims. No cuts are required. A reduction in the rate of growth of public expenditure should not be misperceived as a contraction in the scale of government. After the brakes are put on public spending, big government can continue to grow as long as the economy continues to grow. To reduce fiscal overloading it is simply necessary to put on the brakes sufficiently so that the increase in public expenditure does not exceed the increase in the national product.

To put the brakes on public programmes immediately raises the question: Which programme should grow least, or should the brakes apply to all programmes equally? The multiplicity of public programmes does not mean that all are equally important. The first priority of government is simply stated: do what you must. The sine qua non activities of government are relatively few but crucial. If governors fail to defend the national territory against external threats, maintain public order and collect taxes, a government ceases to exist. The programmatic means to achieve these concerns are more or less common throughout the Western world. Equally important, the claims of these programmes upon public resources are relatively small, and the largest programme, military defence, has been declining in relative significance. Ministries of foreign affairs require small amounts of money and personnel. A ministry of justice is law-intensive rather than money- or manpower-intensive, and the police depend upon voluntary co-operation for the enforcement of the great bulk of laws. Tax collectors are a small portion of total employment, and are cost-effective: for every penny spent on tax collection, a government can reckon to get 50 times as much money back. In most Western nations sine qua non programmes account for a small and declining share of public expenditure.

Government programmes intended to mobilize economic resources, for example building roads, dredging rivers, building houses or investing in a new nationwide telecommunications grid, involve very effective means-ends technologies. A government can be confident that if it allocates money for these programmes it will succeed in creating new capital assets. Spending upon physical resources can be justified as an investment in a nation's future, expanding the economic base for future tax revenue. To reduce investment in economic infrastructure would not be sensible in the long run, whatever the short-run arguments for doing so.

But not all programmes to mobilize economic resources result in assets that enhance the national product. Investment can be risky in the public as in the private sector. The capital cost of major roads may be repaid by the resulting savings in transport, but the capital cost of minor roads can only be justified politically, as a contribution to national integration, to national defence or to electoral victory. This is true also of some glamorous high-technology investments. For example, the Anglo-French investment in the supersonic Concorde jet proved to be a technical success but an economic disaster, because the revenue from operating Concorde does not begin to cover its cost. Some programmes classified as economic services are intended not to generate economic growth, but to subsidize producers in declining industries, or marginal producers in agriculture. There are marginal savings that could be made by putting the brakes upon (or even cutting) subsidies to uneconomic producers, but any major changes would risk reducing economic growth, and risk electoral retribution.

Social welfare programmes are likely to be most affected if the brakes are put on public expenditure (Rose, 1983b). They are the biggest programmes of government, and have been growing the most rapidly. Moreover, at the margin we do not know how effective some major welfare programmes are in achieving their goals; we can only be sure about how much they cost. We do not know whether a marginal increase or decrease in spending produces a proportionate increase or decrease in programme benefits or no change. A reduction in programme inputs — say, in the number of public employees or new buildings for welfare services — is not evidence of a reduction in programme outputs. To argue that teachers or social workers who are paid marginally less are less effective workers is to employ a crass mechanical model of welfare production. It is the uncertainty of the connection between programme inputs and outputs that justifies putting the brakes upon some major welfare programmes.

In education the growth of expenditure has been triggered as much by the broadening of educational aims as by demographic expansion (Table 7.4). As long as education concentrated upon relatively narrow aims, such as instruction in reading, writing and arithmetic, its effectiveness was high. But when education expands its aims to include a variety of socialization goals, such as promoting social mobility or reducing inter-class tensions, its effectiveness is lessened, since the school has no monopoly of social influence. When schools begin to compete with family and neighbourhood as influences on social mobility and class relations, they risk becoming ineffectual. A simple criterion for putting the brakes on education spending would be to squeeze first those programmes that are not central to the unique instructional concerns of schools. Education expansion should lose momentum in any event, since the demographic pressures that justified the expansion of schools in the past two decades now imply a contraction in their claims on public resources.

The connection between resource inputs and the health of a nation is even more uncertain. Doctors and hospitals concentrate upon treating people who lack health. The remedial work of restoring health to the unhealthy is very different from a positive health programme. Many of the measures conducive to good health do not involve doctors or hospitals, but require the unpaid co-operation of individuals, for example, attention to diet, exercise, drinking and smoking. Within the health service there is not always agreement among medical experts about the effectiveness of the allocation of resources or treatments for particular illnesses (Culyer, 1982). Medical uncertainties about health treatment imply that putting the brakes on the expansion of health expenditure would not necessarily affect health at the margin. The escalation in health costs in the past has not been accompanied by an equal escalation in good health.

The best example of an effective social policy, with programme outputs directly related to inputs, is the old-age pension. The basic means-ends technology is simple. Government gives money to all persons who can show proof of entitlement to a pension by producing a birth certificate or a record of pension contributions. Government does not specify what old people need, or dictate what they must consume. Instead, it gives the elderly a money income and pensioners are left to spend the money. Within the limits of the market, pensioners can buy what they think most appropriate for their needs and circumstances. The administrative cost of pensions is small, just as the money cost is great. Governments must expect spending on pensions to accelerate rather than decelerate, for the number of elderly is increasing in almost every Western nation (OECD, 1979), and people too old to work cannot be expected to do without some type of income.

Whatever programmes are selected for special attention in cost containment, their proponents are bound to protest. Programme spending has been increasing so steadily in the past that this creates expectations among public employees and their clients. Selecting a given programme to expand by a less than average rate can be viewed as discriminatory. The larger the programme, the greater the number of public employees and programme beneficiaries who can be mobilized to protest against what is misperceived as 'cuts' (Rose, 1980c).

Given the difficulties in selecting education and health programmes to bear disproportionate pressure when braking the growth of public spending, policy-makers may instead impose non-discriminatory across-the-board limitations on all programmes. Across-the-board measures, such as freezing the number of employees or placing cash limits upon spending whatever the rate of inflation, are analytically indiscriminate, making no allowance for differences between programmes. But they are attractive politically, because of the apparent equity of imposing a little restraint upon everybody. This prevents the proponents of any particular programme from claiming that they have been treated less satisfactorily than others (Wildavsky, 1975).

Cash limits are necessary in every fiscal system, for government agencies cannot spend money without ultimately reaching some constraint. In classic budgeting, cash limits were all-important; the budget authorized spending a fixed sum of money, and that was that. As inflation began to erode the purchasing power of money, budgeting in volume terms was developed. Instead of fixing a cash limit for a programme, an agency could be authorized to spend whatever was needed to purchase a fixed volume of programme goods and services, regardless of the price increase. Volume budgeting is intended to bring stability to the programme outputs of government, but it does so by destabilizing the amount of money that government is committed to spend.

British experience illustrates the significance of the two alternative methods of budgeting. In an era of classic public finance without expectation of inflation, cash limits were all-important. In the 1960s, however, the British government turned to volume budgeting as part of a process of planning a steady inertia expansion of government programmes. In 1976 a Labour government introduced cash limits on spending in the face of high inflation, and in 1981 the Conservative government returned to budgeting in current cash instead of volume terms.

Cash limits do not involve a reduction in public spending. In an inflationary period, this year's limit is almost invariably higher than last year's, and next year's limit becomes higher still. Nor do cash limits prescribe which part of a given programme should be squeezed to stay within a limit. Programme managers are left to work out their own procedures for getting by without the supplementary increases that they could expect with volume budgeting. For example, in public transport it may mean fewer trains and buses, and in the postal service fewer mail deliveries.

However, cash limits cannot be enforced easily or across-the-board, given the inertia commitments of the contemporary welfare state. An attempt to be non-selective inevitably ends up becoming selective, since programmes differ in the extent to which spending can be braked or controlled. Pensions and unemployment programmes give individuals an entitlement to benefits as a statutory right. When people live longer or more people become unemployed, then expenditure on such programmes will rise, as long as the individual pension or unemployment benefit remains unaltered. When transfer payments or the wages of public employees are indexed against inflation, increases will exceed any cash limits set below the rate of inflation. An attempt to apply cash limits equally to all programmes will inevitably end up discriminating between expenditure commitments that are capable of control, and uncontrollable open-ended programme commitments.

Government can evade its own expenditure limits through laws that externalize costs and benefits in ways that do not appear in the budget. Tax expenditure — that is, the grant of exemption from the payment of standard taxes to special groups in the population — leaves money in the pockets of individuals and corporations almost as effectively as would a government cash grant. But tax expenditures do not appear in conventional budgets. Equally important, regulations that compel organizations and individuals to spend money to reduce pollution, to buy safety features for their motor car or to continue employing workers who would otherwise be dismissed result in spending for public purposes just as much as money appropriated in the Budget. In the United States, the estimated cost of federal tax expenditures and of regulations is equivalent to one-sixth or more of the federal budget (Schick, 1981b).

Making or increasing charges for particular programme benefits is a positive means of discriminating in favour of some programmes (those provided without charge) and against others (those for which a charge is made, whether nominal or at full cost). Every Western nation makes some charges for each of its major welfare services, but none recovers the cost of the programme from those who directly benefit. The argument for or against charging is often cast in ideological terms between proponents of market as against merit goods (cf. Seldon, 1977; Musgrave, 1969). The relevant question here is: What are the effects of charging for services? Two immediate consequences are that revenue will be increased, even if only slightly, and demand reduced, as some people will not take up a service if a charge is made. In so far as a reduction in demand leads to some reduction in aggregate costs, then charging will make a double contribution to reducing fiscal overload, adding to revenue and subtracting from expenditure. The extent of savings can easily be exaggerated (cf. Parker, 1976), but equally important is the information that budget-makers gain, for charges convey market signals about the strength of demand for different programmes.

A government worried about fiscal overload will not be anxious to promote new programmes, yet without doing so it is confined solely to maintaining what it inherits from its predecessors. The first concern of an overloaded finance ministry will be to avoid new long-term commitments, for it is the inertia increase in such commitments that creates fiscal overloading. In so far as a budget ministry delegates to operating agencies the dis cretion to shift expenditure within overall budget targets, then programme managers may finance new programmes by cutting back others.

One-off measures by definition are non-recurring. The advantage of hosting the Olympic Games is that, whatever its cost, it is non-recurring. The sponsoring country is disqualified from acting as a host again for a quarter-century or longer. The same advantage holds for celebrating a Royal Jubilee or a national centennial. Collective goods, provided at fixed costs regardless of the number of users, also have advantages. For example, a cost-conscious government would be better advised to spend money for an additional television channel, where costs are more or less fixed whatever the number of viewers, than for community theatres, where the cost of providing plays tends to rise in proportion to the number in the audience.

Capital expenditure programmes involving multi-year but non-recurring investment in public facilities can be chosen according to their cost implications for future expenditure. When fiscal overload is the problem, then capital expenditure should favour measures that do not require a high level of recurrent expenditure; for example, roads involve a heavy capital cost but have low maintenance costs, whereas hospitals or universities are expensive to maintain as well as to build. Where charges can be imposed, the case for spending is stronger still, favouring toll motorways or bridges as against city streets; and municipal swimming pools or cinemas, for which an entrance charge is made, as against municipal libraries, provided without charge to users.

Meta-policies (that is, measures that affect more than one programme) are required to meet the meta-problem of fiscal overload. Yet across-the-board responses affecting all programmes equally are not possible, because public programmes are heterogeneous. They are not equal in their claims upon public resources or in the particular mix of resources required, nor are they equal in the nature and scope of their benefits. Meta-policies reduce the pressure upon any one public programme by putting the brakes upon many. Yet reducing the pressure does not mean that the brakes can easily be put on the inertia commitments of public programmes (Christensen, 1982).

Will people accept a reduction in the rate of growth of public spending on select welfare state programmes? Public opinion surveys show that there is a readiness to accept marginal adjustments in welfare state programmes. The bounds of tolerance are fairly wide, because there is considerable individual ambivalence about the major programmes of the welfare state. The conclusion of a wide-ranging review of public opinion towards the welfare state in eight major countries across Europe and the United States is summarized thus by Richard Coughlin:

> Public attitudes toward the broad principles of social policy have developed along similar lines, both of acceptance and rejection. The idea of collective responsibility for assuring minimum standards of employment, health care, income and other conditions of social and economic well-being has everywhere gained a foothold in popular values and belief. And yet the survey evidence suggests a simultaneous tendency supporting individual achievement, mobility and responsibility for one's own lot ... The prevailing ideological climate in each of the eight nations is mixed and is not dominated by extremes of ideology. [Coughlin, 1980: 31; see also Sniderman and Brody, 1977]

Consent: the first priority of government

The rights that citizens value most are priceless rights. The point is made evident in national constitutions. The rights guaranteed are civil and political rights, not welfare rights. Liberty, equality and fraternity are first of all political values, not economic principles. Because fundamental political rights are few and priceless, they do not threaten fiscal difficulties. There is no economic reason for government to withhold political rights from its citizens.

Consent is the first priority of government. Making authority legitimate comes before making people rich. Money means a lot, but it does not mean everything. Contemporary concern with economic difficulties tends to obscure the great political achievement of legitimate representative government. Material goods may complement but cannot substitute for political rights (see Rose, 1971: Chapter 15). In most Western nations basic civil and political rights are taken for granted. Where there is reason to feel insecure, for example because of the prevalence of crime, then citizens can give the maintenance of law and order a higher priority than any welfare state benefit (cf. Barnes, Kaase et al., 1979: 413).

The benefits of the welfare state are far more numerous and claim far more money than civil and political rights, but they are discretionary, not constitutional, programmes. Citizens are entitled to particular welfare state benefits by an ordinary Act of Parliament; they do not enjoy them as an entrenched constitutional right. The rhetoric of everyday party politics tends to blur the distinction between rights guaranteed citizens in a constitution, and entitlements under ordinary statute law. Constitutional rights cannot be revoked or repealed without threatening consent. Statutory entitlements can be changed by the decision of an elected government, just as they were adopted by an elected government.

Whereas the language of rights is the language of obligation, the language of benefits is the language of bargaining. Government will never have enough resources to meet all the demands placed upon it. Nor will individual citizens be surprised if all their demands are not met. By definition, demands are claims that have *not* been met. To confuse rights with entitlements, to assume that every demand must become an entitlement by statute and that every entitlement is an entrenched constitutional right necessary for popular consent, is to make the loyalty of citizens a byproduct of benefits (or bribes) from government.

The importance of political rights as against social benefits can be illustrated by comparing the evolution of public policy in Britain and Germany. The first rights to be proclaimed for individuals in Britain were civil: the rule of law. The second set were political rights; the mass franchise was granted to Englishmen more than a generation before the first faltering steps towards the welfare state. The principles of the welfare state were enshrined in public policy in Britain only some half a century after the introduction of mass suffrage (Marshall, 1950). From 1885 to 1939 Britain was admired throughout Europe as a paragon of political virtues. Englishmen were guaranteed liberty under the law and full political rights, even though welfare benefits were limited.

By contrast, the German state created under Prussian leadership in 1871 gave first priority to social benefits. In 1881 the Hohenzollern Kaiser, under Bismarck's prompting, proclaimed the principle of the 'social monarchy'. Kaiser Wilhelm endorsed the principle of social security legislation to guarantee every family protection in old age and from industrial injury or hardship. But German workers in receipt of welfare benefits did not enjoy political rights, such as the right to vote or strike. From a Prussian perspective, social benefits were seen as an alternative to political rights. The history of Germany since 1870 is a standing warning of the danger of neglecting the primacy of political rights. Three regimes have risen and fallen, notwithstanding the early adoption of advanced welfare programmes in Germany.

Germany was not alone in promoting social welfare programmes as an alternative to political rights. A wide-ranging historical and statistical analysis by Peter Flora and Jens Albers (1981: 72f.) concludes: 'The propensity to introduce social insurance schemes seems to be primarily a function of the type of regime (i.e. non-parliamentary monarchies or liberal democracies) and not the level of enfranchisement.' When allowance is made for different levels of economic development, non-parliamentary monarchies were found more apt to have initiated welfare programmes than liberal parliamentary democracies.

Earlier European experience remains relevant today. In Spain and Portugal, economic booms began under authoritarian regimes of Franco and Salazar, and were carried forward in Greece under a military dictatorship. The annual growth rates of Portugal (6.9 percent), Spain (7.2 percent) and Greece (7.7 percent) under dictatorships in the 1960s and early 1970s were higher than in any other country in Europe (OECD, 1982a: Table 3.1). But economic progress did not slake the thirst for political rights. Notwithstanding lower growth rates since the institution of free elections in the mid-1970s, these Mediterranean countries prefer regimes that grant citizens political and civil rights.

Italy — and even more, Northern Ireland — offer examples of what happens when the rule of law cannot be taken for granted, because of persisting armed challenges to public order and the authority of the regime. In Italy, notwithstanding widespread popular dissatisfaction verging on contempt for politicians and government, there remains strong popular support for strong government action to maintain the lawful institutions of the Republic against terrorists. In Northern Ireland, an armed conflict involving a multiplicity of illegal armies has killed thousands since internal violence erupted in 1971; and the legal state, the United Kingdom, has not been able to meet its minimum responsibility, to maintain public order. The violent and persisting conflict between competing national claimants to Northern Ireland illustrates the aptness of Flora's (1981: 343) remark that 'the idea of the welfare state has rarely been a truly inspiring ideal . . . compared with that of nationalism.'

Within the framework of representative government, elections provide the most straightforward test of the popular standing of politicians responsible for fiscal overload. In so far as failure to sustain treble affluence disappoints voters, the responsible party or parties in office should be defeated in a bid for re-election (cf. Paldam, 1981). In so far as incumbency is today a liability, not an asset, then a series of elections should lead to the rejection of all major parties, as each fails to reduce the fiscal overload; and anti-regime parties should flourish in the resulting vacuum.

In fact, the electorate has shown no tendency to reject parties that bear the responsibility of government, or of turning to anti-regime parties instead. Since 1968 the electoral fortunes of incumbent parties have hardly been affected by the swing from economic affluence to economic recession. In the 20 years from 1948 to 1967, 64 percent of governing parties in Western nations saw their vote fall at their subsequent general election; since 1968 the proportion has been virtually the same, 69 percent (Table 8.2). While the median governing party loses votes, it still holds office. Of all governing parties contesting elections, 64 percent remain in office afterwards, whether their vote goes up or goes down. A governing party can reckon to remain in office almost two-thirds of the time: responsibility for government in a period of fiscal stress is not a long-term electoral liability.

TABLE 8.2
The electoral fate of incumbent parties, 1948-1982

Incumbent parties	1948-67	1968-82
	%	%
Vote up	36	31
Vote down	64	69
Totals	100	100

Source: Rose and Mackie (1983: Table 5.5), updated by the authors.

Moreover, the popular vote for anti-regime parties has fallen rather than risen in the face of economic difficulties. Important political changes have occurred among parties previously claiming to be anti-regime, especially the French and Italian communist parties. As national economies have become overloaded, communist parties have not been stimulated to greater attacks upon the regime. Instead, they have moderated their positions. In France the Communist Party entered government in 1981 as the weaker party in an electoral alliance with the Socialists, and in Italy the Communist Party formed a tacit alliance to sustain the Christian Democrats in office. In European Community nations overall, votes for anti-regime parties — whether of the extreme left, extreme right, or nationalist — total only a few percent (Rose, 1983b: Table 4).

Studies of the propensity of citizens to protest, sparked off by the manifestation of unconventional protest demonstrations in 1968, have further confirmed the adherence of the great majority of citizens to established constitutional rights and political action within the law. In 1974 a multi-national team of researchers examined public approval of a variety of unconventional protest measures in order to see to what extent protest actions had popular support in Britain, the United States, Germany, the Netherlands and Austria. Individuals were asked to say whether or not they approved of a variety of protest actions inside and outside the law and whether they had ever engaged in such behaviour.

In every Western nation surveyed, a clear majority of citizens endorse lawful protest by petitions and legally recognized demonstrations (Table 8.3), but approval of unconventional protest declines sharply as activities become less conventional and involve law-breaking. The average proportion approving of boycotts is well under half (37 percent), and of rent strikes, occupation of buildings, blocking traffic, unofficial strikes or painting slogans, from 6 to 20 percent. Virtually no one was prepared to express approval of protests involving overt law-breaking, whether damage to property or violence to persons. The limited difference between nations in the approval of some methods of protest is less significant than the low level of actual involvement in protest behaviour. Even signing a petition, a simple and indubitably legal means of registering a voice, has been done by only one-third of citizens.

TABLE 8.3
Popular approval of and participation in political protest

	Approve of protest						Have taken part					
	Brit.	USA	Ger.	Neth.	Aus-tria	Av.	Brit.	USA	Ger.	Neth.	Aus-tria	Av.
	%	%	%	%	%	%	%	%	%	%	%	%
Petitions	72	89	82	92	82	83	22	58	31	21	34	33
Lawful Demo's	65	73	62	80	58	68	6	11	9	7	6	8
Boycotts	35	52	36	42	22	37	5	15	4	2	5	6
Rent strikes	23	20	13	31	13	20	2	2	1	1	3	2
Occupying building	14	15	6	42	6	17	1	2	0	2	0	1
Blocking traffic	14	7	12	22	17	14	1	1	2	1	1	1
Unofficial strikes	13	13	9	20	7	12	5	2	1	1	2	2
Painting slogans	2	4	7	11	7	6	0	1	1	2	1	1
Damaging property	1	1	1	1	2	1	1	1	0	1	0	1
Personal violence	2	2	3	2	3	2	0	1	0	0	0	0

Source: Barnes, Kaase et al. (1979: Tables A-2, A-3).

The great bulk of citizens are ready to vote and to discuss politics casually (see Barnes, Kaase et al., 1979: 541f., 555f.), but they do not approve of or take part in unconventional political protest. Furthermore, the majority of people approve of judges giving severe sentences to people who do break the law, and to the police use of force, if need be, to break up unlawful demonstrations. Political authority collapses if, and only if, citizens are prepared to condone unconstitutional action intended to overthrow the existing regime. In economic boom times or in a recession, citizens can advance causes by peaceful actions. A regime can and must adapt its programmes and actions to maintain popular consent and effectiveness. To treat every demand for political change as an attempt to undermine a political regime is a fundamental definitional error: it is to deny a regime the power to maintain itself by adaptation.

The Euro-Barometre survey of popular opinion in the countries of the European Community provides an unusual wealth of evidence to test whether or not the economic difficulties resulting in fiscal overload have caused support to rise or fall for democratic means of political action. Respondents are asked to choose between three alternative attitudes toward social change: valiant defence against all subversive forces; gradual reform; and revolutionary action to induce change. While a question so phrased can indicate only a very generalized predisposition to collective action, because it has been asked repeatedly since 1970 it can test the extent to which economic events have increased support for radical change by revolutionary means.

Consistently, year after year and in country after country, the Euro-Barometre survey finds that more than 90 percent of the population reject revolutionary action. In 1970 rejection of revolutionary action averaged 95 percent across the European Community. In 1982 the proportion was unchanged (Table 8.4). Nor is there any substantial difference between countries: in 1970 the 'low' for defence of established society was 92 percent in Italy, and in 1982, 90 percent in Belgium. During a decade of economic difficulties unprecedented since the Second World War, the proportion endorsing revolutionary action has everywhere remained very low; minor changes reflect statistical sampling fluctuations.

In so far as economic difficulties have encouraged a change in popular attitudes towards society, Europeans have become more conservative. In 1970 an average of 16 percent stated that they believed that society must be strongly defended against subversive forces. This was a higher percentage than approved of most unconventional forms of political protest. By 1982 the proportion of Europeans approving firm action to defend their society against subversion had doubled to 33 percent. Whereas in 1970 the active opponents of subversion outnumbered the proponents of revolutionary action by a margin of three to one, by 1982 they outnumbered them by a margin of six to one. Moreover, when asked their fears about the decade ahead, Europeans expressed greater anxiety about a rise in crime and terrorism (71 percent) than about unemployment (66 percent) (*Euro-Barometre* no. 17, 1982: 34).

TABLE 8.4
Popular attitudes towards social change, 1970-1982

Country	Defend against subversion			Reform			Revolutionary action		
	1970	1982	Change	1970	1982	Change	1970	1982	Change
	%	%	%	%	%	%	%	%	%
Belgium	16	22	−6	80	68	−12	4	10	+6
Denmark[a]	41	38	−3	55	60	+5	4	2	−2
France	13	27	+14	82	68	−14	5	5	0
Germany	22	45	+23	76	52	−24	2	3	+1
Ireland[a]	25	32	−7	67	59	+8	8	9	+1
Italy	12	23	+19	80	69	−11	8	8	0
Luxembourg	29	34	−5	70	63	−7	1	3	+2
Netherlands	16	36	+20	78	59	−19	6	5	−1
Britain[a]	27	36	+9	65	58	−7	8	6	−2
Greece[b]	—	33	—	—	60	—	—	7	—
Community average[c]	16	33	+17	79	62	−17	5	5	0

a. As these countries were not members of the European Community in 1970, the figures cited are for the first survey available, November 1976.

b. Greece not included in European Community surveys until 1980.

c. A weighted average based upon the population of the Community, with don't knows, averaging 7 percent, omitted.

Source: *Euro-Barometre* no. 18, December 1982: Table 17.

When the broad mass of opinion is examined — and this is the opinion that counts in a democratic political system — the conclusion is clear: consent for established institutions of governance is everywhere strong. Moreover, the consent is not uncritical. The median person in the European Community has a reformist inclination rather than a rigid adherence to the status quo. The challenges to authority briefly evidenced at the time of the so-called student revolt in the late 1960s have not since swelled into a torrent of disaffection, in response to economic difficulties. The regimes that have been most severely challenged in Europe have been dictatorships. In Spain, Portugal and Greece authoritarian regimes have been succeeded by regimes based upon popular consent. In Czechoslovakia and Poland, challenges to authoritarian communist regimes have failed not because of a lack of popular support, but because of Soviet coercion. The contrast between Eastern and Western Europe today reflects the importance of distinguishing between government with and without widespread popular consent.

The first priorities of people
People have many roles; in the course of a single day an individual can be a spouse, a parent, a son or daughter, a producer, a consumer, a friend and even a citizen. Non-political roles are far more numerous in society than political roles, and ordinary people spend far more time in non-political than in political activities. To describe a person as a citizen is normal in political analysis, but civic roles are not the most important roles of ordinary people. Political involvement is occasional and intermittent. This fundamental fact should always be borne in mind when analysing popular attitudes towards problems of governing. It explains why the priorities of governors will not be the same as the priorities of ordinary people in everyday life.

Ordinary people learn from experience, and people learn from things that go wrong as well as from what works. The process of political learning may be disjointed, but cumulatively the experience of what government does and does not do is much more than a process of 'random bumping' (cf. Heclo, 1974: 308). When Western economies were booming, more people expected their conditions to improve rather than worsen. But the pattern was not the same in every country, nor did everyone expect his or her own condition to improve. Both national and individual circumstances influence what people expect of the future (see Rose, 1980b: 159;ff. Katona et al., 1971: 44ff.).

In the course of time there are swings towards pessimism and toward optimism in every country as national conditions change

(Table 8.5). At no time do people in every Western nation have the same expectation of conditions getting better or worse; national differences remain important. At the beginning of 1972 Americans were the most optimistic about the immediate future; the proportion expecting conditions to improve outnumbered those expecting conditions to worsen by a margin of 35 percent. By contrast, in Germany the proportion expecting conditions to worsen was 23 percent greater than those expecting better conditions. In major Western nations overall optimists outnumbered pessimists, but the margin was limited to 12 percent. Even after years of increasing affluence, in 1972 the median person expected conditions to remain much the same in the coming year as in the year preceding.

TABLE 8.5
Expectations for the coming year, 1972-1983

	1972	1975	1979	1983	Change, 1983-1972
	(% replying change for better minus % replying worse)				
America	+35	n.a.	−22	+18	−17
Britain	+14	−50	−8	+13	−1
France	+7	−48	−19	−24	−31
Germany	−23	−42	+11	−9	+14
Italy	n.a.	−44	−30	−29	(+15)
Sweden	+25	+25	+30	−13	−38
Average	+12	−32	−8	−7	−19

Question: So far as you are concerned, do you think that 19— will be better or worse than 19—?
Sources: Rose (1980b: Table 4); and *Gallup Political Index* no. 269, January 1983: 14.

At the beginning of 1975 pessimism was widespread among major Western nations. Pessimists outnumbered optimists by a margin of 32 percent overall, and in Britain by a margin of 50 percent. Pessimistic expectations were well founded: 1975 was *annus horrendus* in the Western world. The national product actually contracted in every major Western nation except Sweden. By the beginning of 1979, pessimism had begun to moderate.

After a decade of economic difficulties, including rising unemployment and inflation as well as fiscal overload, ordinary people have learned to adjust their expectations. At the start of 1983 the balance of opinion tilted only slightly towards pessimism. The median person expected the coming year to be much the same as the year before; the proportion expecting conditions to get worse outnumbered optimists by a margin of 7 percent, a change from a decade previously. National differences remain noteworthy: at the start of 1983 America and Britain were relatively optimistic, and Swedes relatively pessimistic, a shift from four years previously. In the past decade optimism has risen in Germany and Italy, and pessimism has grown in France and Sweden.

Ironically, theories of frustration and rebellion used to predict an increase in popular protest against government (Gurr, 1970) can today be cited to explain why government maintains popular consent. Government is meeting popular expectations today, as it did in the affluent 1960s — but the expectations it meets have changed. Today, people pessimistically expect rising prices, rising unemployment and more strikes, as well as greater economic difficulties. Government can and does meet these pessimistic expectations, not because policy-makers actively wish to make the economy worse, but because they cannot find a way to do better.

The longer the fiscal overload continues, the more likely government is to benefit from the politics of *reprieve* (Rose, 1980c: 224ff.). Reprieve promises relief. If most people expect the economy to deteriorate and conditions do not change, relief should follow if the economy has done better than expected. Since Western economies are still continuing to expand, albeit more slowly than before, there is scope for a positive increase in public and private spending. As long as governors can prevent their economies from contracting in the years ahead, this can strengthen subjective satisfaction. As long as recession is anticipated, a slowly expanding economy will exceed popular expectations.

In any event, individuals in Western nations are not primarily concerned with maximizing their material advantages. If this were the case, then people would be prepared to leave their own country to seek work in a society where higher pay was offered. Notwithstanding the free movement of labour within the European Community, this rarely happens. Governments pour large sums of money into sub-economic programmes intended to minimize interregional movement within a country. Even if individuals wished to maximize money earnings, their positions in the life-cycle will set a ceiling on such ambitions. Having a family brings about an abrupt fall in a household's money income if a wife forsakes a job to do so. Yet the satisfactions of family life may outweigh the simple economic calculus of maximizing income.

What should we expect ordinary citizens to do in the face of contemporary economic uncertainties? One theory is that individuals will increase their investment in political action, pressing more demands upon government and making greater efforts to get government to do what is popular. But in so far as citizens have learned from experience about the limitations of government (failure would be far too strong a word), then we should expect people to invest less time and effort in political activity, and to devote more to their other roles in society.

When government cannot provide all the material benefits a citizen wants, there is a positive incentive for an individual to return to the market to see whether it is possible to earn money there to meet family needs. But making more money is disproportionately difficult when an economy is growing slowly. If the economy is not growing at all, then any increase in earnings for one person must be offset by a fall in earnings for another. Economic stagnation places a limit upon the extent to which individuals can improve their conditions, whether by their personal effort or by acting collectively through trade unions, whose bargaining position is weakened by rising unemployment.

When opportunities for extra earnings in the official economy are few, then individuals may turn to the unofficial economy seeking to increase their take-home pay by evading tax. But the greater the economic difficulties in a society, the more likely the unofficial economy is to contract, for there is less cash about to pay for goods and services in the cash-only economy.

At this juncture individuals can turn their backs upon the national economy as well as upon government, maintaining individual consumption by activities within the household. For most of history in most of the world, the majority of goods and services that families have consumed have been produced within the home, and this remains true in most of the non-Western world today (Hill, 1979). A fall in take-home pay in the official economy need not mean a fall in living standards, in so far as, at the margin, people are able to produce at home what they formerly bought. Household repairs can be undertaken by the householder rather than purchased in the official or unofficial economy. Clothes can be made or repaired at home rather than discarded when a new season's fashion reaches the market. To respond to difficulties in the official economy by drawing upon household resources does not threaten the authority of government. In a mixed society, where the state does not control all activities, it is a mark of social resourcefulness.[1]

Individuals can turn to domestic resources to improve their welfare independently of government. The state is a major source of welfare in society, but it is not a unique resource. Profit-making and non-profit associations make some provision for pensions, education and health care, supplementing or complementing government programmes. Families care for each other within the home and across generations. The role of family, neighbours and friends is greatest in the provision of personal social services, such as care for the elderly or assistance to the handicapped. Many measures required to improve health can be taken only by individuals for themselves. The growth of the welfare state to some extent simply transferred responsibility from the home or market to the state; it did not automatically increase total welfare in society. It is possible for individuals and families to compensate for the brakes being put on some contemporary welfare state programmes by drawing upon their own domestic resources (Rose, 1983c).

From the point of view of the individual, life satisfaction rather than political or economic satisfaction comes first. Individuals have national pride and national loyalties, but they have stronger ties to their face-to-face communities, and especially to their own families. A sophisticated social scientist could argue that in contemporary society everything, even the most elemental of family actions, like the birth of a child, has political and economic causes and consequences, indirectly if not directly. But to argue that the totality of social activities is of concern to the state is to depart from the values of contemporary Western nations, which presuppose a private as well as a public sector in the mixed society. It is to espouse a totalitarian view of the integration of state and society.

The autonomy of individual satisfaction vis-a-vis political and economic events is strikingly demonstrated by a succession of surveys carried out in European Community countries before and after the sharp increase in economic difficulties in the mid-1970s (Table 8.6). In September 1973, shortly before the OPEC oil price led to economic difficulties, 79 percent of people reported that they were satisfied with their lives. The responses given were moderate, for more people reported that they were fairly satisfied than very satisfied. Among the minority dissatisfied with life, the proportion not at all satisfied was trivial — 4 percent. In the decade since, there have been ample political and economic events to generate dissatisfaction, but this has not affected ordinary people. There has been no change in overall life satisfaction; the limited movement observed is well within the range of sampling fluctuations. In 1982, 77 percent reported themselves satisfied with their lives — more than in 1976, and virtually the same as in 1973 or 1978. Significantly, levels of life satisfaction do not vary with satisfaction with the workings of democracy. In 1982 political satisfaction differed greatly between Germany (66 percent) and Italy (19 percent), but overall life satisfaction did not.

TABLE 8.6
Life satisfaction in the European Community, 1973-1982

	1973 (Sept.)	1976	1978	1982	Change, 1982-1973
	(Responses for all member countries of EEC)				
	%	%	%	%	%
Very satisfied	21	20	22	22	+1
Fairly satisfied	58	55	57	55	−3
Satisfied	79	75	79	77	−2
Not very satisfied	16	18	15	17	−1
Not at all satisfied	4	6	5	5	+1
Dissatisfied	20	24	20	22	+2

Sources: European Community surveys, as reported in Rose(1980: Table 1); and *Euro-Barometre* no. 17, 1982: Table 10. Don't knows are not more than 2 percent of responses.

While there are differences between nations in the degree to which citizens report themselves satisfied with their lives, within each country in the European Community the overall level of life satisfaction has remained high in a decade of difficulties. The independence of individual life satisfaction from national economic circumstances is dramatically illustrated by worldwide surveys of life satisfaction in non-Western as well as Western nations. Consistently, the surveys report high levels of life satisfaction, whether the national standard of living is among the highest or lowest in the world (Easterlin, 1974; Heald, 1982).

The explanation for a high level of life satisfaction in the face of political and economic difficulties is simple yet important: the greatest concerns of individuals tend to be insulated from political and economic events. If we could do a content analysis of what ordinary people talk about, we would almost certainly find that ordinary people talked more about the weather or sport than about politics, and phatic communion was more common than reasoned analysis of society's problems.

The actions of big government *do* affect how ordinary people live. The mixed economy welfare state guarantees an income for pensioners and the unemployed, as well as directly or indirectly sustaining millions of jobs in the national economy. Welfare state services such as education, health and housing *are* immediately important in the lives of millions of people. But the activities of big government, however important they appear to politicians, journalists and social scientists, are not the most immediate concerns of ordinary people in everyday life.

Society's major political and economic institutions are out of sight and out of mind of ordinary individuals. Time and again, when people are asked to evaluate their satisfaction with different domains of life, the same responses recur. Individuals report that they are most satisfied with their family, friends, the place they live, their health and their job, and least satisfied with those things for which major institutions of society are formally responsible, such as government and the economy. Individuals determine their life satisfaction principally from face-to-face relationships, and not from the impersonal activities of big government.

Note

1. The emphasis here upon the domestic economy, as against the unofficial economy, is thus a modification of consequences hypothesized in Rose and Peters (1978a), reflecting both the author's further reflections and the depression in the black economy induced by continued economic recession (cf. Rose, 1983a).

REFERENCES

Aaron, Henry (1978), *Politics and the Professors*, Washington DC, Brookings Institution.

Abel-Smith, B. (1973), 'Social Security and Taxation', in B. Crick and W.A. Robson (eds), *Taxation Policy*, Harmondsworth, Penguin, 171-182.

Aberbach, Joel D., R. Putnam, and B. Rockman (1981), *Bureaucrats and Politicians in Western Democracies*, Cambridge, Mass., Harvard University Press.

Aberbach, Joel D. and Bert A. Rockman (1976), 'Clashing Beliefs within the Executive Branch: the Nixon Administration Bureaucracy', *American Political Science Review*, 70 (2): 456-468.

ACIR (1980), *The Federal Role in the Federal System: A Crisis of Confidence and Competence*, Washington, DC, Advisory Commission on Intergovernmental Relations, A-77.

ACIR (1981), *The Federal Role in the Federal System: the Dynamics of Growth*, Washington, DC, Advisory Commission on Intergovernmental Relations, A-78.

Aharoni, Yair (1981), *The No-Risk Society*, Chatham, NJ, Chatham House.

Albers, Jens (1981), 'Government Responses to the Challenge of Unemployment: the Development of Unemployment Insurance in Western Europe', in Flora and Heidenheimer, 1981: 151-183.

Allison, Graham T. (1971), *Essence of Decision: Explaining the Cuban Missile Crisis*, Boston, Little, Brown & Co.

Anderson, Charles W. (1978), 'The Logic of Public Problems', in D. Ashford (ed.), *Comparing Public Policies*, London and Beverly Hills, Sage Publications, 19-41.

Ardant, G. (1975), 'Financial Policy and Economic Infrastructure of Modern States and Nations', in Charles Tilly (ed.), *The Formation of National States in Western Europe*, Princeton University Press, 164-242.

Atkinson, A.B. and J.E. Stiglitz (1980), *Lectures on Public Economics*, New York, McGraw-Hill.

Bacon, Roger and Walter Eltis (1976), *Britain's Economic Problem: Too few Producers*, London, Macmillan.

Barker, Anthony (ed.) (1982a), *Quangos in Britain: Government and the Networks of Public Policy-Making*, London, Macmillan.

Barker, Anthony (1982b), 'Governmental Bodies and the Networks of Mutual Accountability', in Barker, 1982: 3-33.

Barnard, Chester I. (1938), *The Functions of the Executive*, Cambridge, Mass., Harvard University Press.

Barnes, Samuel, Max Kaase et al. (1979), *Political Action: Mass Participation in Five Western Democracies*, London and Beverly Hills, Sage Publications.

Baumol, W.J. (1967), 'Macro-economics of Unbalanced Growth: the Anatomy of Urban Crisis', *American Economic Review*, 57: 415-426.

Beck, Morris (1976), 'The Expanding Public Sector: Some Contrary Evidence', *National Tax Journal*, 29: 15-21.

Beck, Morris (1979), 'Public Sector Growth: A Real Perspective', *Public Finance*, 34: 313-355.

Beck, Nathan (1982), 'Parties, Administration and American Macroeconomic Outcomes', *American Political Science Review*, 76 (1): 83-93.

Bell, Daniel (1973), *The Coming of Post-Industrial Society*, New York, Basic Books.

Bibby, John F., Thomas E. Mann and Norman J. Ornstein (1980), *Vital Statistics on Congress*, Washington, DC, American Enterprise Institute.

Blades, Derek (1982), 'The Hidden Economy and the National Accounts', *OECD Economic Outlook: Occasional Studies* (June): 28-45.

Blondel, J. (1973), *Comparative Legislatures*, Englewood Cliffs NJ, Prentice-Hall.

Blondel, Jean (1982), *The Organization of Governments*, London and Beverly Hills, Sage Publications.

Blondel, Jean et al. (1969), 'Legislative Behaviour: Some Steps towards a Cross-National Measurement', *Government and Opposition*, 5 (1): 67-85.

Borthwick, R.L. (1981), 'The Floor of the House', in S.A. Walkland and M. Ryle (eds), *The Commons Today*, London, Fontana, 64-86.

Bowen, Elinor R. (1982), 'The Pressman-Wildavsky Paradox', *Journal of Public Policy*, 2 (1): 1-22.

Braun, Rudolf (1975), 'Taxation, Sociopolitical Structure and State-Building: Great Britain and Brandenburg-Prussia', in C. Tilly (ed.), *The Formation of National States in Western Europe*, Princeton University Press, 243-327.

Braybrooke, David and C.E. Lindblom (1964), *A Strategy of Decision*, New York, Free Press.

Brittan, Samuel (1975), 'The Economic Consequences of Democracy', *British Journal of Political Science*, 5 (2): 129-159.

Buchanan, J.M. and R.E. Wagner (1977), *Democracy in Deficit*, New York, Academic Press.

Burton, Ivor and Gavin Drewry (1981), *Legislation and Public Policy: Public Bills in the 1970-74 Parliament*, London, Macmillan.

Butler, D.E. and A. Ranney (eds) (1978), *Referendums*, Washington, DC, American Enterprise Institute.

Butler, D.E. and Anne Sloman (1980), *British Political Facts 1900-1979* (5th ed.), London, Macmillan.

Caiden, G.E. and H. Siedentopf (eds) (1982), *Strategies for Administrative Reform*, Lexington Mass., Lexington Books.

Caiden, Naomi (1980), 'Negative Financial Management: a Backward Look at Fiscal Stress', in C. Levine and I. Rubin (eds), *Fiscal Stress and Public Policy*, London, Sage, 135-158.

Cameron, David (1978), 'The Expansion of the Public Economy: a Comparative Analysis', *American Political Science Review*, 72 (4): 1243-1261.

Castles, Francis G. (ed.) (1982a), *The Impact of Parties: Politics and Policies in Democratic Capitalist States*, London and Beverly Hills, Sage Publications.

Castles, Francis G. (1982b), 'The Impact of Parties on Public Expenditure', in Castles, 1982a: 21-96.

CEEP (Centre Europeen de l'Enterprise Publique) (1981), *Public Enterprise in the European Economic Community*, Brussels, CEEP.

Christensen, J.G. (1982), 'Growth by Exception: or The Vain Attempt to Impose Resource Scarcity on the Danish Public Sector', *Journal of Public Policy*, 2 (2): 117-144.

Clarke, Sir Richard (1971), *New Trends in Government*, London: Civil Service College Studies 1, Her Majesty's Stationery Office.

Clarke, Sir Richard (1973), 'The Long-term Planning of Taxation', in B. Crick and W.A. Robson (eds), *Taxation Policy*, Harmondsworth, Penguin, 153-170.

Coleman, James S. (1974), *Power and the Structure of Society*, New York, W.W. Norton.'

Collier, David and Richard Messick (1975), 'Prerequisites versus Diffusion; Testing Alternative Explanations of Social Security Adoption', *American Political Science Review*, 69 (4): 1296-1315.

Cooper, Joseph, D.W. Brady and P.A. Hurley (1977), 'The Electoral Basis of Party Voting: Patterns and Trends in the US House of Representatives, 1887-1969', in L. Maisel and J. Cooper (eds), *The Impact of the Electoral Process*, London, Sage Electoral Studies Yearbook, vol. 3, 133-166.

Cornford, James (ed.) (1975), *The Failure of the State*, London, Croom-Helm.

Coughlin, Richard M. (1980), *Ideology, Public Opinion and Welfare Policy*, Berkeley, University of California Institute of International Studies Research Series no. 42.

Council of State Governments (1982), *The Book of the States, 1982-83*, Lexington, Ky., Council of State Governments, vol. 24.

Crecine, J.P. (1969), *Governmental Problem-solving: a Computer Simulation of Municipal Budgeting*, Chicago, Rand McNally & Co.

Culyer, A.J. (1982), 'Reassessing the Role of Government in the Health Sector: a Sceptical Essay', Kiel, Institut fuer Weltwirtschaft Conference on Reassessing the Role of Government in the Mixed Economy, 23-25 June.

Dahl, Robert A. (1970), *After the Revolution*, New Haven, Conn., Yale University Press.

Dahl, Robert A. and E.R. Tufte (1974), *Size and Democracy*, Stanford University Press.

Damgaard, Erik (1982), 'The Public Sector in a Democratic Order: Problems and Non-Solutions in the Danish Case', Rio de Janeiro, International Political Science Association World Congress, 9-14 August.

Davies, B. (1968), *Social Needs and Resources in Local Government*, London, Michael Joseph.

Dempster, Michael and Aaron Wildavsky (1978), 'On Change: or, There is No Magic Size for an Increment', *Political Studies*. 27: 371-389.

Di Palma, Giuseppe (1977), *Surviving without Governing — Italian Parties in Parliament*, Berkeley, University of California Press.

Dogan, Mattei (ed.) (1975), *The Mandarins of Western Europe*, Beverly Hills, Sage Publications.

Dogan, Mattei and Dominique Pelassy (1981), *Sociologie Politique Comparative*, Paris, Economica.

Downs, Anthony (1965), 'Why the Government Budget is Too Small in a Democracy', in S. Phelps (ed.), *Private Wants and Public Needs*, New York, W.W. Norton.

Downs, Anthony (1967), *Inside Bureaucracy*, Boston, Little, Brown.

Drewry, Gavin (1972), 'Reform of the Legislative Process: Some Neglected Questions', *Parliamentary Affairs*, 25 (4) 286-302.

Easterlin, Richard (1974), 'Does Economic Growth Improve the Human Lot — Some Empirical Evidence', in Paul A. David and Melvin W. Reder (eds), *Nations and Households in Economic Growth*, New York, Academic Press.

Easton, David (1965), *A Systems Analysis of Political Life*, New York, John Wiley.

Egeberg, Morten (1980), 'The Fourth Level of Government: On the Standardization of Public Policy within International Regions', *Scandinavian Political Studies*, 3 (3) 234-248.

Ehrmann, Henry W. (1976), *Comparative Legal Cultures*, Englewood Cliffs, NJ, Prentice-Hall.

Eliasson, Gunnar and B.C. Ysander (1981), *Picking Winners or Bailing Out Losers?* Stockholm, Industrial Institute for Economic and Social Research Working Paper no. 37.

Euro-Barometre (semi-annual), Brussels, European Commission.

Flora, Peter (1975), *Quantitative Historical Sociology*, Paris and the Hague, Mouton, *Current Sociology*, 22 (2).

Flora, Peter (1981), 'Solution or Source of Crises? The Welfare State in Historical Perspective' in W.J. Mommsen (ed.), *The Emergence of the Welfare State in Britain and Germany*, London, Croom-Helm, 343-389.

Flora, Peter and J. Albers (1981), 'Modernization, Democratization and the Development of Welfare States in Western Europe', in Flora and Heidenheimer, 1981: 37-80.

Flora, Peter and Heidenheimer, Arnold J. (eds) (1981), *The Development of Welfare States in Europe and America*, New Brunswick, NJ, Transaction Books.

Frears, John R. (1981), 'Parliament in the Fifth Republic', in W.G. Andrews and S. Hoffmann (eds), *The Fifth Republic at Twenty*, Albany, NY, SUNY Press, 57-78.

Galbraith, J. Kenneth (1958), *The Affluent Society*, Boston, Houghton-Mifflin.

Goode, Richard (1977), 'The Economic Definition of Income', in Joseph A. Pechman (ed.), *Comprehensive Income Taxation*, Washington, DC, Brookings Institution, 1-36.

Goodsell, Charles T. (1983), *The Case for Bureaucracy*, Chatham, NJ, Chatham House.

Goodwin, Craufurd D. (ed.) (1975), *Exhortation and Controls: the Search for a Wage-Price Policy 1945-71*, Washington, DC, Brookings Institution.

Gough, Ian (1982), *The Political Economy of the Welfare State*, London, Macmillan.

Gregory, Roy (1971), *The Price of Amenity*, London, Macmillan.

Griffith, J.A.G. (1974), *Parliamentary Scrutiny of Government Bills*, London, Allen and Unwin.

Gunlicks, Arthur B. (ed.) (1981), *Local Government Reform and Reorganization: an International Perspective*, Port Washington, NY, Kennikat Press.

Gurr, T.R. (1970), *Why Men Rebel*, Princeton University Press.

Gustafsson, Gunnel (1980), 'Modes and Effects of Local Government Mergers in Scandinavia', *West European Politics*, 3 (3): 339-357.

Hague, D.C., W.J.M. Mackenzie and A. Barker (eds) (1975), *Public Policy and Private Interests: the Institutional Compromise*, London, Macmillan.

Hanf, K.W. and Scharpf, F.W. (eds) (1978), *Interorganizational Policy Making: Limits to Coordination and Central Control*, London and Beverly Hills, Sage Publications.

Hayek, F.W. von (1944), *The Road to Serfdom*, London, Routledge & Kegan Paul.

Heald, Gordon (1982), 'A Comparison between American, European and Japanese Values', paper to annual meeting of WAPOR, Hunt Valley, Maryland, 21 May.

Heclo, Hugh (1974), *Modern Social Politics in Britain and Sweden*, New Haven, Conn., Yale University Press.

Heclo, Hugh (1975), 'Frontiers of Social Policy in Europe and America', *Policy Sciences*, 6 (4).

Heclo, Hugh (1978), 'Issue Networks and the Executive Establishment', in A.S. King (ed.), *The New American Political System*, Washington, DC, American

Enterprise Institute, 87-124.

Heclo, Hugh (1981), 'Toward a New Welfare State?' in Flora and Heidenheimer, 1981: 383-406.

Heller, Peter S. (1981), 'Diverging Trends in the Shares of Nominal and Real Government Expenditure in GDP', *National Tax Journal*, 34 (1): 61-74.

Herber, Bernard P. (1967), *Modern Public Finance*, Homewood, Ill., Richard D. Irwin Inc.

Hibbs, Douglas A. and H.J. Madsen (1981), 'Public Reactions to the Growth of Taxation and Government Expenditure', *World Politics*, 33 (3): 413-435.

Hill, T.P. (1979), 'Do It Yourself and GDP', *The Review of Income and Wealth*, 25 (1): 31-40.

Hine, David (1981), 'Thirty Years of the Italian Republic', *Parliamentary Affairs*, 34: 63-80.

Hoebel, Edward A. (1954), *The Law of Primitive Man*, Cambridge, Mass., Harvard University Press.

Hogwood, Brian W. (1982), 'Quasi-government in Scotland', in Barker, 1982a: 69-87.

Hogwood, Brian W. and B. Guy Peters (1982), *Policy Succession*, Brighton, Harvester Press.

Holden, Matthew (1966), 'Imperialism in Bureaucracy', *American Political Science Review*, 60: 943-951.

Hood, C.C. (1976), *The Limits of Administration*, London and New York, John Wiley.

Hood, C.C. (1982), 'Governmental Bodies and Government Growth', in Barker, 1982a: 44-68.

Hood, C.C. and A. Dunsire (1981), *Bureaumetrics*, Farnborough, Gower.

Hood, C.C. and W.J.M. Mackenzie (1975), 'The Problem of Classifying Institutions', in Hague et al., 1975: 409-424.

Huntington, Samuel P. (1974), 'Post-industrial Politics: How Benign Will it Be?' *Comparative Politics*, 6 (2): 163-191.

Inglehart, Ronald (1977), *The Silent Revolution*, Princeton University Press.

Inter-Parliamentary Union (1976), *Parliaments of the World*, London, Macmillan.

Johnson, Nevil (1982), 'Accountability, Control and Complexity', in Barker, 1982a: 206-218.

Jordan, A. Grant (1981), 'Iron Triangles, Woolly Corporatism and Elastic Nets', *Journal of Public Policy*, 1 (1): 95-123.'

Justitiedepartementet (1980), *Can You Bring up Children Successfully without Smacking and Spanking?* Stockholm, Justice Department.

Kamlett, M.S. and D.C. Mowery (1980), 'The Budgetary Base in Federal Resource Allocation', *American Journal of Political Science*, 24: 804-821.

Katona, G., B. Strumpel and E. Zahn (1971), *Aspirations and Affluence*, New York, McGraw-Hill.

Kay, J.A. and M.A. King (1980), *The British Tax System* (2nd ed.), London, Oxford University Press.

Keman, Hans (1982), 'Securing the Safety of the Nation-State', in F.G. Castles (ed.), *The Impact of Parties*, London, Sage Publications, 177-221.

Keohane, R.O. and J.S. Nye (1977), *Power and Interdependence*, Boston, Little Brown & Co.

King, A.S. (1973), 'Ideas, Institutions and the Policies of Government', *British Journal of Political Science*, 3 (3 and 4): 291-313 and 409-423.

Kochen, Manfred and K.W. Deutsch (1980), *Decentralization*, Cambridge, Mass., Oelgeschlager, Gunn and Hain.

Kohl, Juergen (1979), *Staatsausgaben in Westeuropa: Ansaetze zur empirischen Analyse der langfristigen Entwicklung der Oeffentlichen Ausgaben*, Mannheim, PhD dissertation.

Kuhnle, Stein (1981), 'The Growth of Social Insurance Programs in Scandinavia', in Flora and Heidenheimer, 1981: 125-150.

Laegereid, Per and Johan P. Olsen (1981) 'The Storting — A Last Stronghold of the Political Amateur', Madrid: Centro de Investigaciones Sociologicas Conference on The Role of Parliamentarians in Contemporary Democracies, 15-16 December.

Larkey, Patrick, D., Chandler Stolp and Mark Winer (1981), 'Theorizing about the Growth of Government', *Journal of Public Policy*, 1 (2) 157-220.

Leemans, A.F. (1976) (ed.), *The Management of Change in Government*, The Hague, Martinus Nijhoff.

Lewis, Alan (1982), *The Psychology of Taxation*, Oxford, Martin Robertson.

Lilley, William III and James C. Miller III (1977), 'The New Social Regulation', *Public Interest*, no. 47: 49-61.

Lindbeck, Assar (1971), *The Political Economy of the New Left*, New York, Harper & Row.

Lindbeck, Assar (1976), 'Stabilization Policy in Open Economies with Endogenous Politics', *American Economic Review*, 66 (2).

Lindberg, Leon (1982), 'Economists as Policy Intellectuals and Economics as a Policy Profession', Twelfth World Congress of the International Political Science Association, Rio de Janeiro.

Lindblom, C.E. (1965), *The Intelligence of Democracy*, New York, Free Press.

Lindblom, C.E. (1977), *Politics and Markets*, New York, Basic Books.

Lowi, T.J. (1969), *The End of Liberalism*, New York, W.W. Norton & Co.

Mackenzie, W.J.M. (1967), 'The Civil Service, the State and the Establishment', in B. Crick (ed.), *Essays On Reform*, London, Oxford University Press, 182-202.

Mackie, T.T. and Hogwood, B.W. (1983), *Cabinet Committees in Executive Decision-Making*, Glasgow, University of Strathclyde Studies in Public Policy, no. 111.

Mackie, T.T. and Richard Rose (1982), *The International Almanac of Electoral History* (2nd ed.), London: Macmillan.

Maddison, Angus (1981), *Les Phases du Developpement Capitaliste*, Paris, Economica.

March, James G. and Herbert A. Simon (1958), *Organizations*, New York, John Wiley.

March, M.S. (1982), 'Colorado's Sunset Review 1976-1981: An Experiment in State Regulatory Reform', *Policy Studies Review*, 1 (3): 491-502.

Marshall, T.H. (1950), *Citizenship and Social Class*, Cambridge University Press.

Martin, John (1982), 'Public Sector Employment Trends in Western Industrialized Economies', in International Institute of Public Finance, *Public Finance and Public Employment*, Detroit, Wayne State University Press, 29-46.

Mayhew, David R. (1974), *Congress: The Electoral Connection*, New Haven, Conn., Yale University Press.

Mazmanian, Daniel and Paul Sabatier (1980), 'A Multivariate Model of Public Policymaking', *American Journal of Political Science*, 24: 439-468.

Merryman, John H. (1969), *The Civil Law Tradition*, Stanford University Press.

Merryman, John H., David S. Clark and Lawrence M. Friedman (1971), *Law and Social Change in Mediterranean Europe and Latin America*, Stanford University Studies in Law and Development/SLADE.

Meyer, Jack A. (ed.) (1982), *Meeting Human Needs*, Washington, DC, American Enterprise Institute.

Musgrave, R.A. (1969), *Fiscal System*, New Haven, Conn., Yale University Press.

Musolf, Lloyd D. and Harold Seidman (1980), 'The Blurred Boundaries of Public Administration', *Public Administration Review*. March/April: 124-130.

NAPA Study Panel (1981), *Report on Government Corporations*, Washington DC, National Academy of Public Administration.

Newton, Kenneth (1980), *Balancing the Books: Financial Problems of Local Governments in West Europe*, London and Beverly Hills, Sage Publications.

Niskanen, W.A. (1971), *Bureaucracy and Representative Government*, Chicago, Aldine-Atherton Press.

O'Connor, James (1973), *The Fiscal Crisis of the State*, New York, St Martin's Press.

OECD (1976), *Public Expenditure on Education*, Paris, OECD Studies in Resource Allocation no. 2.

OECD (1977), *Towards Full Employment and Price Stability* (the McCracken Committee Report), Paris, OECD.

OECD (1978), *Public Expenditure Trends*, Paris, OECD Studies in Resource Allocation no. 5.

OECD (1979), *Demographic Trends 1950-1990*, Paris, OECD.

OECD (1980), *The 1979 Tax/Benefit Position of a Typical Worker in OECD Member Countries*, Paris, OECD.

OECD (1981), *Long-Term Trends in Tax Revenues of OECD Member Countries 1955-1980*, Paris, OECD.

OECD (1982a), *Historical Statistics, 1960-1980*, Paris OECD Economic Outlook.

OECD (1982b), *Employment in the Public Sector*, Paris, OECD.

Olson, Mancur (1982), *The Rise and Decline of Nations*, New Haven, Conn., Yale University Press.

Page, Edward (1982), *Laws and Orders in Central-Local Government Relations*, Glasgow, University of Strathclyde Studies in Public Policy no. 102.

Paldam, Martin (1981), 'A Preliminary Survey of the Theories and Findings on Vote and Popularity Functions', *European Journal of Political Research*, 9 (2): 181-199.

Parker, R.A. (1976), 'Charging for the Social Services', *Journal of Social Policy*, 5 (4): 359-373.

Parry, Richard (1981), 'Territory and Public Employment: a General Model and a British Example', *Journal of Public Policy*, 1 (2): 221-50.

Peacock, Alan (1982), 'Reducing Government Expenditure Growth: a British View', Kiel: Institut fuer Weltwirtschaft Conference on Reassessing the Role of Government in the Mixed Economy, 23-25 June.

Peacock, Alan and Jack Wiseman (1961), *The Growth of Public Expenditure in the United Kingdom*, Princeton University Press.

Pempel, T.J. (ed.) (1977), *Policymaking in Contemporary Japan*, Ithaca, NY, Cornell University Press.

Pempel, T.J. (1981), 'The Japanese Parliament', Madrid: Centro de Investigaciones Sociologicas Conference on the Role of Parliamentarians in Contemporary Democracies, 15-16 December.

Peters, B. Guy, John C. Doughtie and M.K. McCulloch (1977), 'Types of Democratic Systems and Types of Public Policy', *Comparative Politics*, 9 (3): 327-355.

Plattner, Marc F. (1979), 'The Welfare State vs. the Redistributive State', *The Public Interest*, no. 55: 28-48.

Pressman, Jeffrey and Aaron Wildavsky (1973), *Implementation*, Berkeley, University of California Press.

Pryor, Richard (1968), *Public Expenditures in Communist and Capitalist Nations*, London, Allen and Unwin.

Quermonne, Jean-Louis (1980), *La Gouvernement de la France sous la Ve Republique*, Paris, Dalloz.

Reorganization Project of President Carter (1977), 'Current Inventory of Organizational Units within the Executive', Washington, DC, Executive Office of the President; duplicated.

Robinson, A. and Cedric Sandford (1983), *Tax Policy-making in the United Kingdom*, London, Heinemann.

Rokkan, Stein (1970), *Citizens, Elections, Parties*, Oslo, Universitetsforlaget.

Rose, Richard (1968), 'Modern Nations and the Study of Modernization', in S. Rokkan (ed.) *Comparative Research across Cultures and Nations*, Paris, Hague and Mouton, 118-128.

Rose, Richard (1971), *Governing without Consensus: an Irish Perspective*, London, Faber and Faber.

Rose, Richard (1974), 'Coping with Urban Change', in R. Rose (ed.), *The Management of Urban Change in Britain and Germany*, London and Beverly Hills, Sage Publications, 3-25.

Rose, Richard (1975), 'Overloaded Government: the Problem Outlined', *European Studies Newsletter*, 5 (3): 13-18.

Rose, Richard (1976a), 'On the Priorities of Government', *European Journal of Political Research*, 4: 247-289.

Rose, Richard (1976b), *Managing Presidential Objectives*, New York, Free Press.

Rose, Richard (1978), *What is Governing? Purpose and Policy in Washington*, Englewood Cliffs, NJ, Prentice-Hall.

Rose, Richard (1979), 'Ungovernability: Is There Fire Behind the Smoke?', *Political Studies*, 27: 351-370.

Rose, Richard (1980a), *Do Parties Make a Difference?* London, Macmillan.

Rose, Richard (1980b), 'Ordinary People in Extraordinary Economic Circumstances', in R. Rose (ed.), *The Challenge to Governance: Studies in Overloaded Polities*, London, Sage, 151-174.

Rose, Richard (1980c), 'Misperceiving Public Expenditure: Feelings about Cuts', in C. Levine and I. Rubin (eds), *Fiscal Stress and Public Policy*, London, Sage, 203-230.

Rose, Richard (1980d), 'Government against Sub-Governments: a European Perspective on Washington', in R. Rose and E. Suleiman (eds), *Presidents and Prime Ministers*, Washington, DC, American Enterprise Institute, 284-347.

Rose, Richard (1982a), *Understanding the United Kingdom*, London, Longmans.

Rose, Richard (1982b), *Policy Research and Government Research*, Glasgow, University of Strathclyde Studies in Public Policy no. 100.

Rose, Richard (1983a), *Getting By in Three Economies: The Resources of the*

Official, Unofficial and Domestic Economies, Glasgow, University of Strathclyde Studies in Public Policy no. 110.

Rose, Richard (1983b), 'Elections and Electoral Systems: the Alternatives for Choice', in V. Bogdanor and D.E. Butler (eds), *Democracy and Elections*, Cambridge University Press.

Rose, Richard (1983c), 'The State's Contribution to the Welfare Mix: Implications for Political Choice', Glasgow, University of Strathclyde, unpublished.

Rose, Richard (ed.) (forthcoming), *Public Employment in Western Nations*, Cambridge University Press.

Rose, Richard and Terence Karran (1983), *Increasing Taxes, Stable Taxes or Both? The Dynamics of United Kingdom Tax Revenues since 1948*, Glasgow, University of Strathclyde Studies in Public Policy no. 116.

Rose, Richard and T.T. Mackie (1983), 'Incumbency in Government: Asset or Liability?' in H. Daalder and P. Maire (eds), *Western European Party Systems*, London & Beverly Hills, Sage Publications, 115-137.

Rose, Richard and Edward Page, (1982), 'Chronic Instability in Fiscal Systems', in R. Rose and E. Page (eds), *Fiscal Stress in Cities*, Cambridge University Press.

Rose, Richard and B. Guy Peters (1978a), *Can Government Go Bankrupt?* New York, Basic Books.

Rose, Richard and B. Guy Peters (1978b), *The Juggernaut of Incrementalism*, Glasgow, University of Strathclyde Studies in Public Policy no. 24.

Rose, Richard and Derek W. Urwin (1975), *Regional Differentiation and Political Unity in Western Nations*, London, Sage Contemporary Political Sociology Series no. 06-007.

Rose, Richard and Denis Van Mechelen (forthcoming), *The Growth of Laws in the United Kingdom*, Glasgow, Centre for the Study of Public Policy.

Rosenthal, Alan and Rod Forth (1978), 'The Assembly Line: Law Production in the States', *Legislative Studies Quarterly*, 3 May.

Salamon, Lester (1981), 'The Question of Goals', in Szanton, 1981: 58-84.

Savas, E.S. (1982), *Privatizing the Public Sector*, Chatham, NJ, Chatham House.

Scharpf, Fritz W. (1981), *The Political Economy of Inflation and Unemployment in Western Europe*, Berlin, International Institute of Management/WZB IIM/LMP 81-21.

Schattschneider, E.E. (1960), *The Semi-Sovereign People*, New York, Holt, Rinehart & Winston.

Schick, Allen (1981a), 'The Coordination Option', in Szanton, 1981: 85-113.

Schick, Allen (1981b), 'Off-budget Expenditure: an Economic and Political Framework', Paris, OECD, duplicated.

Schindler, Peter (1981), 'Parliaments- und Wahlstatistik fur die l.bis 8. Wahlperiode des Deutschen Bundestages', *Zeitschrift fuer Parlamentsfragen*, 5-21.

Schmidt, Manfred G. (1982), 'The Role of the Parties in Shaping Macroeconomic Policy', in Castles, 1982a: 97-176.

Schmitter, P.C. and Lehmbruch, G. (1980), *Trends toward Corporatist Intermediation*, London and Beverly Hills, Sage Publications.

Schumpeter, Joseph A. (1952), *Capitalism, Socialism and Democracy* (4th ed.), London, Allen and Unwin.

Schwerin, Don (1980), 'The Limits of Organization as a Response to Wage-Price Problems', in R. Rose (ed.), *The Challenge to Governance*, London, Sage, 71-106.

Seldon, Arthur (1977), *Charge*, London, Maurice Temple Smith.
Seldon, Arthur (1979), 'Microeconomic Controls — Disciplining by Price', in A. Seldon (ed.), *The Taming of Government*, London, Institute of Economic Affairs Readings, no. 21, 67-89.
Sharkansky, Ira (1980), 'Policy-Making and Service Delivery on the Margins of Government', *Public Administration Review*, March/April: 116-123.
Smith, Adrian (1981), 'The Informal Economy', *Lloyds Bank Review*, July: 45-61.
Sniderman, P.M. and R.A. Brody (1977), 'Coping: the Ethics of Self-Reliance', *American Journal of Political Science*, 21 (3): 501-552.
Social Trends (annual), London, Central Statistical Office.
Statesman's Year-book (annual), London, Macmillan.
Surrey, Stanley S. (1973), *Pathways to Tax Reform: The Concept of Tax Expenditures*, Cambridge, Mass., Harvard University Press.
Szanton, Peter (ed.) (1981), *Federal Reorganization: What Have We Learned?* Chatham, NJ, Chatham House.
Tarschys, Daniel (1975), 'The Growth of Public Expenditures: Nine Modes of Explanation', *Scandinavian Political Studies Yearbook*, no. 10: 9-31.
Tarschys, Daniel (1977), 'The Soviet Political System: Three Models', *European Journal of Political Research*, 5 (3): 287-320.
Tarschys, Daniel (1981), 'Public Policy Innovation in a Zero-growth Economy: a Scandinavian Perspective', in Peter R. Baehr and Bjorn Wittrock (eds), *Policy Analysis and Policy Innovation*, London and Beverly Hills, Sage Publications, 9-25.
Tarschys, Daniel (1982), 'Curbing Public Expenditures: a Survey of Current Trends', Paris, OECD, duplicated.
Taylor, Charles L. (1981), 'Limits to National Growth', in R. Merritt and B. Russett (eds), *From National Development to Global Community*, London, Allen and Unwin.
Taylor, Charles, L. and Michael C. Hudson (1972), *World Handbook of Political and Social Indicators* (2nd ed.), New Haven, Conn., Yale University Press.
Tilly, Charles (ed.) (1975), *The Formation of National States in Western Europe*, Princeton University Press.
Treasury, H.M. (1982), *The Government's Expenditure Plans, 1982-83 to 1984-85*, Cmnd 8494-II, London, HMSO.
Treasury, H.M. (1983) *The Government's Expenditure Plans, 1983-84 to 1985-86*, Cmnd 8789-I, II London, HMSO.
United States Budget (1982), *Budget of the United States Government: Fiscal Year 1983*, Washington, DC, US Government Printing Office.
Vernon, Raymond and Y. Aharoni (eds) (1981), *State-owned Enterprise in the Western Economies*, London, Croom-Helm.
Wagner, Adolf (1877, 1890), *Finanzwissenschaft*, Parts I, II, Leipzig, C.F. Winter.
Wallace, H., W. Wallace and C. Webb (eds) (1977), *Policy-making in the European Communities*, London, John Wiley.
Walsh, A.H. (1978), *The Public's Business*, Cambridge, Mass., MIT Press.
Warneryd, K.E. and B. Walerud (1982), 'Taxes and Economic Behaviour: Some Interview Data on Tax Evasion in Sweden', *Journal of Economic Psychology*, 2 (3): 182-212.
Wassenberg, A.F.P. and J. Kooiman, (1980), 'Advice and the Reduction of Overload', in R. Rose (ed.), *Challenge to Governance*, London, Sage, 127-150.
Wayne, Stephen (1978), *The Legislative Presidency*, New York, Harper & Row.

Weidenbaum, Murray (1970), *The Modern Public Sector*, New York, Basic Books.

Weidenbaum, Murray (1981), *Business, Government and the Public* (2nd ed.), Englewood Cliffs, NJ, Prentice-Hall.

Weisbrod, Burton A. (1977), *The Voluntary Non-profit Sector*, Lexington, Mass., Lexington Books.

Wildavsky, Aaron (1975), *Budgeting*, Boston, Little, Brown.

Wildavsky, Aaron (1979), *Speaking Truth to Power: the Art and Craft of Policy Analysis*, Boston, Little, Brown.

Wilensky, Harold (1981), 'Leftism, Catholicism and Democratic Corporatism', in Flora and Heidenheimer, 1981: 345-382.

Williams, Philip (1958), *Politics in Post-War France* (2nd ed.), London, Longmans.

Wolf, Charles (1979), 'A Theory of Non-market Failure', *Journal of Law and Economics*, 22: 107-139.

Young, Hugo (1982), 'Wreckers or Obedient Servants? The Other Side of the Treasury Men', *The Times*, 25 February.

INDEX

Richard Rose

brings a unique perspective to writing about questions of big government. In the past quarter-century he has authored or edited more than two dozen books in the field of comparative politics, including *Presidents and Prime Ministers*, *Do Parties Make a Difference? Electoral Behavior*, *Fiscal Stress in Cities*, *Governing without Consensus* and *Can Government Go Bankrupt?* In addition to contributing to press and television on both sides of the Atlantic, he has been a visiting fellow at such think-tanks as the Brookings Institution and American Enterprise Institute, Washington DC, and the European University Institute, Florence. As Professor of Public Policy at the University of Strathclyde, Glasgow, he has a unique interdisciplinary vantage point for analysing the problems and opportunities of contemporary governments.